100 CLASSIC HIKES IN
NEW ENGLAND

100 CLASSIC HIKES IN

NEW ENGLAND

Maine / New Hampshire / Vermont / Massachusetts / Rhode Island / Connecticut

Jeffrey Romano

THE MOUNTAINEERS BOOKS

THE MOUNTAINEERS BOOKS
is the nonprofit publishing arm of The Mountaineers Club, an organization founded in 1906 and dedicated to the exploration, preservation, and enjoyment of outdoor and wilderness areas.

1001 SW Klickitat Way, Suite 201, Seattle, WA 98134

© 2010 by Jeffrey Romano

First edition, 2010

Manufactured in China

Copy Editor: Jane Crosen, Crackerjack Editorial Services
Cover and Book Design: The Mountaineers Books
Layout: Peggy Egerdahl
Cartographer: Pease Press Cartography

All photographs by the author
Cover photograph: *Autumn view of Eagle Lake from North Bubble, Acadia National Park*
Frontispiece: *The Bondcliff Trail is one of New England's remotest paths.*

Maps shown in this book were produced using *National Geographic's* TOPO! software. For more information, go to www.nationalgeographic.com/topo.

Library of Congress Cataloging-in-Publication Data
   Romano, Jeffrey.
      100 classic hikes in New England : Maine, New Hampshire, Vermont, Massachusetts, Connecticut, Rhode Island / Jeffrey Romano.—1st ed.
            p. cm.
      Includes index.
      ISBN 978-1-59485-100-1 (ppb)
      1. Hiking—New England—Guidebooks. 2. Trails—New England—Guidebooks. 3. Backpacking—New England—Guidebooks. 4. New England—Guidebooks. I. Title.
      GV199.42.N38R66 2010
      796.510974—dc22
                                    2009034021

   ISBN 978-1-59485-100-1

CONTENTS

HIKE NUMBER AND NAME	DIFFICULTY[1]	SEASON[2]	FEATURES
Half-Day Hikes			
2. Block Island North	Moderate	All year	Coastal bluffs, beaches
3. Block Island Greenway	Moderate	All year	Coastal bluffs, wildlife, natural splendor
4. Sachuest Point	Easy	All year	Coastal, wildlife
5. Ninigret Refuge	Easy	All year	Coastal, wildlife
6. Bluff Point	Easy	All year	Coastal, history, family-friendly
7. Stepstone Falls	Easy	All year	Waterfall, history, family-friendly
10. Devils Hopyard	Easy–Moderate	All year	Waterfall, geology, family-friendly
11. Wolf Den	Moderate	All year	Geology, history
13. Great Blue Hill	Moderate–Strenuous	All year	Views, geology, scenic ridges
14. Walden Pond	Easy	All year	Ponds, history, family-friendly
15. Hellcat Interpretive Trail	Easy	All year	Sand dunes, wildlife
16. South Pawtuckaway	Moderate	All year	Views, wildlife
17. Ragged Mountain	Moderate	All year	Views, ledges
18. Talcott Mountain	Moderate	All year	History, ledges
19. Peoples Forest	Moderate	All year	Ledges, wetlands
20. Holyoke Range	Moderate	All year	Ledges, history
21. Mount Tom	Moderate–Strenuous	All year	Views, ledges
23. Wachusett Mountain	Moderate–Strenuous	All year	Views, geology
24. Mount Watatic	Moderate	All year	Views, ledges
28. Mohawk Mountain	Moderate	All year	Views, history
29. Rands View	Moderate	All year	Views, geology
34. Monument Mountain	Moderate	All year	Views, history, cliffs
35. Mohawk Trail	Moderate–Strenuous	All year	History, old-growth
36. Spruce Hill	Moderate	All year	Views, wildlife, family-friendly
42. Ludlow Mountain	Moderate	All year	Views, tower
44. Deer Leap	Moderate	All year	Views, old-growth
45. Rattlesnake Cliffs	Moderate–Strenuous	All year	Views, waterfalls
46. Mount Independence	Easy	All year	History, lake, family-friendly
50. Big Deer Mountain	Moderate	All year	Views, pond
53. Smugglers Notch	Moderate	June–October	Views, pond
54. Devils Gulch	Moderate	All year	Geology, pond
55. Mount Pisgah	Moderate–Strenuous	All year	Views, geology, cliffs
56. Mount Israel	Moderate	All year	Views, ledges
58. Welch and Dickey	Moderate–Strenuous	All year	Views, family-friendly, ledges
59. Greeley Ponds	Moderate	All year	Ponds, wildlife
68. Crawford Notch	Moderate	All year	Views, waterfalls, cliff
77. Camden Hills	Moderate	All year	Ocean views, cliff
78. Bald Rock Mountain	Moderate	All year	Views, family-friendly
80. The Beehive and Great Head	Moderate–Strenuous	May–November	Ocean views, ladders

HIKE NUMBER AND NAME	DIFFICULTY[1]	SEASON[2]	FEATURES
Half-Day Hikes			
81. Cadillac Mountain	Moderate–Strenuous	May through November	Ocean views, geology
85. Schoodic Mountain	Moderate	April–November	Views, pond
87. Quoddy Head	Moderate	All year	Ocean views, wildlife
94. Mount Kineo	Moderate–Strenuous	May through October	Lake, views
98. Katahdin Lake	Moderate	May through October	Views, lake
99. South Turner	Strenuous	May through October	Views, pond, wildlife
Day Hikes			
1. Great Island	Moderate–Strenuous	All year	Coastal, beaches
8. Arcadia Loop	Moderate–Strenuous	All year	Geology, ponds
9. Walkabout Trail	Moderate	All year	Lakes, wildflowers
12. Breakneck Pond	Moderate–Strenuous	All year	Ponds, wildflowers
22. Tully Mountain and Lake	Moderate–Strenuous	All year	Views, lake, waterfalls
25. Mount Monadnock	Strenuous	April–November	Views, ledges
26. Mount Cardigan	Strenuous	All year	Views, ledges
27. Macedonia Ridge Trail	Moderate–Strenuous	All year	Views, geology, scenic ridges
30. Mount Frissell	Moderate–Strenuous	All year	Views, wildflowers, includes Connecticut's highest point
31. Bear Mountain	Strenuous	All year	Views, cascades, natural splendor
32. Alander Mountain	Moderate–Strenuous	All year	Views, waterfalls
33. Mount Everett	Strenuous	All year	Views, pond, waterfalls
41. Mount Ascutney	Moderate–Strenuous	All year	Views, cascades
43. Baker Peak and Griffith Lake	Moderate–Strenuous	All year	Views, pond
47. Bread Loaf Mountain	Moderate–Strenuous	May–October[3]	Views, pond
48. Mount Abraham (VT)	Moderate–Strenuous	May–October[3]	Views, alpine
49. Camels Hump	Strenuous	All year[3]	Views, geology
51. Worcester Range	Strenuous	All year[3]	Views, ledges
52. Mount Mansfield	Strenuous	All year[3]	Views, geology, Vermont's highest peak
57. Mount Whiteface	Strenuous	All year	Cliffs, views
61. Mount Chocorua	Moderate–Strenuous	All year	Views, waterfalls
62. Mount Moosilauke	Strenuous	All year	Views, alpine
63. Cannon Mountain	Strenuous	All year	Views, lake
65. Mount Garfield	Moderate–Strenuous	May through October	Views, ledges
66. Zeacliff	Moderate–Strenuous	May through October	Views, ponds, waterfalls
70. Davis Path	Moderate–Strenuous	All year	Views, history
71. Nancy Brook Scenic Area	Moderate–Strenuous	All year	Waterfalls, ponds
72. South and Middle Moat	Moderate–Strenuous	All year	Views, ledges
76. East Royce Mountain	Moderate–Strenuous	All year	Views, waterfalls

HIKE NUMBER AND NAME	DIFFICULTY[1]	SEASON[2]	FEATURES
Day Hikes			
79. Isle au Haut	Moderate–Strenuous	May–October	Ocean views, wildlife
82. The Bubbles and Pemetic	Moderate–Strenuous	April through November	Views, ponds
83. Sargent Mountain	Moderate–Strenuous	April–November	Views, geology
86. Cutler Coast	Moderate–Strenuous	All year	Ocean views, wildlife, natural splendor
90. Tumbledown Mountain	Strenuous	May through October	Views, geology, pond
92. Mount Abraham (ME)	Strenuous	May through October	Views, alpine
95. Big Moose Mountain	Moderate–Strenuous	May–November	Views, history
96. Gulf Hagas	Moderate–Strenuous	May through October	Waterfalls, geology
97. Doubletop Mountain	Strenuous	May–October	Views, ponds
Long Day Hikes			
37. Monroe State Forest	Strenuous	All year	Old-growth, cascades
38. Mount Greylock	Strenuous	All year	Views, waterfalls, Massachusetts' highest peak
64. Franconia Ridge	Very strenuous	All year	Alpine, waterfalls, scenic ridges
67. Mount Washington	Very strenuous	May–October	Views, alpine, waterfalls, New Hampshire's highest peak
73. Carter Dome	Strenuous	All year	Views, geology
74. Mount Adams	Very strenuous	June through October	Alpine, geology, waterfalls, natural splendor
75. Baldfaces	Strenuous	All year	Views, ledges
84. Frenchboro	Moderate–Strenuous	May–November	Ocean views, ledges
91. Saddleback Mountain	Strenuous	All year	Alpine, geology, ponds, scenic ridges
100. Mount Katahdin	Very strenuous	June through October	Alpine, waterfalls, geology, Maine's highest peak
Short Backpacks			
40. Stratton Pond and Mountain	Moderate–Strenuous	All year[3]	Views, pond, wildlife
69. Webster Cliff–Dry River	Strenuous	May through October	Views, wilderness
88. Mahoosuc Notch	Very strenuous	June through October	Geology, views, pond
93. Bigelow Range	Strenuous	May through October	Alpine, ponds
Extended Backpacks			
39. Glastenbury Mountain	Moderate–Strenuous	All year[3]	Views, wilderness
60. Pemigewasset Wilderness	Strenuous	May through October	Views, wilderness
89. Grafton Loop	Strenuous	All year	Views, waterfalls

Key:

[1] Difficulty: Estimation based on length of hike, elevation change, and terrain

[2] Season to hike: Based primarily on road access; hike descriptions include other seasonal considerations.

[3] Vermont asks hikers to avoid high elevations during mud season (mid-April to Memorial Day).

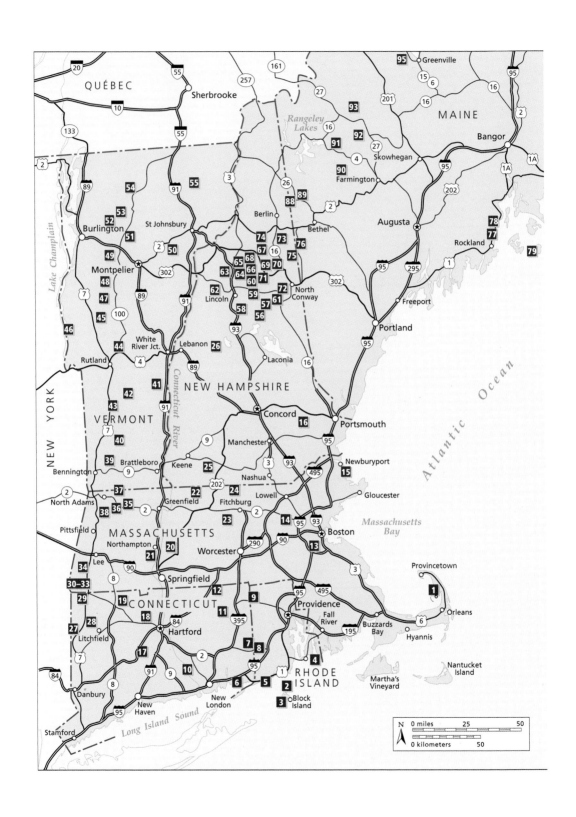

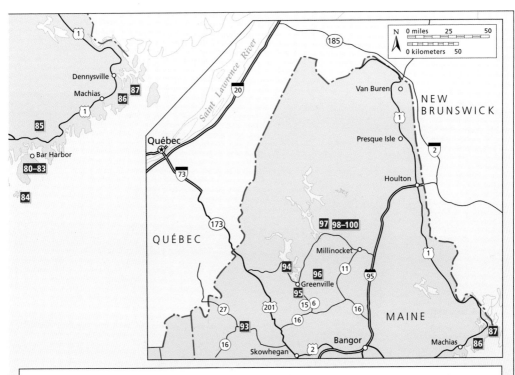

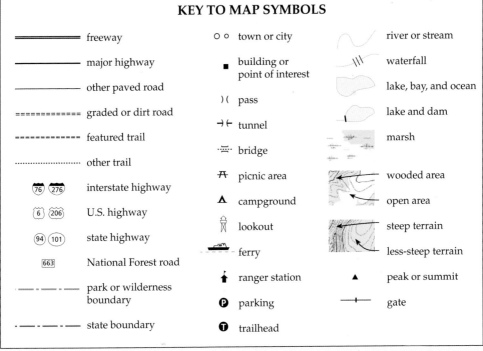

KEY TO MAP SYMBOLS

——————— freeway	o o	town or city		river or stream
———— major highway	■	building or point of interest		waterfall
——— other paved road	)(	pass		lake, bay, and ocean
============= graded or dirt road	→←	tunnel		lake and dam
- - - - - - featured trail	⋯≍⋯	bridge		marsh
·············· other trail	⼎	picnic area		wooded area
⑦⑥ ②⑦⑥ interstate highway	▲	campground		open area
⑥ ②⑥ U.S. highway	🗼	lookout		steep terrain
⑨⑭ ⑩⑪ state highway	⛴	ferry		less-steep terrain
663 National Forest road	☗	ranger station	▲	peak or summit
– · — park or wilderness boundary	Ⓟ	parking	—+—	gate
· — · — state boundary	Ⓣ	trailhead		

ACKNOWLEDGMENTS

I would be remiss in failing to acknowledge the many people who played a part in the evolution of this book, especially those who joined me on the trail, posed for photographs, and reviewed draft material. I wish to thank Richard Romano, Judy Romano, Craig Romano, Doug Romano, Rich Knox, Andy Walsh, Fred Michaud, and Pat Sirois. In addition, extra-special thanks are due to my wife Maria and son Anthony. Both provided the essential support needed to make this book a reality. Thank you for your patience during the long weekends away (see you next Mother's Day!), frantic hours writing, and the constant preparation. I hope you remember most the many adventures we enjoyed together, of which I have fond memories: skipping stones at Sterling Pond, scrambling up Monadnock's rocky ridge, weaving through the Tumbledown tunnel, watching the sunset from Block Island, startling the Black Racer at Stepstone Falls, and gazing upon the moose of Sandy Stream.

Opposite: *The Nature Conservancy's Clay Head Preserve, Block Island*

INTRODUCTION

The 100 classic hikes described in this guidebook showcase the breadth and diversity of New England's picturesque landscapes: from the sandy beaches of Long Island Sound to the lofty summits of the White Mountains, from the sweeping ridges of the Berkshires to Maine's rocky coastline, from the traprock cliffs of the Connecticut River Valley to the lush forests of Vermont. Taking advantage of the patchwork of conserved lands protected over the past century, the book showcases the region's premier hiking destinations that include national parks, forests, and wildlife refuges; state parks, public lands, and wildlife management areas; and land trust reserves.

Arriving at the 100 classic hikes in New England was a challenge—there are so many trails and destinations from which to choose. In addition to capturing the region's varied landscape, the final list includes hikes with diverse degrees of difficulty, multiple interesting features (natural and/or historic), and, when possible, opts for trailheads that offer a multitude of options (from short half-day hikes to overnight backpacks).

New England is noteworthy for a number of reasons, not the least of which is the cycle of the seasons. Exploring these hikes covered in snow, sprouting with wildflowers, buzzing with songbirds, and afire with foliage will undoubtedly lead you to discover what I did long ago: New England is a hiker's paradise that beckons the adventurer throughout the year. I look forward to crossing paths with you en route to one of New England's 100 Classic Hikes!

CLIMATE

New England's climate is as diverse as its seasons. While each season offers unique attractions, all four require different considerations.

Spring Hiking

Spring hiking can be deceptively winter-like. Warm weather at lower elevations and in southern parts of New England does not mean spring has arrived everywhere. In fact, it is not unusual for snow and ice to be abundant throughout April and May (sometimes into June) in northern New England, especially in elevations over 3000 feet. Proper equipment like snowshoes, crampons, and warm clothing may be necessary additions to your backpack. When considering a spring hike, keep in mind that slopes melt faster, especially south-facing slopes, and that flat areas, particularly when shaded by evergreens, stay snowy longer.

While winter-like in some respects, spring can also be like summer. The sun's rays, for example, can burn as quickly in April as in August. Adding to the sunburn threat is the reflection of light off snow and the lack of leaves to provide shade. Be sure to add sunscreen to your pack by March. Insects are also a concern on spring hikes. The arrival of the swarming, biting, and eye-, mouth-, and ear-filling blackflies usually begins in late April in the southern areas described in this book. By Memorial Day most places have ushered in their arrival. Although short-lived, the blackfly season can be frustrating. Spring also marks the start of tick season, and the blood-sucking parasites seem to be spreading farther north each year (see the "Ticks and Insects" section for additional information).

Finally, spring can also be very spring-like, and nothing says spring more than water. A constant issue on many spring hikes is the number of and size of water crossings. It is hard to hike in New England without encountering running water. To ensure that the worst-case scenario is only wet boots, it is essential to use caution at all stream crossings and be prepared to turn around if necessary. The increased water also creates muddy trails that lead to wet feet and increased erosion. To avoid mud, pick hikes in the southern and coastal areas earlier in the spring and slowly work your way north.

Opposite: *Mounts Carrigain and Nancy (l–r) from the icy summit of Mount Crawford*

Gray jays are friendly inhabitants of northern New England.

Summer Hiking

Few things put a damper on a summer hike more than swarming insects. Clouds of mosquitoes lurking in shady, moist areas and deerflies circling on the hottest, most humid days of July can be annoying and painful. To ease the situation, be prepared with effective bug repellent; avoid low, wet areas; and remind yourself that without the insects we would not be blessed with so many different and colorful songbirds.

Summer heat and humidity are other factors to consider. This combination, most common in July, quickly saps your energy. Try to start hikes early in the day and make sure to drink plenty of fluids. Heat and humidity may also trigger thunderstorms. Many of the hikes in this book describe trails with a lot of exposure. These are excellent hikes when the weather cooperates, but are potentially very dangerous when lightning is in the air. Storms most frequently hit later in the day, but often come on suddenly. Be alert and seek cover quickly at the sound of thunder. Lastly, heat and humidity tend to mix with smog from the Midwest, diminishing views that can be far more impressive at other times of the year. If you are looking for the optimum summer day, wait for the day after a strong thunderstorm, which is often followed by cooler, cleaner air from Canada.

Autumn Hiking

While autumn hiking can be very enjoyable, remember that the days shorten quickly. Conditions may tempt you for long adventures, but be prepared to finish before the sun sets. Unlike the summer, in autumn once the sun goes down the temperatures quickly follow. In addition, it is not uncommon to experience winter-like conditions during the day, especially in northern New England. Be sure to have plenty of warm clothing, including a hat and gloves. The cool temperatures often make water crossings more difficult, too. When crossing rocks that look icy, step on sections slightly submerged by water rather than wet spots exposed to the open air.

A final consideration for the autumn is that while excellent for hiking, it is also prime hunting season throughout the region—for deer and a variety of other wildlife (Note: Not all hunting takes place in autumn; consult with each state's fish and wildlife agency for specific information on hunting laws, schedules, and regulations). Many of the trails described in this book occur in areas open for hunting. Although it is quite uncommon to encounter hunters near hiking trails, it is good policy to wear bright colors such as blaze orange (required in some places). To avoid hunters altogether, head for Connecticut, Massachusetts, or Maine on Sunday, when hunting is prohibited.

Winter Hiking

Before choosing a winter hike, it is important to keep in mind that many trailheads are inaccessible from November to May. Before heading to a particular hike, make sure to check on the accessibility of the access road and/or be prepared to change plans.

The margin for error in the winter hiking is slim. It is a good policy to carry more than what you think you will need: clothes, water, and food. It is especially helpful to have dry clothes in case you get wet. In winter, the sun sets around 4:00 PM–4:30 PM in January and slowly grows later and later. On cloudy days or on northern, forested slopes, it can get darker even earlier.

Finally, always bring and expect to use snowshoes. Surprisingly, many hikers shy away from using snowshoes and focus more on ice axes and crampons. While ice axes and crampons are essential in certain circumstances, they are needed infrequently, even while climbing 4000-footers. On the contrary, snowshoes are required on the vast majority of winter hikes. When choosing snowshoes, opt for narrow oval-shaped ones with metal grips below. This design will allow maximum control and maneuverability, particularly in mountainous terrain.

USING THIS BOOK

This book is designed to introduce you to 100 of New England's best hiking destinations. Extra care was used to choose those locations that not only exemplify the region's most scenic features, but also those that offer you the greatest variety of trip choices. While each recommended hike includes a description of one specific itinerary, more than 80 percent of the hikes provide information on other optional excursions (of various lengths and difficulties) from the same trailhead or a nearby starting point. Rather than an end, use this book as an introduction to New England's most special places.

Information Blocks

Each hike begins with an information block that provides helpful facts. Use this information to decide whether the hike makes sense for you.

The **Distance** refers to the length of the entire described hike and is always followed with information as to whether the journey is round-trip (using the same route both ways) or a loop. In other words, a hike that leads 2.3 miles to the final destination and then returns along the same 2.3 miles of trail will be listed as 4.6 miles round-trip. If, on the other hand, the hike returns on a different trail or trails, it will be listed as a 4.6-mile loop.

When referring to the **Hiking time**, please bear in mind that this is an estimate for the average hiker based on experience. You may find the estimates are too high or too low. Use the estimate as a tool, rather than a way to judge success or failure.

Each hike is also evaluated based on degree of **Difficulty** (easy, moderate, strenuous, or very strenuous). This subjective tool seeks to categorize the hikes based on their length, elevation gain, exposure, steepness, and terrain.

To provide a better sense of the terrain, refer to the **Low point** and **High point**. Keep in mind that the low point may or may not be the starting point.

The **Season** listing is another subjective tool meant to be a guide—not an absolute. Anyone who has lived in New England knows that the weather can be quite unpredictable. The amount of snow and ice on a given trail or access road varies from year to year. In most cases, hikes that have trailheads accessible twelve months a year are listed as year-round destinations. However, some hikes with year-round-accessible trailheads are recommended only for times of the year when snow and/or ice are typically not a factor. This does not mean that with proper equipment and experience these hikes are not possible other times of the year.

With each hike you will find a category titled **Information** that includes the name of the respective **landowner** most responsible for the management of the trail or trails along the described route (some hikes take place on lands owned and managed by more than one organization, individual, or governmental entity). While the vast majority of land in New England is held privately, most of the hikes in this book occur exclusively on publicly owned and managed lands. However, the book also includes hikes accessible over private roads, hikes crossing sections of private land, and hikes on conservation land owned by nonprofit conservation organizations. Each landowner and manager associated with hikes in this book has unique missions and regulations. For your enjoyment, and to ensure that others that follow can enjoy these same special places, it is important to know and obey all regulations and to be especially considerate of private landowners. For the most up-to-date information on fees, trail conditions, camping requirements, and regulations, call the respective landowner or visit their website. Contact information for landowners can be found in the book's appendix.

While every hike includes a map outlining the trails and various other important features, the information block also includes a list of one or more **USGS maps** that cover the area. It is important to note that in many cases the USGS topographic maps may be out-of-date in regards to trails, roads, and other man-made features; however, they provide a good illustration of the area's natural features. For additional mapping material, visit the website of or contact the landowner listed under the **Information** category. For many of the hikes in this book, the landowner offers a useful complimentary map.

At the end of the information block is a section titled **Getting there** that provides driving directions to the parking areas connected with the trailhead or trailheads outlined for the hike. In a few cases this section also includes ferry and shuttle directions that are essential for accessing the trailhead.

OUTDOOR ETIQUETTE

With more folks enjoying hiking and backpacking each year, the need for outdoor ethics has never been greater. Few things on a hike are more frustrating, for example, than encountering improper or inconsiderate campers. It is amazing how often tents are perched on the banks of a stream or right off a trail. Similarly, watching a mountainside erode due to hikers taking short-cuts, or having a peaceful day in the woods interrupted by a loud group of people inconsiderate to the enjoyment of others, can leave a sour taste after an otherwise glorious day in the outdoors. In some cases these types of activities violate the rules that govern a particular area; but more important, these activities diminish the experiences of other hikers.

Leave No Trace

To ensure that we all can enjoy the same opportunity to renew our spirits in the wilds of New England, it is essential for each of us to commit to basic outdoor ethical principles. The Leave No Trace Center for Outdoor Ethics, a national nonprofit organization dedicated to promoting and inspiring responsible outdoor recreation through education, research, and partnerships, has developed seven simple principles all hikers should follow. They are:

Plan Ahead and Prepare

This includes knowing applicable regulations and special concerns for each area visited; being prepared for extreme weather, hazards, and emergencies; scheduling trips to avoid times of high use; and understanding how to use a map, guidebook, and compass.

Travel and Camp on Durable Surfaces

This means using established trails and camp-sites, rock, gravel, dry grasses, or snow. Remember that good campsites are found, not made, and should never be located closer than 200 feet from wetlands. Also, walking single file in the middle of the trail, even when wet or muddy, minimizes erosion. Remaining on the trail is especially important for the high-elevation hikes described in this book that use trails surrounded by fragile vegetation.

Dispose of Waste Properly

We should all follow the basic rule of waste disposal: pack it in and pack it out. When depositing solid human waste, dig a small hole 6 to 8 inches deep at least 200 feet from water, camp, and trails. Cover and disguise the hole when finished. Avoid washing yourself or your dishes within 200 feet of streams or lakes and use small amounts of biodegradable soap.

Leave What You Find

You are not the first to visit any of these places and likely will not be the last. Preserve the experience for others who follow: examine, but do not touch, cultural or historic structures and artifacts; leave rocks, plants, and other natural objects as you find them; avoid introducing or transporting nonnative species; and do not build structures or furniture or dig trenches.

Minimize Campfire Impacts

Lightweight stoves and candle lanterns leave less impact than campfires. Where fires are permitted, use established fire rings, fire pans, or mound fires, and keep fires small. Only use sticks from the ground that can be broken by hand. When done, burn all wood to ash, and then scatter cool ashes. Put campfires out completely.

Respect Wildlife

Wildlife is best observed from a distance and should never be fed. Feeding wildlife damages their health, alters natural behaviors, and exposes them to predators and other dangers. Protect wildlife and your food by storing rations and trash securely. Control pets at all times, or leave them at home.

Be Considerate of Other Visitors

Respect other visitors and protect the quality of their experience. Be courteous and yield to other users on the trail. Let nature's sounds prevail—avoid loud voices and noises.

SAFETY

Before beginning your next New England hiking adventure, it is important to prepare adequately for a number of potential hazards. Taking the necessary precautions to avoid or minimize exposure to the following safety concerns will help to ensure a more pleasurable outdoor excursion and allow you to experience countless future hikes throughout the region.

Lightning

Lightning storms are a common occurrence throughout New England. While most electrical storms occur from May to August, thunderstorms are possible any time of the year. Since many of the hikes described in this book occur on exposed ridges and along other high locations, the threat of being struck by lightning should not be underestimated.

To minimize your risk of being injured or killed by lightning, you should take a number of precautions. First, be aware of the day's weather forecast and avoid hikes with a lot of exposure when the threat of thunderstorms is great. Second, pay attention to the sky and do your best to avoid being caught on exposed ridges, open areas, or above tree line. Third, if a storm hits, it is wise to spread out so if one person is struck, others can help. Lastly, if you don't have time to get to a lower elevation or out of an open area: squat down to reduce your height, minimize your contact with the earth (only your feet should touch the ground), and avoid metal objects.

Hypothermia

Hypothermia is literally the lowering of your body's core temperature. While most often a threat during colder months, hypothermia can strike any time of the year. To protect yourself or a fellow hiker from succumbing to hypothermia, it is important to understand the early warning signs, which include poor judgment, a slight sensation of chilliness, and trouble using your hands for simple tasks. Should these early signs go unnoticed or unaddressed, hypothermia can lead to more serious conditions such as uncontrolled shivering, unconsciousness, and even death.

The best way to prevent hypothermia is to wear clothes that keep you warm even when they are wet and to dress in layers. Be sure to wear good wind and rain gear, because your body loses heat three times as fast when it is wet. Finally, it is important to eat and drink properly. Even when the temperature is cold, drinking plenty of water is critical to your health. Avoid alcohol and caffeine, because both can contribute to hypothermia. When eating, opt for many small meals.

Weather above Tree Line

When choosing a hike that climbs above tree line, like Katahdin, Saddleback, Abraham, and the Bigelows in Maine; Mansfield, Abraham, and Camels Hump in Vermont; or Moosilauke, Franconia Range, the Pemigewasset Wilderness,

Opposites attract

and the Presidential Range in New Hampshire, weather should be of increased concern. The weather in all of these areas can be ferocious and, in most cases, there is no safe shelter once you are above tree line.

Pay attention not only to the existing conditions but also to the afternoon forecast that day and any incoming systems noted in the weather report. Remember that weather conditions above tree line are not reflective of conditions in the lowlands. Expect a minimum drop in air temperature of three degrees Fahrenheit for each 1000 feet in elevation gain, combined with the wind chill from increased velocity as you climb. Plan for the best possibilities, but be prepared to change plans to accommodate weather conditions. Do not try to outsmart the weather or push hesitant members of your party if conditions are not ideal. The mountain will be there another day, and hopefully you will get a chance to try again; this decision will be made all the sweeter by the fact that you have exercised discipline and shown respect for the elements.

Water

Unless faced with extreme dehydration, you should not drink any water before treating it. In fact, the most clean mountain streams could be home to microscopic viruses and bacteria, such as giardia, that can wreak havoc with your digestive system. Treating water can be as simple as boiling it, chemically purifying it with iodine tablets, or pumping it through one of the many commercially available water filter and purifier systems. Drinking untreated water is a mistake you will remember for a long time, and one that will provide you ample time to "sit down" to think about the poor decision you made.

Wildlife

New England is not known as a hiking destination fraught with dangerous wildlife encounters. However, there are a few animal species that can potentially be problematic. Male moose during the fall rutting season and female moose with young can be aggressive if their space is violated. Since they typically do not go looking

A harbor seal enjoys the midday sun off Block Island.

for trouble, do not be overly enthusiastic about getting their photo, and you should remain safe. Similarly, black bear sows with their young are another situation of possible concern; however, more often than not they sense your presence first and are long gone before you arrive. Lastly, some of the southern hikes in this book occur in rattlesnake country. Pay attention to where you step and place your hands. If bitten, you should seek immediate medical attention.

In the end, you should not let your fear of wildlife deter you from a hiking adventure. Use common sense with all animals (view from a distance, do not feed them, and respect their space), and you will likely avoid threatening encounters. In fact, the animal you are most apt to be threatened by on a hike will be an unleashed dog, and that can just as easily occur on a walk around your neighborhood.

Ticks and Insects

While many tend to fear an attack from a larger animal, the animals most likely to injure you on a hike are the smallest ones you will encounter. The most common antagonists are blackflies, mosquitoes, deerflies, ticks, and yellow jackets. Since their presence varies depending on the region, the time of year, and the current conditions, you will not encounter each of these on every New England hike during the year's warmer months. Still, it is likely you will encounter at least one of them if you go for a hike between April and October.

Frequently, encounters with these critters are manageable with little effort. However, if their numbers are high, you suffer allergic reactions to any of them, and/or your tolerance is low, consider using insect repellents, hats, long pants, or commercially available gear to help ease the annoyance, threat, and pain inflicted by them. To avoid picking up ticks, which carry Lyme and other diseases, it is helpful to tuck clothes in and wear light colors. In addition, after every hike, you should do a thorough scan of your body to ensure no ticks are present and use fine-tipped tweezers to quickly and thoroughly remove any ticks you find.

Getting Lost and Found

While the hikes described in this book are located on well-developed trails in areas frequently used by hikers, the possibility of being lost, injured, or stranded after dark is something to consider. The best advice is that you should not rely on technology to save you. For example, cell phones cannot receive signals in many regions covered in this book, and even if they did, their batteries may run out of juice. If you find yourself lost or injured, it is much safer to rely on basic outdoor skills, preparedness, common sense, and a few simple rules: It is always safer to hike with companions; if you choose to hike alone, be sure to let someone else know of your plans; study the area you are visiting beforehand to have a better understanding of the topography; keep all hiking groups together; and always carry and know how to use the Ten Essentials (see the following section).

BEFORE YOU GO

Before hitting the trails, it is prudent to be prepared with proper gear. While it is often tempting to head up the trail with less, you never know what may occur: injury, change of weather, illness, etc. The bottom line for any hike is to bring more than you think you will need; the worst that could happen may be building stronger back and shoulder muscles. For any hike, it is wise to include the following Ten Essentials:

1. **Extra clothing:** Even on the hottest days of summer, at a minimum you should carry a rain jacket and a water-resistant layer of clothing. During colder times of the year or while venturing above tree line, lots of additional layers are a must, including warm hats and gloves. The highest locations described in this book can experience winter-like conditions throughout the year.
2. **Extra food and water:** Hiking is a strenuous activity that burns calories quickly. Fill your pack with high-energy food and more than you expect to eat. In addition, begin each hike with at least two quarts of water per person, even during colder months. Few things put more of a damper on an otherwise enjoyable hike than headaches resulting from dehydration and/or hunger.
3. **Sunglasses and sunscreen:** Sun protection is a must throughout the year. In fact, the

low angle of the sun and the reflection off snow and ice can make sunglasses very important during colder months. Sunscreen is also necessary, especially from March to October. Late winter through mid-spring can be your most vulnerable time of the year, when the sun is strong and bare trees provide little protection.

4. **Knife:** A knife or multi-tool with pliers is a handy device to carry. While neither may be necessary 99 percent of the time, the one time either is needed you will be happy to have brought one along.

5. **First-aid kit:** Cuts, stings, twisted ankles, and other ailments are distinct possibilities even for the most prepared hiker. Bandages, pain relievers, and ointments can help to significantly alleviate many injuries in a pinch. Knowledge of first-aid procedure can also help instruct how to react in certain emergency situations to ensure an injured party receives the necessary help.

6. **Firestarter:** Having something that will catch fire, even when sticks and brush are wet, can be a huge help in an emergency, such as having to spend the night in the woods.

7. **Matches in a waterproof container:** Like a firestarter, dry matches can make a big difference in an emergency situation.

8. **Flashlight or headlamp:** If you are forced to spend the night outdoors or when still on the trail after sunset, artificial light can be a big help in returning to the trailhead safely.

9. **Map:** Having a map of the area and knowing how to read it provides options in the case of emergency. For example, often there are multiple trails in an area that provide shorter or easier alternatives. Know where you are and how to most quickly get some place safely in an emergency.

10. **Compass:** While the trails in this book are generally well marked and easy to follow, harsh weather and snow can sometimes obscure the way. If for some reason you lose your way, the use of a compass can be a valuable tool in safely returning home.

In addition to these ten items, there are other gear considerations to make. Many of the hikes in this book and throughout the region take place on rocky terrain. To provide optimum comfort and effectiveness, choose sturdy boots with good ankle protection. It is also desirable to seal the boots with waterproof material. There are a number of commercially available products that will cause water to bead up and run off boots, leaving your feet dry. Gaiters that wrap around your lower leg are also handy for keeping water and debris out of your boots. When choosing socks, avoid cotton, because it is not the best material to wear when wet.

Last but not least, carrying a camera and binoculars can add a lot of enjoyment to a hiking adventure. Similarly, bringing books that help in the identification of birds, wildlife, trees, mushrooms, and wildflowers can add many new dimensions to a hiking adventure.

A NOTE ABOUT SAFETY

Safety is an important concern in all outdoor activities. No guidebook can alert you to every hazard or anticipate the limitations of every reader. Therefore, the descriptions of roads, trails, routes, and natural features in this book are not representations that a particular place or excursion will be safe for your party. When you follow any of the routes described in this book, you assume responsibility for your own safety. Under normal conditions, such excursions require the usual attention to traffic, road and trail conditions, weather, terrain, the capabilities of your party, and other factors. Keeping informed on current conditions and exercising common sense are the keys to a safe, enjoyable outing.

—The Mountaineers Books

SOUTHEASTERN NEW ENGLAND

Surf crashing into Block Island's Black Rock Beach

This most populated area of New England extends from Cape Cod, west across gently rolling terrain, north into southern New Hampshire, and south to Long Island Sound. Scattered throughout the densely developed landscape are countless pockets of conservation treasures that highlight the region's sandy coastline, centuries-old history, lush hardwood forests, and quirky geologic remnants.

Southeastern New England's predominantly easy-to-moderate hikes are ideal for family excursions, bird-watching adventures, picnicking, and seascape photography. While beautiful and accessible throughout the year, many of this region's hikes are more enjoyable from October to May when crowds and traffic are less overwhelming.

1 GREAT ISLAND

Distance: 8 miles loop
Hiking time: 6 hours
Difficulty: Moderate–Strenuous
Low point: 0 feet
High point: 75 feet
Season: Year-round
USGS map: Wellfleet, MA
Information: Cape Cod National Seashore

Getting there: From Route 6 in Wellfleet, 1.4 miles north of the lookout tower, turn west onto Main Street toward Wellfleet Center. In 0.3 mile bear left on East Commercial Street and continue 0.7 mile to the town pier. Follow the pavement as it swings right, and drive 2.5 miles on Chequessett Neck Road to the parking area on the left.

The Cape Cod National Seashore draws countless beachgoers to its sandy expanses and bike enthusiasts to its paved paths; however, the park also includes miles of hiking trails. The most challenging and rugged, by far, is the Great Island Trail. Jutting southward on the west side of Wellfleet Harbor, Great Island has a storied past of Native American settlers, European whalers, and small communities long since swallowed by the shifting seas. Today, Great Island is an oasis of seabirds, fiddler crabs, pitch pine forests, and towering sand dunes. For optimum enjoyment, venture here during low to mid-tide; parts of the trail, particularly near Jeremy Point, may be underwater at high tide.

From the parking area, a well-groomed path descends gently to the water's edge. Here,

View of Middle Meadow marsh and Great Beach Hill from the tavern site

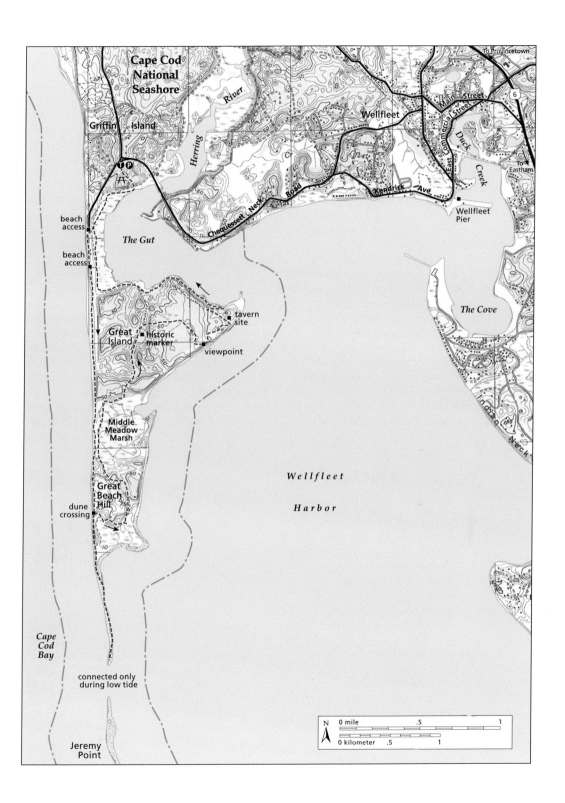

Cape Cod
National
Seashore

To Provincetown

Griffin Island

Herring   River

Wellfleet

Main   Street

East Commercial Street

6

To
Eastham

Duck   Creek

beach
access

The Gut

Chequessett Neck   Road

Kendrick   Ave

Wellfleet
Pier

beach
access

The Cove

tavern
site

Great
Island

historic
marker

viewpoint

Middle
Meadow
Marsh

Wellfleet

Harbor

Great
Beach
Hill

dune
crossing

Cape
Cod
Bay

connected only
during low tide

Jeremy
Point

N

0 mile   .5   1

0 kilometer   .5   1

The Gut, a small bay adjacent to Wellfleet Harbor, provides a scenic backdrop. Sweeping right, the trail leads toward the colorful sand dunes and the first of two beach access points. Turn right, cut through the sculpted sands, and emerge upon a seemingly endless beach. Follow the shoreline south for roughly 2 miles. For easier travel, wear sturdy sandals. During low tide the exposed flats make an excellent, albeit wet, footway. From April to August, keep your eyes open for diminutive piping plovers (dogs are prohibited during this time). The National Park Service fences off nest sites to protect these endangered shorebirds.

After strolling past the base of Great Beach Hill, look for a small gap in the dunes that leads to the inland path back. South of this point, it is possible to explore the sandbar for another mile or so. Jeremy Point, which used to be permanently connected, is only accessible during low tide. While exploring this area, watch carefully for additional shorebird nesting sites—the territory-defending least tern and the orange-billed American oystercatcher often rear their young here.

From the beach, the inland trail skirts east toward Wellfleet Harbor. As you walk, armies of fiddler crabs scurry along the path, darting into tiny holes. Wrapping around the point, turn north and climb up the pine-shaded hillside. The path descends to and then circles around Middle Meadow Marsh. Be sure to remain on the trail to minimize potential contact with ticks and poison ivy. Up a small incline, level off and journey through pleasant forest surroundings. Beyond a historic marker on the right (a Mayflower descendant once lived here), reach a trail junction. Turn right and follow the narrow path that leads to an excellent viewpoint of Wellfleet Harbor, and beyond to a spot where a tavern once served customers from 1690 into the 1740s. East of the tavern monument a spur branches a few dozen feet to the edge of a scenic bluff.

The route proceeds west to a grassy opening, high above The Gut. Swing right and descend to the beach. Follow the shoreline left back to the main trail, and then bear right and continue to wind around the bright blue waters on your journey back. If you have time, visit the nearby Marconi observation area (located in Wellfleet on the opposite side of the Cape Cod peninsula) or venture south to the Park Service's Salt Pond Visitor Center in Eastham to learn about other recreational opportunities within the seashore.

2 BLOCK ISLAND NORTH

Distance: 5.9-mile loop
Hiking time: 4 hours
Difficulty: Moderate
Low point: 0 feet
High point: 110 feet
Season: Year-round
USGS map: Block Island, RI
Information: The Nature Conservancy; Rhode Island National Wildlife Refuge Complex

Getting there: There are a number of ferry services that connect Block Island to the mainland. During the summer, ferries run from New London, Connecticut; Newport, Rhode Island; and Montauk, New York. A year-round ferry connects Galilee, Rhode Island (near Point Judith), with the village of Old Harbor on Block Island. Visit www.blockislandinfo.com for the latest information. In the summer, bringing a car can be problematic (there are auto, bike, and moped rentals available), but off-season it is more practical.

Once on the island, head for the intersection of Ocean Avenue and Dodge Street in Old Harbor. From here, follow Corn Neck Road north 2.5 miles. Turn left onto West Beach Road. Drive past the transfer station and park at the end of the road.

Block Island is a good place to see migratory songbirds.

Block Island, famous for weddings, has long been tamed. Scattered about the island are large hotels and summer homes. Yet, for the seasoned hiker, Block Island offers 28 miles of trails and 17 miles of beaches to explore. In addition, more than 43 percent of the island is permanently protected from development. This 5.9-mile loop around North Light showcases the best of what Block Island has to offer: views of majestic homes, wild expanses of sand, and stunningly beautiful ocean bluffs.

Begin the journey by heading north along West Beach. Lightly used, this delightful sandy shoreline stretches 1.5 miles to the northern tip of the island, which continues to grow each year with eroded debris washed ashore from other parts of the island. Past rocks popular with sunning seals, you'll parallel a border with the Block Island National Wildlife Refuge. Please stay off the dunes and away from the seagull nest sites that are abundant in the area. As you approach the end of the land, a route leads right through the dunes to a historic lighthouse, built in 1867. Today, North Light houses a maritime museum.

Departing the lighthouse to the east, follow a sandy road leading to an open beach. Walk along the soft soil for 0.5 mile, where a small parking area lies near a monument commemorating the arrival of the island's first settlers in 1661. Follow the paved road 0.1 mile and join a dirt road that leads left.

Past a few houses, the narrow lane swings right and soon arrives at the northern end of the Clay

Near the highpoint of Clay Head Nature Trail

Head Nature Trail. Leading nearly 2 miles past scenic, oceanside vistas, this path winds pleasantly across The Nature Conservancy's 190-acre Clay Head Preserve. Note the abundant array of unmarked and red-signed trails that depart the main route throughout. One area is appropriately referred to as "The Maze." While it is difficult to get too lost, because civilization remains near, it is possible to wander aimlessly. To avoid this predicament, simply remain on the blue-signed nature trail that remains closest to the bluff's edge.

Up and over a 110-foot hill, there are incredible views of the seaside surroundings. Dropping to the right, the path leads through a wetland area before returning to additional viewpoints in an area famous for its flowering daffodils. Soon, the trail descends on an increasingly sandy footpath and reaches a popular beach access point. Veer right, hike past Clayhead Swamp, and arrive at a parking area. To return to your car, walk the dirt road 0.4 mile to Corn Neck Road. Turn left and then immediately right onto West Beach Road. It is 0.5 mile from here to the West Beach parking area.

3 BLOCK ISLAND GREENWAY

Distance: 5.8 miles loop
Hiking time: 4 hours
Difficulty: Moderate
Low point: 0 feet
High point: 190 feet
Season: Year-round
USGS map: Block Island, RI
Information: Block Island Conservancy

Getting there: For directions to Block Island, refer to Hike 2. From the junction of Old Town Road and Center Road in the southern half of Block Island, drive south on Center Road 0.4 mile toward the airport. On the right, use the small parking area for Nathan Mott Park.

In 1972, the Block Island Conservancy was formed to "maintain habitat for birds and animals, to protect the views of hills rolling to the sea, [and] to provide walking trails and quiet recreation to islanders and visitors." In the intervening three-and-a-half decades, the Block Island Land Trust, The Nature Conservancy, and the state of Rhode Island have joined with this initial effort to produce tremendous results. Nowhere on Block Island are land protection successes more evident than in the meandering paths that form the Greenway. The Greenway trails cover 15 miles of terrain on the island's southern half, including Rodmans Hollow, a glacial outwash that was one of Block Island's earliest conservation victories.

Descending west from the kiosk, the path leads across a grassy meadow and over a small knoll. Down into the heart of the "Enchanted Forest," a long wooden staircase rises to a trail junction. To the right the path journeys north toward New Harbor. Turn left and follow the signs to "Turnip Farm." Swing right where a path diverges left to Old Mill Road and make your way to a large field. Listen for the guttural call of the ring-necked pheasant and the more melodious "drink your teaaaa" emanating from resident rufous-sided towhees.

Turn right and parallel a stone wall. Soon a spur leads north to an outlook. Continuing straight, enter the Elaine Loffredo Memorial Preserve. Named for a victim of TWA flight 800, the

View from the bluff above Black Rock Beach

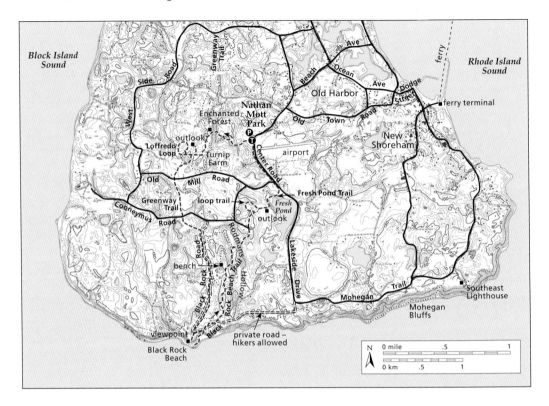

preserve trail loops quickly around and returns to the start. From the outlook spur, follow the main trail south and then turn right, where a sign points to "West Side Road." Remain on this path as it bends left, passes a private house, and arrives at Old Mill Road.

Continue straight across the pavement and rise through an open field. The trail soon bends right over a stone wall, and reaches Cooneymus Road. Carefully cross this busy thoroughfare and join the path on the far side as it leads east and soon ends on Black Rock Road (no vehicle traffic allowed). Follow this way south for nearly a mile, past two entrances to the Rodmans Hollow Preserve, until it reaches the land's end. To the right a path leads a few hundred feet to a dramatic bluff with excellent ocean views. Turning left, the grassy path reaches a small private parking area. Here a rough trail descends steeply to Black Rock Beach. This is a quiet place to enjoy the spectacular scenery, but please watch your step.

From the beach access trail, follow the dirt drive north. Turn right on a wider road. After passing over a small rise, arrive at a trailhead on the left. Follow this route north into Rodmans Hollow. At a junction stay right and climb up a small hill to a second intersection. To the left a path leads quickly to a bench with excellent views. This area is especially vibrant in May, when the shadbush is flowering. Take the trail east, descending steeply into the heart of the hollow. Bear right onto the Fresh Pond Trail. Ascending out of the depression, the route passes through a development and gradually leads to the edge of the large pond. Wrapping around the north shore, the trail ends on Lakeside Drive. Turn left and walk 0.4 mile up Center Road to reach the Nathan Mott Park parking area.

If you are looking for an additional area to explore, consider visiting nearby Mohegan Bluffs and Southeast Light. Both offer exceptional views of Block Island.

4 SACHUEST POINT

Distance: 2.5-mile loop
Hiking time: 1.5 hours
Difficulty: Easy
Low point: 0 feet
High point: 30 feet
Season: Year-round
USGS maps: Sakonnet Point, RI; Newport, RI
Information: Rhode Island National Wildlife Refuge Complex

Getting there: From Route 138A in Middletown (just east of the Newport line), drive east 1 mile on Purgatory Road. Bear right at a sign for Sachuest Beaches and continue 0.4 mile to another intersection. Stay right and drive 1.1 miles past the refuge entrance to a visitor center and parking area.

Open year-round during daylight, the 242-acre Sachuest Point National Wildlife Refuge is an oasis for migratory birds and an inviting winter home for the multicolored harlequin duck. For the better part of four centuries, the area was farmed and grazed; during the Second World War the U.S. Navy established a rifle range and communications center; today Sachuest Point, surrounded by popular sand beaches, is a quieter destination for those seeking a more wild experience on the Rhode Island shore. In addition to nature viewing, the refuge provides a scenic 2.5-mile loop with countless scenes of crashing surf.

Approaching Island Rocks, a winter home for harlequin ducks

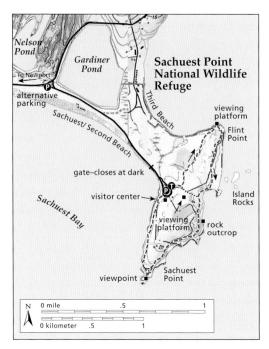

Sachuest Point National Wildlife Refuge

Sachuest enjoys one of New England's higher concentrations. Use the platform's scope to get a closer look at these beautiful creatures.

Continuing south along the shore, wrap around a cobble beach to shore access number 6, where you can cautiously meander to a scenic rock outcrop—an excellent lounging location. To the south, the trail slices through an open field where an interpretive sign describes resident songbirds. After entering thickets, arrive at a three-way intersection. Follow the short spur left as it emerges onto rocky Sachuest Point with its excellent views of the Rhode Island shore including the famous Newport Cliffs.

The 0.6-mile journey back follows the eastern shore of Sachuest Bay. Enjoy the many surf views as the waves flow toward alluring sandy beaches. Check out the visitor center before leaving; it is open from 10:00 AM to 4:00 PM on weekends throughout the year and every day (except Wednesday) during warmer months. The nearby beaches, while popular for swimming, are also excellent places to explore from late autumn to spring. Also, the nearby Cliff Walk in Newport, paved and very popular, provides excellent views of the ocean and incredibly large mansions.

From the parking area's east side, follow a short path south to a viewing platform. Here, you can gaze upon the distant waters and, perhaps, spot a northern harrier gliding over the gentle terrain. Returning to the trailhead, follow the main path east to a junction. Straight ahead, you can quickly reach the shoreline; however, for now turn left to enjoy a longer journey. Winding along the edge of a field, the path slowly swings right and arrives at Flint Point and a second viewing platform. Perched atop the small structure, you can survey the large bay and rocky shoreline for sandpipers.

Follow the level trail south past the first of eight ocean access points. Only use these well-marked locations to approach the water. The route quickly reaches a third viewing platform near Island Rocks, a collection of small near-shore islands. This is an excellent location to spot harlequin ducks—blue, white, and chestnut-colored birds that nest in Canadian streams but winter along the North Atlantic's turbulent coast.

Rocky Sachuest Point is surrounded by water on three sides.

A sandy beach along the Grassy Point Nature Trail

5 NINIGRET REFUGE

Distance: 4.5-mile loop
Hiking time: 2.5 hours
Difficulty: Easy
Low point: 0 feet
High point: 25 feet
Season: Year-round
USGS map: Quonochontaug, RI
Information: Rhode Island National Wildlife Refuge Complex

Getting there: From Westerly, take Route 1 east. After entering Charlestown, continue 3.3 miles (1.7 miles past the exit to East Beach) and turn right into the west entrance of Ninigret National Wildlife Refuge. Follow the driveway straight a few hundred feet to a large parking area.

Once the home of the Charlestown Naval Auxiliary Landing Field, today Ninigret National Wildlife Refuge consists of 409 acres of diverse habitat. With more than 4 miles of trails to explore grasslands, shrub lands, wooded swamps, freshwater ponds, and the state's largest saltwater pond, the refuge is an ideal spot to discover many resident and migratory birds. This flat, 4.5-mile loop traverses the entire refuge. Although you will occasionally stumble across a former runway,

it is amazing to witness how quickly nature reclaims previously developed landscapes.

Begin on the Foster Cove Loop Trail as it departs the northwest corner of the parking area. Circling in a southerly direction, the well-trodden path descends past a forested wetland on the left and soon arrives at a viewpoint of the cove. Approach the water quietly and perhaps stumble upon some feeding waterfowl. The route continues past a second view of the cove and in 0.5 mile arrives at a junction where the Foster Cove Loop bears left. Continue straight and join the Cross Refuge Trail as it emerges onto an old runway. To the right, the runway leads 0.4 mile to a fishing access point.

Hike across the runway and reenter a more natural backdrop. The trail cuts between small freshwater ponds that provide excellent wildlife viewing opportunities. Winding around the wet ground, the path enters a landscape dominated by grass and shrubs. Stay on the wide swath to minimize potential contact with ticks, but enjoy the many birds serenading the trail.

Across a second runway, the path straightens and in 0.3 mile reaches a sign for the Grassy Point Nature Trail. Turn right and follow the gravel path as it swings through the forested terrain. At a T intersection bear right and join the scenic path as it meanders down the narrowing peninsula before arriving at the Grassy Point viewing platform. Along the way there are markers describing the human and natural history of the area, as well as many views of the large saltwater Ninigret Pond.

Return along the Grassy Point Nature Trail and follow it to a small loop in the refuge's northeast corner. Circling a small wetland, the loop provides additional views of Ninigret Pond and the opportunity to spot egrets, herons, and other shorebirds. Head past the east entrance parking area and turn left, rejoining the Cross Refuge Trail (alternatively, the paved Charlestown Runway Trail leads 0.8 mile back to the parking area but provides little shade). Follow the Cross Refuge Trail back to the Foster Cove Loop's eastern half. After paralleling the old runway, the flat path soon ends at the trailhead.

For additional hikes in the area, consider the nearby 8-mile Vin Gormley Trail. (See the USGS map.) It leaves from the Burlingame State Park Campground and circles Watchaug Pond on trail and road. Also, nearby 3-mile East Beach, a very popular swimming beach fronting Ninigret Pond, provides an excellent location for sandy, oceanside walking during colder months.

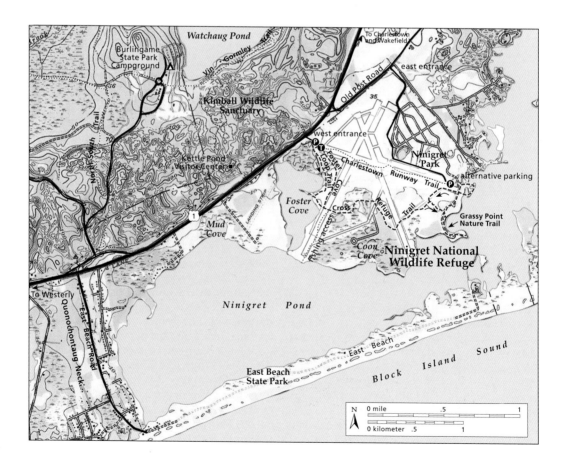

Undeveloped Bluff Point Beach is nearly one mile long.

6 BLUFF POINT

Distance: 4.5-mile loop
Hiking time: 3 hours
Difficulty: Easy
Low point: 0 feet
High point: 115 feet
Season: Year-round
USGS map: New London, CT
Information: Connecticut Department of Environmental Protection

Getting there: From Interstate 95 in Groton, take Exit 88 and head south 1.1 miles on Route 117. Turn right onto Route 1, drive 0.2 mile to a traffic light, and then turn left onto Depot Road. Continue 0.3 mile and stay straight. Go under the railroad tracks and drive 0.3 mile to a large parking area.

At 800 acres, Bluff Point State Park is the largest piece of conservation land on Connecticut's shore. While purchased by the state in 1963, the point was acquired in 1644 by John Winthrop, Jr., one of Connecticut Colony's first governors. This 4.5-mile loop circles past Winthrop's former homestead before arriving at scenic bluffs that line the rocky point. Before returning to the trail-

head, enjoy a pleasant half-mile diversion along an undeveloped sandy beach. For those seeking further adventure, Bluff Point State Park also offers additional miles of unmarked paths along the quiet shores of Mumford Cove.

The trail begins near a picnic area, beyond the gate. Quickly arrive at the start of the loop and stay left. Rising abruptly up the slope, the woods road soon levels under a canopy of towering trees, where paralleling stone walls offer a glimpse into an agrarian past. Nearly 1 mile from the start, arrive at the Winthrop homestead. Today, all that remains are portions of the stone foundation. Here, an unmarked route leads east toward Mumford Cove. It follows an old road 0.4 mile to an interesting rock formation, swings

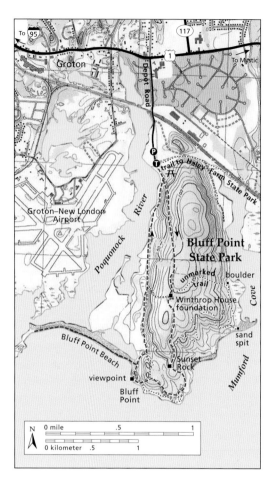

right to a spur that leads to a quiet sand spit, and then winds over undulating landscape for 0.75 mile before returning to the main trail.

Remaining on the more popular and straightforward route, bear right at the homestead area. After passing a connector to the lower path diverging west, the upper trail leads easily down the wide footway. In 0.5 mile reach a short spur right to Sunset Rock, exposed granite that is now shaded by the surrounding trees. Beyond the interesting geologic feature, arrive at the first of many unmarked paths that lead left to the water's edge. Follow the main trail as it winds west around the point to the top of scenic bluffs more reminiscent of the Maine coast than Connecticut.

Dropping north, the trail leads to the eastern end of 1-mile-long Bluff Point Beach. Occasionally, soft footing may slow you down; however, journeying at least 0.5 mile along the picturesque extension of the point provides an excellent perspective of the bluff and offers ideal locations for picnicking.

The 1.2-mile return trek to the parking area exclusively follows the lower trail. The terrain is generally flat with countless views of the adjoining marshland. In this area, you are most likely to notice the nearby airport. Fortunately, the occasional noise does little to undermine the abundant natural beauty.

7 STEPSTONE FALLS

Distance: 3.4 miles round-trip
Hiking time: 2.5 hours
Difficulty: Easy
Low point: 175 feet
High point: 330 feet
Season: Year-round
USGS map: Voluntown, CT
Information: Rhode Island Division of Parks and Recreation

Getting there: From the junction of Routes 3 and 165 in Exeter, follow Route 165 west 2.8 miles and then turn right onto Frosty Hollow Road (near church—see map for Hike 8). Follow this dirt road 1.5 miles, then turn left onto Austin Farm Road (not maintained in winter). Drive 2.2 miles to the parking area on the right.

Located in the northwest corner of Arcadia Management area, Stepstone Falls is Rhode Island's most scenic waterfall. A wonderful choice for visitors of all ages, this hike is enjoyable year-round, but is especially alluring in the spring with water rushing, wildflowers bursting into bloom, hungry deer browsing, and abundant songbirds warbling. In addition to its many natural charms, the journey also highlights numerous historical features including two mill sites, stone walls, and the remains of a quarry. (Note: The state has specific blaze-orange requirements for visitors during hunting season, and road access may be limited during winter.)

Begin along the Ben Utter Trail (which coincides with Rhode Island's North–South Trail) and follow

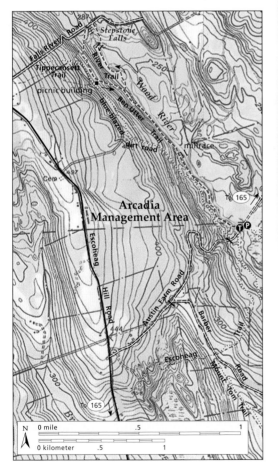

Springtime at Stepstone Falls, Rhode Island's highest waterfall

its yellow blazes through a wooden fence. Remaining close to the Wood River's west bank, the gentle path provides ample views of the sparkling water crashing over fallen logs and around small rocks. A bridge leads over a boggy area and soon the trail approaches a former mill site. Climb rock steps up the remains of soil once used to dam the river, and then descend back to the water's edge where the mill's stone remnants are evident.

Continuing upstream, the trail swings left to a junction with a blue-blazed dirt road frequently used by horseback riders. Veer right and proceed across a level area flanked by mountain laurel. Ahead, the path crosses an old millrace on a small bridge that leads to the structure's dilapidated foundation and drained pond. After a second bridge leads over the race once again, follow the stone-lined former waterway as it winds back to the main river.

Rising left, the route leaves the rushing waters and enters a quieter forest backdrop. Skirting along the bottom of a rock-filled slope, arrive at a junction. Turn right onto the white-blazed River Trail, which quickly drops into a marshy grove. Wrapping around reflective pools of water, the trail reaches the Wood River one last time. With the sound of Stepstone Falls crashing nearby, cross the large wooden bridge to the east side

and head upstream. While not extremely high, the falls are impressive for their abrupt drop and abundant water. There are numerous places to sit and enjoy the scenery, including a number of granite slabs locally quarried.

Follow the River Trail to Falls River Road. (This dirt road is open year-round and provides alternative access to the area, reached by taking Escoheag Hill Road off Route 165.) An arched bridge leads to a parking area. Rejoin the Ben Utter Trail (it coincides with the blue-blazed Tippecansett Trail) and rise gradually south to the site of a picnic building that has seen better days. Here the Tippecansett Trail leaves right to Camp Yawgoog on the Connecticut border. Stay on the Ben Utter Trail as it turns sharply left beyond the picnic area (do not go straight) and descends quickly to the River Trail junction. Retrace your steps from here.

8 ARCADIA LOOP

Distance: 12.6-mile loop
Hiking time: 8 hours
Difficulty: Moderate–Strenuous
Low point: 130 feet
High point: 460 feet
Season: Year-round
USGS map: Hope Valley, RI
Information: Rhode Island Division of Parks and Recreation

Getting there: From the junction of Routes 3 and 165 in Exeter, follow Route 165 west 2.5 miles and turn left into the small parking area.

At more than 14,000 acres, the Arcadia Management Area is Rhode Island's largest public land unit. Popular year-round, it is managed for multiple uses including hiking, fishing, hunting, mountain biking, and horseback riding. This 12.6-mile circuit uses the area's best hiking trails en route to Arcadia's most interesting natural features. The gently rolling terrain allows for a relaxing pace. For those seeking shorter excursions, this all-day loop can easily be broken into three or more half-day adventures. (Note: The

state has specific blaze-orange requirements for visitors during hunting season.)

Begin south on the Arcadia and Mount Tom Trails. Quickly, the Arcadia Trail diverges left. Remain on the Mount Tom Trail and turn right. Rise gradually past stone walls through an intersection of woods roads that includes the North–South Trail, a 75-mile path that begins at East Beach (see Hike 5) and ends at the Massachusetts border. After crossing Summit Road, the trail rises over a low hill, passes small wetlands, and arrives at a large parking area near the banks of the Wood River. Follow the driveway to Route 165 and turn left. After crossing the river, head south into a second parking

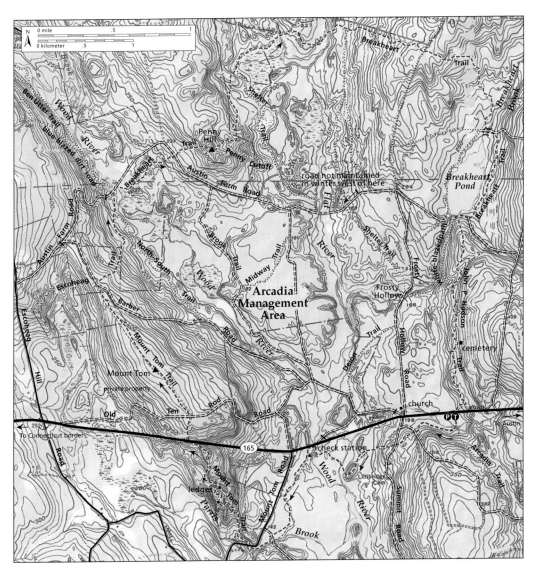

area, near a check station. Stay on the Mount Tom Trail as it departs southwest through an actively managed pine stand. The route turns sharply left and follows a dirt road 0.1 mile. Bear right before crossing a bridge and proceed along the banks of Parris Brook, a peaceful, flowing stream.

Once across paved Mount Tom Road, the day's most difficult section ensues. Rising rapidly up steep ledge-covered slopes, the path reaches the first of many pleasant viewpoints. Continue

carefully, up and around the uneven terrain past many interesting geologic formations. A sudden descent leads to busy Route 165. Cross with care—it is hard to see oncoming traffic from the west—and rejoin the path as it climbs quickly to a four-way intersection. To the left a road leads to private property, while to the right Old Ten Rod Road descends toward the check station. Continue north past the indiscernible, 460-foot high point of Mount Tom and an assortment of glacial erratics. The level trail soon drops to Barber Road.

Breakheart Pond is an excellent place to picnic.

Cross the dirt road and follow the Escoheag Trail as it gradually descends northeast. After intersecting the North–South Trail and reaching Austin Farm Road, turn right over the Wood River (past Hike 7's start), and pick up the Breakheart Trail as it enters the forest on the right. Briefly following the running water, the path swings left and ascends a long esker. Continue straight over Austin Farm Road and begin a short but steady climb to a small ledge atop Penny Hill. While the views are limited, the topography is interesting.

Descend steeply only to climb more easily to a second knoll. Here the Penny Cutoff leads right. Remain on the Breakheart Trail as it swings north.The path drops moderately past a junction with the Shelter Trail before arriving at the first of two Flat River crossings. Over the next

1.5 miles, the trail traverses undulating terrain before heading south along Breakheart Brook. Upon reaching a dirt road, bear sharply left and cross the meandering brook over a wooden bridge. Up a small rise, turn right onto another woods road and head south. Paralleling the side of Breakheart Pond, the path does not approach the water just yet. Continue right at another intersection of woods roads and hike west to reach the pond's south shore. As you approach the outlet and a small dam there are excellent views of the expansive pond. This is also a nice location to picnic and enjoy the area's serenity.

The final leg of the day's circuit is along the John P. Hudson Trail. This yellow-blazed route leads south up an evergreen-draped ridge—to the right a white-blazed path follows the brook more closely. After cresting the hillside, join a woods road briefly, but quickly bear right, reaching the south end of the white-blazed alternative. Continue south through an area thick with mountain laurel. Past a small cemetery and a short spur right to the site of a former fire tower, the trail drops to a parking area. Cross Route 165 to return to your car.

If you are looking for shorter excursions along this loop, consider parking at the check station and combining the Mount Tom Trail with Barber Road (roughly 6 miles); parking at Breakheart Pond and combining the Breakheart and Shelter Trails with Austin Farm Road (roughly 5.5 miles); or parking at the John P. Hudson Trailhead and combining that trail with the white-blazed-trail alternative (roughly 3 miles). There are countless other possibilities with the many trails and roads in the area. (Note: Many of the roads have gates that are open at certain times of the year, allowing vehicular access.)

9 WALKABOUT TRAIL

Distance: 8-mile loop
Hiking time: 5 hours
Difficulty: Moderate
Low point: 560 feet
High point: 720 feet
Season: Year-round
USGS map: Thompson, CT
Information: Rhode Island Division of Parks and Recreation (fee)

Getting there: From the Rhode Island–Connecticut border, follow Route 44 east 2.4 miles (or from the junction of Routes 100 and 44 in Chepachet, take Route 44 west 4.4 miles), then turn north on the George Washington Management Area road. Drive 0.3 mile, then left into a large parking area near a forest building, campground, and sandy beach.

The Walkabout Trail was created in 1965 by more than 300 Australian soldiers. These young men found themselves in Rhode Island with little to do for more than a month until the destroyers their country had purchased were ready to ship off and head "Down Under." The state's Division of Forestry asked the Aussies if they were interested in helping develop the 3489-acre George Washington Management Area. They responded positively, and today, thanks to their

Parts of Wilbur Pond suggest northern New England.

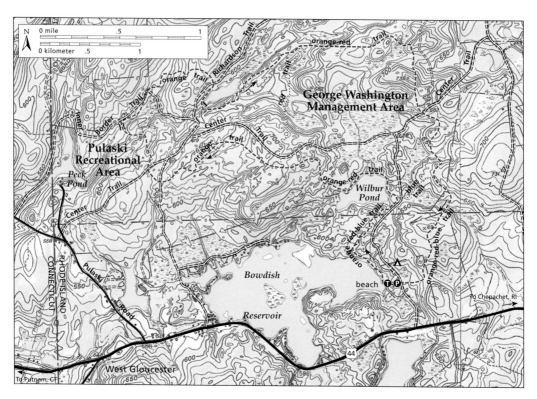

efforts, visitors to this rural corner of Rhode Island can enjoy a trail network that includes three interconnected loops of 2, 6, and 8 miles. Whichever length you choose, the dense forests, gently rolling terrain, scattered boulders, and wildlife-filled wetlands provide an ideal backdrop to connect with the "spirits of the land" much as aboriginal Australians have for centuries while on their walkabouts (didgeridoos are optional).

The loop begins at a large rock with a plaque commemorating the trail. Following the eastern shore of Bowdish Reservoir, the orange-, red-, and blue-blazed trail meanders easily to a ledge with nice views of the shimmering water. Swinging right, gradually climb past impressive boulders and campsites. After approaching a dirt road for a second time, the 2-mile blue-blazed loop veers right. Continue on the orange-and-red-blazed trail as it makes its way quickly to the banks of Wilbur Pond.

Hugging the shoreline, the route visits many interesting vistas of the scenic water body, which, save for the campsites on the far shore, leaves you with an impression of greater remoteness. Returning to higher, drier terrain, make your way under the growing canopy. Beyond a small, forested wetland the 6-mile red-blazed trail departs north. Stay left and follow the orange blazes. The relaxing journey winds through pine saplings and down easy grades before reaching the first of five dirt road crossings. In the winter many of these roads are used by cross-country skiers.

Continue straight and then straight again over a more heavily used road (the Center Trail). Descending past a gate, the wider route leads through a darkening hemlock grove. Be sure to follow the orange markings while swinging left, then cross a small stream with the help of a long wooden bridge. Beyond, turn sharply right at a sign that points left to the Pulaski Recreational Area. Paralleling the small stream at first, the trail leads gradually to a third road crossing and then enters more hilly terrain. Upon crossing the Richardson Trail (a fourth dirt road), follow the orange blazes right toward the shore of a wildlife marsh frequented by waterfowl. At the south end, the trail bears left and leads across an earthen dam.

Up a small hill, bear left along more marshland. Soon, the red trail rejoins from the right and the two continue up the day's most significant rise. The brief climb ends at a well-used sitting rock. Down the far side, make your way through an ever-increasing array of mountain laurel. The footing here can be wet, but logs laid perpendicularly across the path ease the way. After a final road crossing, the route rises and reconnects with the blue trail. From here the three colors lead gently for nearly a mile back to the parking area.

10 DEVILS HOPYARD

Distance: 2.7 miles loop
Hiking time: 2 hours
Difficulty: Easy–Moderate
Low point: 170 feet
High point: 450 feet
Season: Year-round
USGS map: Hamburg, CT
Information: Connecticut Department of Environmental Protection

Getting there: Take Exit 70 off Interstate 95 in Old Lyme. Follow Route 156 north 8.7 miles. Turn right onto Route 82 and in 0.2 mile turn left at sign for Devils Hopyard State Park. Drive 3.4 miles and turn right. Take immediate left into parking area for Chapman Falls.

Tucked away in south-central Connecticut, 860-acre Devils Hopyard State Park is a perfect destination for a relaxing family hike. This 2.7-mile circuit is packed with fascinating natural features and just enough challenge to reward young hikers with a sense of accomplishment. With a

A covered bridge leads hikers safely over the Eightmile River.

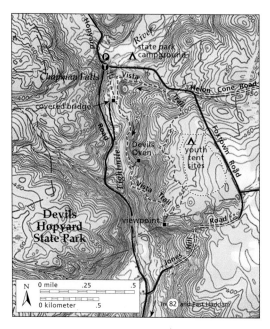

Evergreen trees tower over the Vista Trail.

maze of additional trails located in the park's western half and camping facilities available, the park has plenty to keep you busy throughout any weekend. While visiting, try to figure out which of many explanations is the true origin of the park's name: perhaps the mispronunciation of a local farmer named Dibble who grew hops for beer, or a fable used to describe how an angry, pitchfork-packing deity stamped the deep potholes in the river upon dampening his long, pointy tail.

The hike begins on the banks of the recently designated Wild and Scenic Eightmile River. Cross Helon Cone Road, join a wide path, and quickly reach a view of Chapman Falls. Cascading down a steep rock ledge, the falls are a popular attraction. A few hundred feet ahead, a spur leads left to its base. Make your way down the hill to a picnic area. Here a picturesque covered bridge leads across the river to the start of the Vista Trail, a 2.3-mile loop.

Turn right and proceed under the shady canopy of towering evergreens. The trail weaves up, over, and around numerous boulders and rock outcrops. Occasionally the route is a bit unclear because of the trampled ground surrounding it. However, it does not veer too far up the hill;

when in doubt, search for one of many orange blazes. After approaching the peaceful, meandering river for a final time, begin an easy climb to a signpost. To the left, an extremely steep, but very short, climb ends at the Devils Oven, a dark hole in the rock face. Carefully return to the main trail.

Continuing south, begin the most difficult climb of the hike. The 0.4-mile ascent leads out of the darker evergreen forest, soon cresting atop a brighter, oak-dominated ridge. With the hammering of woodpeckers in the air, follow a short spur south to a ledge with bucolic views of nearby forested hillsides. Back on the main path; turn right onto a stretch of flat terrain. Weaving along the ridge, cross two small streams. Stay right at the second one and climb briefly to an intersection where a path leads right to a youth camping area. Remain on the Vista Trail.

Once through a pine grove and over a stone wall, begin a final 0.5-mile descent along a small, bubbling brook. Past clusters of mountain laurel in the narrowing valley, the path levels off where an overgrown trail leads to a view of Chapman Falls. The Vista Trail swings south and quickly returns to the covered bridge. Retrace your steps past the falls to the parking area.

11 WOLF DEN

Distance: 4.2-mile loop
Hiking time: 2.5 hours
Difficulty: Moderate
Low point: 320 feet
High point: 710 feet
Season: Year-round
USGS map: Danielson, CT
Information: Connecticut Department of Environmental Protection

Getting there: Take Exit 93 off Interstate 395 in Killingly. Follow Route 101 west 4.9 miles. Turn left, just before the intersection with Route 44, onto Wolf Den Drive. In 0.7 mile turn left onto a long driveway. The parking area is located near the Mashamoquet Brook State Park office building on the right.

The famous—some may argue infamous— location where Connecticut's gray wolf met its final demise, Mashamoquet Brook State Park is a tranquil 900-acre oasis in eastern Connecticut. Today's park is an amalgam of three previous independent parks, including Wolf Den State Park, first protected by the Daughters of the

Table Rock, reminiscent of a sacrificial altar, is covered by dense vegetation.

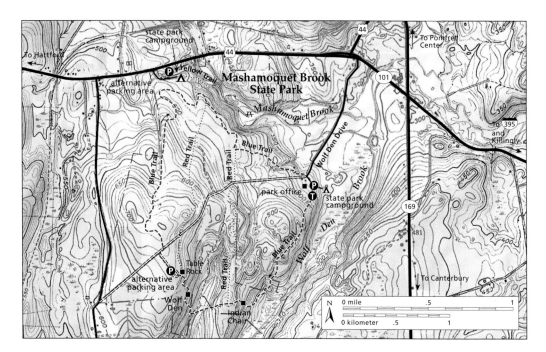

American Revolution in 1899. This 4.2-mile loop snakes around gnarled rock outcrops, gradually descends beneath tall forest stands, and hugs the upper slopes of a steep river valley. It is a moderate half-day journey and an ideal choice throughout the year for hikers of all ages.

The Blue Trail begins south of the parking area near a small sign. Leading left, the grassy route quickly swings right between pine trees. Veer left, cross the stone wall, and begin the first of many short climbs on the hike's first 1.5 miles. While the most difficult section of the hike, this is also the most intriguing. Follow the path as it curves up and over the rolling terrain, passing one quirky geologic feature after another. It is hard to imagine today, but the glacier that moved here—not so long ago—has clearly left its mark on this rocky landscape.

One mile from the parking area, pass Indian Chair, a small seat-shaped rock perched atop a wooded ledge. After crossing a small bridge, the trail climbs quickly and reaches the Wolf Den on the left. Here a plaque commemorates Israel Putnam's 1742 slaying of the state's final wolf. Mr. Putnam proceeded to build upon his lore by becoming a famous major general

during the American Revolution. A final ascent leads to a spur right to Table Rock, a large flattened boulder reminiscent of a sacrificial altar.

From Table Rock, continue on the Blue Trail, which leads through a parking area and down a long dirt driveway. At the main road, turn right and then immediately left back onto an old woods road. At this point a relaxing 1.4-mile stroll ensues. Gradually descending the hilltop, the trail passes an open field on the left and then drops more quickly into a fern-filled forest. The route bends sharply right, crosses a small stream, and reaches a trail junction. To the left a path leads to a campground, a popular picnic area, and swimming holes on Mashamoquet Brook, so named by Native Americans because of its excellent fishing.

Continuing right, follow the trail as it remains on the rim above a steep slope. With the sounds of picnickers echoing from below, press on past two intersections with the Red Trail. Stay left at both junctions. After the second one, the trail parallels a number of stone walls and eventually reaches Wolf Den Drive. Cross the road and follow the driveway back to the parking area.

12 BREAKNECK POND

Distance: 7.4-mile loop
Hiking time: 5 hours
Difficulty: Moderate–Strenuous
Low point: 640 feet
High point: 990 feet
Season: Year-round
USGS maps: Southbridge, MA; Eastford, CT; Westford, CT
Information: Connecticut Department of Environmental Protection (fee)

Getting there: Take Exit 74 from Interstate 84 in Union. From the south, turn right off the exit and quickly turn right again onto Route 171. From the north, take the first two lefts from the exit, then drive over the interstate and turn right onto Route 171. Once on Route 171, drive 2.3 miles south and bear left at a junction with Route 190, remaining on Route 171. In 1.4 miles turn left into Bigelow Hollow State Park. Drive 0.6 mile to a small parking lot on the left near a picnic area.

Tucked away on the northern border of Connecticut, Breakneck Pond is surrounded by a 9000-acre conservation area comprised of Bigelow Hollow State Park and adjacent Nipmuck State Forest. In Algonquin, Nipmuck describes a land "abounding in small ponds and streams." Aptly named, this thickly forested region is also dissected by a series of long, narrow ridges decorated with lichen-draped boulders, carpets of fern fronds, and the gnarled limbs of prolific mountain laurels. One of eastern Connecticut's largest undeveloped spaces, the area offers many trails of various lengths. This recommended circuit is one of the longer options and provides an excellent overview of the region's many natural features.

Begin on the east side of the road near a kiosk. Up a small bank, the trail splits. Stay right on the East Ridge Trail as it follows an old roadway. In 0.2 mile turn right at a small signpost. Up a low rise, veer left onto a grassy road that soon leads through an open area. After returning to the woods

The Ridge Trail snakes through an oak-filled forest.

and beginning to climb, immediately look for the blue-blazed Nipmuck Trail. (Note: Many of the intersections in the park, including this one, lack signs, but the trails are clearly blazed.) Head north, for a 0.8-mile trek through serene forest surroundings. Upon reaching Breakneck Hill Road, turn left to an intersection. Remain on the Nipmuck Trail as it enters the forest to the northwest.

Quickly, the path reaches Breakneck Pond's south shore. Here a splendid 1.6-mile journey begins along the pond's east side. Passing numerous viewpoints and interesting rock formations, the route tunnels under abundant mountain laurel (typically blooming in mid- to late June). After reaching a small lean-to, follow the dirt road north into Massachusetts. Swing

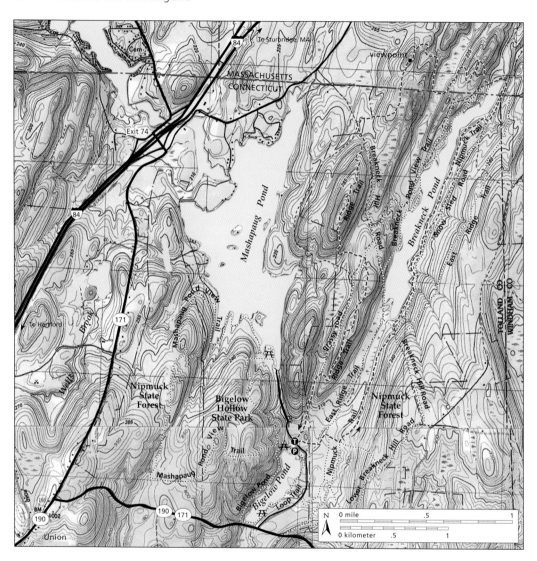

left at the pond's northern tip and take in the final reflections off the deep blue water. Upon crossing a small stream, branch right onto the blue-and-orange-blazed Ridge Trail.

Heading up a small but steep incline, the route winds over ledges to a large beaver pond. Continue south around the wetland, then swing north into a hillside labyrinth of large boulders. Once through, a steep climb ensues to the top of a forested ridge and a pleasant viewpoint of surrounding hillsides. Descend rapidly and pass a spur left that leads to caves and ledges (use

extreme caution if you choose to explore). Beyond, the trail veers sharply right and reaches Breakneck Hill Road. The route follows this road southeast past a small gate and then branches right onto a second road up the hillside. Quickly depart the second road and head southwest onto a narrower pathway. Leading 0.9 mile over a more gradual, sedge-covered ridge, the journey eventually descends to and crosses a grassy road. For the final 1.5 miles, the trail traverses the narrowing ridgeline, descends abruptly to a small stream, and soon reaches the parking area.

13   GREATBLUE HILL

Distance: 3.4-mile loop
Hiking time: 3 hours
Difficulty: Moderate–Strenuous
Low point: 170 feet
High point: 635 feet
Season: Year-round
USGS map: Norwood, MA
Information: Massachusetts Department of Conservation and Recreation

Getting there: Take Exit 3 off Interstate 93 in Milton. Drive north on Blue Hill River Road for 0.5 mile, and then turn right onto Hillside Street. Continue 0.6 mile to parking area on right (across from reservation headquarters). Additional parking is available near Houghtons Pond 0.3 mile south.

The highest point in the 7000-acre Blue Hills Reservation, Great Blue Hill offers expansive views east to the Atlantic Ocean, north to the Boston skyline, and west across the hills and ponds of southeastern New England. The Blue Hills, named by European sailors who spotted their rolling silhouettes on the horizon, were home to

Great Blue Hill's stone tower offers excellent views of Boston.

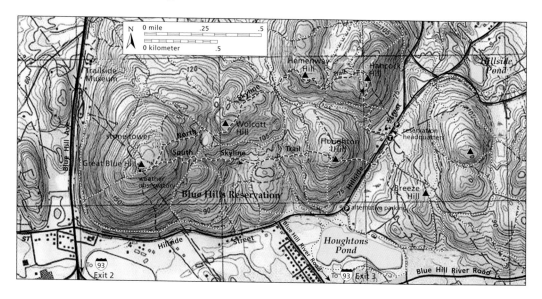

generations of Native American inhabitants. In fact, Massachusetts means "people of the great hills." After centuries of European settlement, the state decided to acquire the hilly terrain in 1893 and set it aside as one of Massachusetts' first public outdoor recreational areas. Today, the popular reservation, less than 10 miles from downtown Boston, offers more than 125 miles of hiking trails. This 3.4-mile loop is a rocky, challenging introduction to an area that begs further exploration.

After carefully crossing Hillside Street, head up the paved road to reservation headquarters. Here, you can purchase a map of the area clearly outlining the complicated maze of trails in the reservation. On this described hike, the map may help pinpoint your exact location at the many intersections encountered; however, it is not essential, as the entire loop follows the well-marked, blue-blazed Skyline Trail.

Follow the dirt road past the headquarters. Soon, the North Skyline Trail veers right onto a steep rocky slope and ascends to the first of many outcrops atop Hancock Hill. Under the shadow of jets approaching Logan Airport, continue over the rounded summit and descend into a small depression. Swinging right, the path scales the mostly wooded summit of Hemenway Hill, but then drops more rapidly down a ledge-covered

ridge. Watch your footing as you make your way to a major trail intersection.

Continue to follow the blue blazes straight ahead and easily up tree-covered Wolcott Hill. Another tricky descent leads to a forested wetland. Catch your breath for the final push to the summit ridge. Aided by rock steps, the initial climb slowly eases through a shady grove of evergreens. Emerge onto a series of ledges that leads to an interesting stone bridge, picnic area, and stone observation tower. A curling flight of stairs winds to an excellent view of Boston.

Follow the blue blazes south across the bridge and past a stone marker for the South Skyline Trail, to the summit weather observatory. Sitting on the 635-foot high point of Great Blue Hill, the observatory has a gift shop and museum that welcomes visitors for a small fee.

Return to the South Skyline stone marker and begin a steep, rocky descent. Past numerous viewpoints, the trail winds over a ledge back into a denser forest. A relaxing stretch ensues, across moderately undulating terrain. After paralleling a small stream, the path cuts through an interesting boulder. A final climb leads to limited views atop Houghton Hill. Carefully make your way down a final steep section that leads back to Hillside Street. Cross the road and follow it left to the parking area.

14 WALDEN POND

Distance: 2.5-mile loop
Hiking time: 1.5 hours
Difficulty: Easy
Low point: 145 feet
High point: 270 feet
Season: Year-round
USGS map: Maynard, MA
Information: Massachusetts Department of Conservation and Recreation (fee)

Getting there: From Main Street in downtown Concord, follow Walden Street south 1.3 miles. Go straight at intersection with Route 2 and continue 0.3 mile to the Walden Pond State Reservation parking area on the left. Parking is limited and access is restricted when the lot fills. Call in advance (978-369-3254), especially on summer days, to check status.

Perhaps the most famous kettle hole in the world, Walden Pond is the former home of Henry David Thoreau. This 2.5-mile circuit includes much of the popular Pond Path that circles Walden Pond, but also includes a brief diversion to a quieter corner of the reservation, where turtles sun on fallen logs and thrushes sing beside a shady cliff. In 1854, Thoreau wrote in *Walden*, "All change is a miracle to contemplate; but it is a miracle which is taking place every instant." While much has changed since 1845, the year Thoreau built a modest cabin near the pond's shore, the 462-acre forested reservation that surrounds the 100-foot-deep pond remains an evolving natural treasure in the heart of New England's most populated region.

Near the parking area are a nature museum, a replica of the Thoreau cabin, and signs to illustrate the natural and human history of the land. To reach the trailhead, carefully cross Walden Street and descend to the Main Beach area—this sandy spot and nearby Red Cross Beach are popular with swimmers. Join the Pond Path on the right. Immediately, the Sherwood Trail veers right. Along with the Ridge Trail, the two offer a quieter alternative route toward the Thoreau cabin site. Following the Pond Path, emerge onto Red Cross Beach and nice views of the glistening water.

The route reenters the forest and meanders pleasantly near the pond's edge, soon encountering an understandable but unfortunate element that surrounds much of the path—a recently installed metal fence that ensures all hikers remain on the trail and approach the pond only at designated spots. This is not the natural world that Thoreau knew, but neither was the heavily eroded shoreline that is slowly recovering.

Upon reaching Thoreau's Cove and a view of Wyman Meadow, grab the right spur that climbs to the former cabin site. All that remains now is a pile of rocks and a memorial to recognize Thoreau's importance to the area. Returning to the Pond Path, continue along the water's edge to Ice Fort Cove. Located near the railroad line,

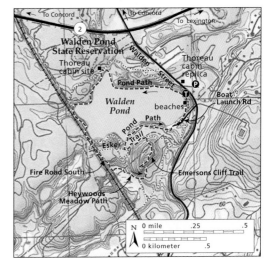

Walden Pond, a kettle hole carved by receding glaciers more than 10,000 years ago

this spot housed an excursion park built in 1866. Ascend the low ridge beyond the cove and pass near the active rail tracks.

After descending past Long Cove, leave the more crowded trail behind and proceed straight up the hill onto Fire Road South. A short, level jaunt is followed by a steep drop to the banks of Heywoods Meadow. Turn left and parallel the shore of this lush, wildlife-filled wetland. Roughly halfway around the meadow, follow an unmarked trail leading left, just before a large boulder. A short but steep climb soon ends atop Emersons Cliff. Though the views are limited, the lack of noise is welcome. Head north down the slope to the Esker Trail.

Turn left and follow this woods road for 0.1 mile. After the Esker Loop bears left, take the short trail right that connects to the Pond Path. Turn right and remain on this trail as it leads back to the Main Beach.

15 HELLCAT INTERPRETIVE TRAIL

Distance: 2 miles round-trip
Hiking time: 1 hour
Difficulty: Easy
Low point: 0 feet
High point: 30 feet
Season: Year-round
USGS maps: Newburyport, MA; Ipswich, MA
Information: Parker River National Wildlife Refuge (fee)

Getting there: From Route 1 in downtown Newburyport, follow Water Street (becomes Plum Island Turnpike) east 3.6 miles. Turn right on Sunset Drive, which is the first right after crossing Plum Island River. Drive 0.5 mile to the Parker River National Wildlife Refuge entrance. During warmer months, the refuge sometimes fills to capacity and entry is restricted, typically for several hours. Arrive early to avoid this inconvenience. The trail is located 3.5 miles on the right, just before the pavement ends.

The most famous bird-watching destination in New England, Parker River National Wildlife Refuge is comprised of 4662 acres of diverse seacoast habitats including sprawling sand beaches, ever-changing dunes, and abundant marshes. The combination of habitats and location make the refuge the ideal home and migratory rest stop for more than 300 species of birds. Crowded with birders during peak migration and beachgoers after piping plover nesting is completed (most of the beach remains closed from April to midsummer each year to protect the birds), the refuge is a wonderful year-round destination for those seeking short nature trails with amazing wildlife viewing areas. During colder months, opt for a long hike down the 6.5-mile beach, where crashing surf and scurrying sanderlings offer a soothing respite from the daily grind.

The Hellcat Interpretive Trail is the refuge's longest and provides an excellent introduction to Plum Island's human and natural history. Divided into two separate loops, the 0.8-mile Marsh Trail and the 0.6-mile Dunes Trail, the route is well marked and easily followed. Weaving along boardwalks throughout, the trails are especially intriguing in mid-May when dozens of songbird species can be easily spotted flitting about the vegetation.

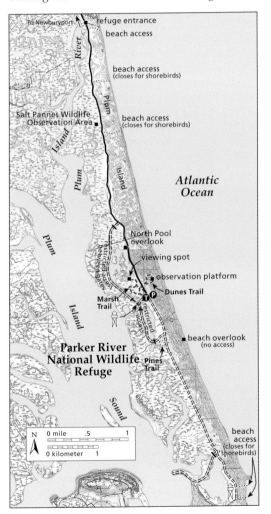

A boardwalk leads to the observation platform on the Dunes Trail.

The snowy egret is one of more than 300 bird species that have visited the refuge.

The highlight of the Dunes Trail, which crosses to the east side of the park road, is the staircase that rises to a long observation platform. From atop the dunes, there are excellent views up and down the island. The Marsh Trail, conversely, swings through a dense maze of tall reeds and remains deep in the vegetation throughout. To the north, a spur branches from the Marsh Trail and leads 0.1 mile to a wildlife viewing spot. A final stopping point on the Hellcat Trail is the lookout tower located to the west on the far side of a dike. This is a nice location to scan the area for herons, egrets, and waterfowl.

In addition to the Hellcat Interpretive Trail, Parker River offers a number of other wildlife viewing areas worthy of exploration: Salt Pannes Wildlife Observation Area is a popular spot for terns and ducks; the 0.3-mile Pines Trail offers nice marshland views; and of course the beach, when open, provides endless opportunities. When hiking along the beach, be sure to use only designated entranceways.

In addition to refuge lands, the southern tip of Plum Island is home to Sandy Point State Reservation. Containing a beach that remains open year-round, Sandy Point's parking area fills up quickly on summer days.

16 SOUTH PAWTUCKAWAY

Distance: 5.8 miles round-trip
Hiking time: 4 hours
Difficulty: Moderate
Low point: 260 feet
High point: 908 feet
Season: Year-round
USGS map: Mount Pawtuckaway, NH
Information: New Hampshire Division of Parks and Recreation (fee)

Getting there: From Exit 5 on Route 101 in Raymond, drive north 0.5 mile, then turn left at the light. In 0.1 mile, veer right onto Route 156. Drive 1.1 miles and then turn left onto Mountain Road. Continue 2.2 miles to the entrance on the left. The trailhead is located 0.4 mile beyond the tollbooth on the north side of Mountain Pond. Park on either side of the road, but pull off the pavement.

Pawtuckaway State Park is 5500 acres of prime conservation land in rapidly developing southern New Hampshire. In addition to a popular swimming area and campground located on the park's namesake 820-acre lake, Pawtuckaway also boasts excellent four-season hiking trails. At 908 feet, the rocky summit and fire tower atop Pawtuckaway's South Mountain provide 360-degree views that include four states. This 5.8-mile trek is an excellent choice for families and a great opportunity to spot resident wildlife.

Begin along the wide Round Pond Trail as it skirts past pleasant scenes of Mountain Pond. Up and over a small rise, stay alert for mountain bikers, and descend to a junction with the Mountain Trail. Swing right, following the signs that point to the fire tower. After crossing a small stream, proceed over the gently rolling terrain. Across a small saddle, the path cuts between two forested wetlands, climbs up and over the mountain's main ridge, and then descends to a trail junction. Turn right here onto the South Ridge Trail.

Ascending gradually at first, the path crosses stone walls, signs of the pastureland that once dominated the area. Weaving up and around the increasingly large ledges, the trail stays left and begins a steep climb up a shady mountain slope. The workout is soon rewarded. As the route

levels, the forest thins. Emerge onto a semi-open ridge with views of Middle Mountain. Just ahead, find the summit fire tower—a popular place on weekend days. The tower provides sweeping views, and the resident ranger offers excellent information on the park's history and natural features. Interestingly, the three Pawtuckaway Mountains are remnants of an ancient caldera.

From the tower, remain on the South Ridge Trail as it leads northeast (rather than the more popular Tower Trail, which descends rapidly to the northwest). This lightly used path curls past an assortment of uniquely shaped rocks and exposed granite. After scaling a small knoll, the path descends quickly to the edge of a quiet beaver pond. Leaving the water's edge, make your way to a three-way intersection. To the right the South Ridge Trail continues to Round Pond. Bear sharply left instead and

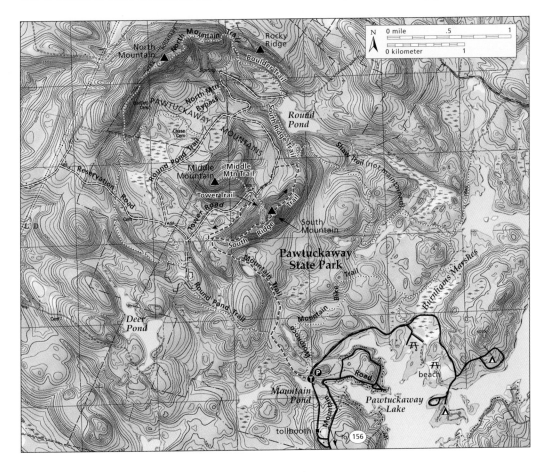

The South Ridge Trail climbs past impressive ledges.

follow the wide path 0.2 mile to Tower Road.

Follow the dirt road southwest 0.3 mile to a large parking area on the left. The first trail leaving left climbs to the fire tower. Take the second one, which descends into a grove of hardwood trees. After leveling off, the path visits a thick marshy area and then ends at the Mountain Trail. Turn left, pass the South Ridge Trail, and return to the parking area.

For a slightly longer hike, add a side trip to the top of Middle Mountain. The trail's beginning is one of the few New Hampshire locations to spot a cerulean warbler. If you are interested in a very long journey, consider following the South Ridge Trail to scenic Round Pond. Pick up the Boulder Trail here and then join the North Mountain Trail. Complete the nearly 10-mile circuit along the Round Pond Trail.

MONADNOCK–METACOMET

Mount Tom's dramatic cliffs rise abruptly from the Pioneer Valley.

Paralleling the Connecticut River Valley, the Monadnock–Metacomet landscape is noteworthy for its isolated mountain peaks (monadnocks), long scenic traprock ridges, and bucolic countryside. Along the region's river valleys, mill towns and large cities serve as regional hubs and cultural centers for numerous rural communities.

A handful of long-distance trails link the region's patchwork of public and private conserved lands. For more than 200 miles, the Sunapee–Ragged–Kearsarge Greenway, the Monadnock–Sunapee Greenway, and the Monadnock–Metacomet–Mattabesset Trail connect central New Hampshire with southern Connecticut. Similarly, the Wapack and Midstate Trails join to form a shorter 115-mile-corridor to the east. Offering rewarding four-season hiking, the region is especially attractive in spring and late fall when northern destinations are engulfed in winter-like conditions.

17 RAGGED MOUNTAIN

Distance: 6.1-mile loop
Hiking time: 4 hours
Difficulty: Moderate
Low point: 220 feet
High point: 761 feet
Season: Year-round
USGS map: Meriden, CT
Information: Connecticut Forest and Park Association

Getting there: Follow Route 71 (Chamberlain Highway) north from Meriden. Drive 3.7 miles past the Meriden–Berlin line and stay left, joining Route 71A. Continue 1.2 miles and then turn left onto West Lane. The trailhead is located 0.6 mile on the right. (Note: This popular trailhead is located near a residential area; please be considerate of the local homeowners and observe all parking regulations.)

At 761 feet, Ragged Mountain in central Connecticut forms one of the most dramatic of the state's many traprock ridgelines. The mountain's western cliff face, a popular hangout for rock climbers, provides an impressive panorama of rolling countryside. Surrounded by more than 500 acres of conservation land secured through donations to The Nature Conservancy and the Berlin Land Trust, and purchased with financial support from the federal Land and Water Conservation Fund,

Ragged Mountain's summit is a popular place for rock climbers.

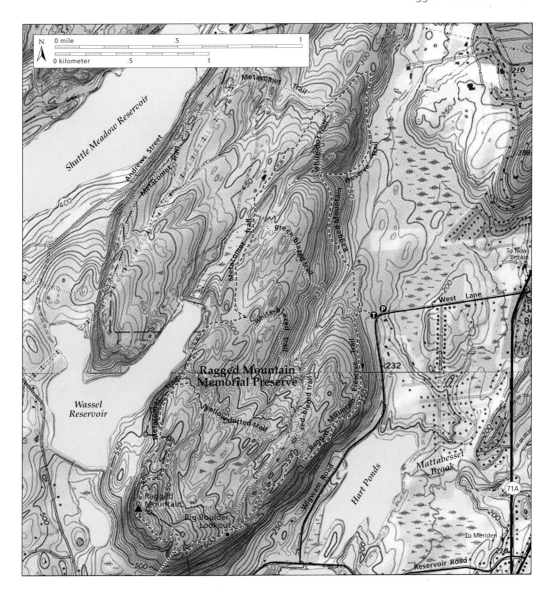

Ragged Mountain exhibits numerous rock outcrops with splendid aerial views of shimmering waters. Beginning from the West Lane trailhead, five paths connect to the Metacomet Trail, offering countless loop possibilities. This 6.1-mile circuit visits Ragged Mountain's most scenic spots, offering a challenge for hikers of all ages.

From the large "Ragged Mountain Memorial Preserve" sign, head 0.1 mile up the wide path to an area where four trails intersect. Stay to the far left and pick up the south branch of the Ragged Mountain Preserve Trail (blue-blazed with a red dot). Follow the 1.7-mile red-dotted trail up a short incline. Beginning on an old woods road, the trail eventually swings right and then left up to the first of many viewpoints. Looking across the Hart Ponds and south toward Meriden, the forested landscape forms a peaceful backdrop. Proceed over the uneven terrain. After passing a noteworthy, precipitous drop and the well-framed Big Boulder Lookout, the path rises to a junction with the Metacomet Trail.

Swing northwest and follow the blue-blazed path into a small notch. Scramble up the other side and make your way to Ragged Mountain's main ridgeline. Turning sharply right, the path soon reaches the wide-open summit atop an impressive cliff face. Here, enjoy the day's most expansive views, including the Hartford skyline to the north. Watch your step as you continue north—the summit area is often draped with ropes and other climbing gear. In fact, the cliff area is owned by the Ragged Mountain Foundation, a nonprofit that supports rock climbing.

Quickly returning to the shady forest, the Metacomet Trail descends gradually. Veer left and ascend a series of small inclines that lead to a lower ledge with excellent views of Wassel Reservoir. Drop past a junction, where a blue-blazed, yellow-dotted path leads right, and continue north, paralleling the water's edge.

Another climb leads to a flat ridge before descending abruptly right. Now on level terrain, proceed straight to a T intersection. To the right an infrequently marked white-blazed route leads 1 mile back to the parking area. If you have the energy continue left on the Metacomet Trail as it gradually winds past a green-blazed trail diverging right and soon reaches the northern branch of the Ragged Mountain Preserve Trail.

Turn right for the final 1.6-mile trek back to the trailhead. Descending slowly to the northeast at first, the path quickly swings south and drops off the ridge. Hike along the flat trail toward the side of a small stream. Here, the Ragged Mountain Preserve Trail turns sharply right and ascends to the top of a small seasonal waterfall. Continue south along the ridge. Eventually the route drops to a larger streambed. Make your way across to reach the four-way intersection that began the loop and the parking area beyond.

18 TALCOTT MOUNTAIN

Distance: 3.8-mile loop
Hiking time: 3 hours
Difficulty: Moderate
Low point: 415 feet
High point: 940 feet
Season: Year-round
USGS map: Avon, CT
Information: Connecticut Department of Environmental Protection

Getting there: From the junctions of Routes 185 and 178 in Bloomfield, follow Route 185 west 1.1 miles and turn right. Beginning in Simsbury at the junctions of Routes 202 and 185, follow Route 185 east 1.7 miles and turn left. After entering Penwood State Park, drive 0.1 mile and park on the right.

Rising above Hartford, Talcott Mountain and the rocky ridges north and south of it are prominent features protruding above the more gentle Connecticut River Valley landscape to the east. While similar to its mountainous neighbors, Talcott also stands apart thanks to the 165-foot Heublein

Tower that sits upon its summit. Built in 1914 by Hartford resident, German-born hotelier and restaurateur Gilbert Heublein, the tower provides one of the finest views in the Nutmeg State.

From the parking area, take your time crossing Route 185 to a sign for the Metacomet Trail. (One of Talcott Mountain's summits is named King Philip, the English name for Metacomet, a seventeenth-century Wampanoag sachem who battled New England colonists for two bloody years.) Start on this historic trail and gradually ascend along the Talcott Mountain State Park boundary. In 0.5 mile, swing right under a powerline and soon begin a modest descent to the

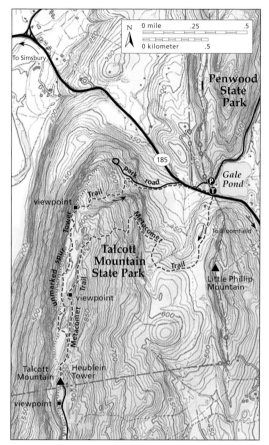

leading to the top. On a clear day, much of Connecticut can be seen as well as New Hampshire's Mount Monadnock to the north and the sparkling waters of Long Island Sound to the south. Hartford's skyline is especially impressive from this aerial location.

Before descending, check out the tower's many displays. Its history includes two noteworthy guests in the early 1950s: World War II hero and future president Dwight D. Eisenhower, as well as head of the Screen Actors' Guild and president-to-be Ronald Reagan. Also, just south of the tower check out the picnic area and a scenic viewpoint to the west.

For the return trip, follow the Tower Trail north. The wide pathway drops gradually for about a mile. For the most scenic descent, pick up the narrower spur that branches left. This more dramatic path follows closer to the edge of

north. Follow the wide trail to the base of the mountain, then proceed aggressively up a series of switchbacks. The terrain levels as the path turns abruptly left. Now on a narrower and more interesting route, weave along the spine past numerous ledges, including one with sweeping western views.

Soon, the Metacomet Trail intersects the more popular Tower Trail. Continue left 0.1 mile to the white monolith atop the summit. The Heublein Tower, maintained by a nonprofit preservation society, is open Thursday through Sunday in the summer and daily from Labor Day to the end of October. Access is free—donations accepted— and it is well worth climbing the many staircases

The Heublein Tower provides a spectacular view of Connecticut.

the mountain's western ledges before rejoining the main trail. Watch your step along the way and beware of the precipitous cliffs. The Tower Trail reaches a final viewpoint and then descends steeply 0.3 mile, ending at a large parking area.

Turn right and follow the paved park road back to Route 185. Turn right again and quickly reach the parking area. On return trips, use this location to explore Penwood State Park. The Metacomet Trail and other paths traverse this 800-acre preserve that offers many additional hiking opportunities.

19 PEOPLES FOREST

Distance: 4.8-mile loop
Hiking time: 4 hours
Difficulty: Moderate
Low point: 475 feet
High point: 1120 feet
Season: Year-round
USGS maps: New Hartford, CT; Winsted, CT
Information: Connecticut Department of Environmental Protection

Getting there: From the junction of Routes 44 and 181 in Barkhamsted, follow Route 181 north 1.1 miles. Stay on Route 181 and turn right across the Farmington River. Immediately turn left onto East River Road and drive 2.4 miles to the parking area on the left.

With the adjacent American Legion Forest, the Peoples Forest combines to form an impressive array of conserved lands on both sides of the Wild and Scenic Farmington River. Connecticut acquired the first portions of both forests in the mid-1920s. The American Legion Forest was donated to the state with the hope of demonstrating proper forest management. Around the same time, the Connecticut Forest and Park Association spearheaded an effort to assemble the Peoples Forest. Today, visitors flock to the area for swimming, fishing, and exploring the more than 10 miles of hiking trails that weave throughout. This nearly 5-mile loop showcases stands of old timber, scenic ledges, and tranquil wetlands.

Begin on the 1.2-mile Jessie Gerard Trail, near an old Native American settlement known as Barkhamsted Lighthouse. Take the left fork as it

Opposite: *Beaver Brook carves its way through the Peoples Forest.*

climbs steeply up 299 stone steps past tumbling water before cresting the ridge. Bear left through the mountain laurel understory and continue to climb steadily past three viewpoints, including Chaugham Lookout, an impressive perch above the Farmington River Valley. The path soon cuts between the large Veeder Boulders, bears right, and ends on Greenwoods Road.

Turn south and follow the road through the Big Spring picnic area. In a few hundred feet the Charles Pack Trail descends east. Follow this yellow-blazed trail under an impressive stand of hemlocks. In 0.5 mile, upon reaching Beaver Brook Road, turn left, cross the rushing stream, and then turn right into another picnic area. The Pack Trail continues east and for 1.5 miles winds up and over many slopes and crosses a handful of forest roads. After dropping toward a large marsh where an old foundation remains, the route makes its way to a crossing of Beaver Brook and ends at an intersection with the Agnes Brown Trail.

Follow the Agnes Brown Trail right and arrive at an unmarked spur to the water's edge—an excellent place to spot wildlife. Proceed along the orange-blazed path across level terrain near the shoreline. Upon reaching the pavement, follow it right 0.1 mile and then enter the forest east. At the pavement a second time, stay right once again, and in a few hundred yards the trail veers left off the road. Climbing over a low ridge and past a hidden wetland, the Agnes Brown Trail heads straight through a third road junction and soon arrives at a four-way intersection.

Follow the blue-blazed Robert Ross Trail right. It gracefully wraps around jagged ledges and at an unmarked intersection reaches the south branch of the Jessie Gerard Trail. Turn left, down the weaving switchbacks. Reach the road in 0.4 mile.

For some hikers or during winter conditions, the lower sections of the Jessie Gerard Trail may be too steep. If so, consider using the west branch of the Agnes Brown Trail, which begins 0.5 mile south of the Jessie Gerard Trail. Two other options are the east branch of the Agnes Brown Trail and the Robert Ross Trail; both begin near the forest's nature center.

20 HOLYOKE RANGE

Distance: 4.2-mile loop
Hiking time: 3 hours
Difficulty: Moderate
Low point: 470 feet
High point: 1106 feet
Season: Year-round
USGS map: Mount Holyoke, MA
Information: Massachusetts Department of Conservation and Recreation

Getting there: From the eastern junction of Routes 9 and 116 in downtown Amherst, take Route 116 south 5.1 miles into The Notch. Turn left into the large parking area.

Mount Norwottuck rises 1000 feet above the Connecticut River Valley on a long ridge of rocky peaks that formed from flowing lava millions of years ago. The centerpiece of Mount Holyoke Range State Park, the 1106-foot mountain is one of several scenic summits that are connected by a 10-mile section of the Metacomet–Monadnock (MM) Trail. A wonderful introduction to this low but prominent mountain range, this 4.2-mile loop includes many views as well as a trip to impressive caves once used as a hideout by defeated elements of the 1786 Shays' Rebellion. Choose this hike throughout the year for pleasant snowshoeing, blooming wildflowers, warbling songbirds, or brilliant foliage.

A hiker descends into the historic Horse Caves.

Pick up the multi-blazed main trail that departs east from the visitor center. The entire loop follows either the white-blazed MM Trail or the red-blazed Robert Frost Trail (a 33-mile route that links many natural features in the Amherst region). Descending quickly, the path leads around a large quarry. After the blue-blazed Laurel Loop diverges left, continue right, proceed under the powerlines, and reach a second intersection—this is the start of the loop. Turning right, follow the MM Trail as it leads swiftly up the hardwood-covered slope. Cresting the ridgeline, the incline lessens as the route swings east. Weave through the open forest for 0.5 mile to Norwottuck's summit. Looking north, there are expansive views beyond the skyline of the

University of Massachusetts to the southern peaks of the Green Mountains. Dropping southward a few dozen feet, the trail reaches a prominent ledge with equally impressive views to the east.

Leaving the summit, the route descends rapidly over loose soil. In no time, reach the top of the Horse Caves. Watch your step as the narrow path squeezes through the rocks and arrives beneath a massive overhang. Here, in the nooks and shadows, disgruntled farmers aligned with Daniel Shays scurried for cover. Their rebellious actions helped to thwart the Articles of Confederation and led to America's present-day Constitution.

From the caves, the trail leads gracefully along the gentle terrain and soon meets up once again with the Robert Frost Trail entering from the

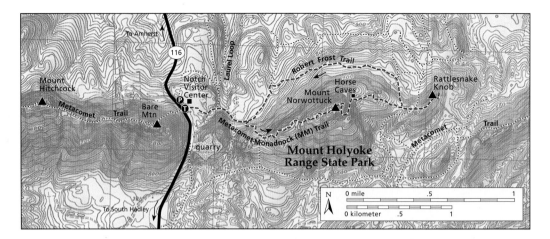

north. Continue east on the two trails as they simultaneously rise past a red town marker and in 0.2 mile arrive at a spur left to Rattlesnake Knob. Follow this short path to two scenic ledges, each with excellent views of the lush countryside.

Returning west to the previous intersection, take the Robert Frost Trail right as it descends from the ridge. In 0.1 mile, continue on the red-blazed path as it turns sharply left. Paralleling the MM Trail to the south, the Robert Frost Trail leads easily through a stately forest filled with scattered boulders. Continue west for roughly a

mile to a small stream. Once across, veer south to rejoin the MM Trail in 0.2 mile. Follow both paths right to return to the parking area.

Additional opportunities to hike in this region are great. From the parking area, the MM Trail leads west, over more rugged terrain, to scenic Bare Mountain in 0.9 mile and Mount Hitchcock in 1.8 miles. Farther east are the Seven Sisters and Mount Holyoke, popular destinations that can also be accessed from Skinner State Park. In total, there are more than 30 miles of trails to explore along the mountain range.

21 MOUNT TOM

Distance: 5.8 miles loop
Hiking time: 4 hours
Difficulty: Moderate–Strenuous
Low point: 550 feet
High point: 1202 feet
Season: Year-round
USGS maps: Easthampton, MA; Mount Tom, MA
Information: Massachusetts Department of Conservation and Recreation (fee)

Getting there: From the south, take Exit 17A from Interstate 91. Pick up Route 5 in Holyoke and head north 3.9 miles to Smiths Ferry Road on the left. From the north, use Exit 18 off Interstate 91 and turn right. Follow Route

5 south 3.5 miles to Smiths Ferry Road on the right. Smiths Ferry Road leads 0.3 mile to the Mount Tom State Reservation entrance and 1.4 miles farther to a parking lot on the right (just beyond a picnic area).

Mount Tom's rugged traprock cliffs provide the most dramatic views in Massachusetts' Pioneer Valley. Its long ridgeline, a popular destination for hawk migration enthusiasts, drops precipitously toward the setting sun. To the east, the 2082-acre Mount Tom State Reservation contains subtler mountain slopes draped in the shadows of tall, distinguished trees. Home to 75 percent of the state's reptile and amphibian species, the reservation offers more than 20 miles of diverse trails available for year-round exploration. This challenging 5.8-mile excursion visits many of the area's most scenic spots and includes the ridge's highest point. However, you could turn around near Deadtop's summit, reduce the trek by 2 miles, and still feel sufficiently invigorated.

Cross Smiths Ferry Road, and hike south on the Keystone Trail. Swinging east over level terrain, the path quickly arrives at Keystone junction. Turn right and follow the Keystone Extension 0.6 mile as it gently swings over low rocky hillsides and past diminutive wetlands. At the day's second four-way intersection, proceed straight on the DOC Trail. Here, a more aggressive climb begins. With increasingly rocky footing, the path levels, offers limited views, and circles around the high point of Whiting Peak, soon ending at the Metacomet–Monadnock (MM) Trail.

Turn left and reach the first of many spectacular vistas on the ridge's western flank. Perched high above Easthampton, the rocky outcrop offers 180-degree views of western Massachusetts. The 1.3-mile journey south to Mount Tom's summit includes consecutive, and often more dramatic, vantage points. While gaining little overall elevation, this section of trail contains frequent minor ups and downs and uneven walking surfaces; however, the payoff is well worth the effort. The most picturesque cliff face is located a few hundred feet west of 1100-foot Deadtop, only 0.3 mile from the DOC Trail junction. (Note: The final section of trail to Mount Tom is on private land, and while the summit offers excellent views, it is covered in communications towers and old buildings.)

The final 1-mile leg of the day's journey begins north along the MM Trail. Ascend the southern side of Whiting Peak and pass yet more scenic viewpoints on the left. The route descends abruptly, at first down a narrow, natural rock staircase and then along a shady, forested slope. As steepness gives way to level ground, continue straight through yet another four-way intersection, and in 0.3 mile reach Smiths Ferry Road. Follow the pavement right 0.1 mile to the parking area.

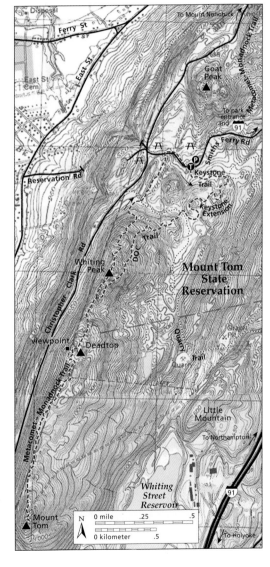

A hiker enjoys the views near Deadtop. (Photo by Maria Fuentes)

22 TULLY MOUNTAIN AND LAKE

Distance: 8.8 miles round-trip
Hiking time: 6 hours
Difficulty: Moderate–Strenuous
Low point: 650 feet
High point: 1163 feet
Season: Year-round
USGS maps: Mount Grace, MA; Royalston, MA
Information: The Trustees of Reservations

Getting there: Take Exit 17 off Route 2 in Athol and turn north onto Route 32. Follow Route 32 north 5.8 miles through the center of Athol into Royalston. Turn right into a parking area 0.1 mile beyond a large dam.

Hidden in north-central Massachusetts, the Tully Lake area is a delightful outdoor destination. The Tully Trail, the area's hiking centerpiece, is a 22-mile circuit connecting a patchwork of state, federal, and private conservation areas that contain small mountains, picturesque falls, and sprawling wetlands. This 8.8-mile trek uses a portion of the long-distance route and forms two hikes in one, both 4.4 miles round-trip. The first hike ventures to Tully Mountain's summit ledges for pleasant views of pastoral landscapes, while the second visits roaring Doanes Falls while circling Tully Lake's glistening waters. Either is alluring separately; however, combined they form a classic adventure especially attractive in the fall. (Note: Parts of the Tully Lake Trail may be underwater during spring or after heavy rain.)

Begin by following the Tully Trail along Route 32 north a few hundred feet. Turn left onto Royalston Road, which descends quickly to a trail sign. Head right up a small rise and across private land. Swinging west, the trail crosses a small stream, then enters a state-owned wildlife management area. Through the dark forest, emerge at a junction of two woods roads, where the narrower trail veers right at a 45-degree angle. Wrap around a boulder-covered ridge, then down to another woods road. The path leads straight through a pleasant white pine grove and soon arrives at a junction. Turn sharply right onto a wider footway and climb steadily north. Curling back to the south, the straightforward ascent

departs the Tully Trail and proceeds straight for the final climb. Beyond the high point, drop a few dozen yards to the top of Tully's impressive summit ledges and 180-degree views of Mount Monadnock, the Wapack Ridge, numerous lakes, and south toward the Quabbin Reservoir.

Retrace your steps 2.2 miles to the parking area to initiate the day's second journey. The loop around the lake descends east 0.1 mile to the water's edge. For 1.6 miles, the Tully Trail winds north and east, while passing various unmarked spurs that lead to the shore. While mostly flat, the path rises over an occasional slope or esker. After approaching Stewart Road, the trail swings south along a narrow peninsula and then veers left to arrive at the Tully Lake Campground. Managed by the membership-based land conservation organization The Trustees of Reservations (TTOR), this overnight facility is a popular destination for hikers and paddlers.

Follow the trail east 0.2 mile as it uses Stewart Road to cross the Tully River. Once across, the Tully Trail swings left into a parking area; stay straight and pick up the Doanes Falls Trail a few

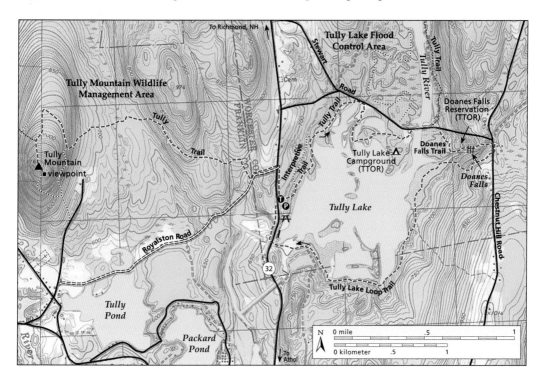

The last of Doanes Falls' many roaring drops

hundred feet on the right. The Doanes Falls Trail climbs aggressively 0.5 mile through a splendid TTOR reservation that showcases the impressive series of cascading falls. Remain on the trail and heed the warnings; swimming is not allowed, but thankfully quiet contemplation, photography, and inspiration are.

Upon reaching Chestnut Hill Road, follow the pavement right 0.1 mile to the rerouted Tully Lake Loop Trail. No longer near the brook, the path winds gradually down the steep hillside and soon levels off. For 1.5 miles the trail hugs the shore; walk quietly to spot resident waterfowl. Follow the well-blazed path over mostly flat terrain. Once through a habitat restoration area and past a disc golf course, climb to the top of the dam. Follow Route 32 north 0.2 mile to reach your car.

23 WACHUSETT MOUNTAIN

Distance: 4.4 miles round-trip
Hiking time: 3 hours
Difficulty: Moderate–Strenuous
Low point: 975 feet
High point: 2006 feet
Season: Year-round
USGS maps: Sterling, MA; Fitchburg, MA
Information: Massachusetts Department of Conservation and Recreation

Getting there: Take Exit 25 off Route 2 in Westminster. Turn south onto Route 140. Drive 2.3 miles and turn right onto Mile Hill Road. In 0.5 mile turn right onto Bolton Road.

The Wachusett Mountain State Reservation parking area is located 0.3 mile on the right (just beyond the trailhead on the left).

The highest mountain in southern New England east of the Connecticut River, Wachusett Mountain, or "Mountain Place," is the heart of a 3000-acre state reservation surrounded by hundreds of acres of additional public and private conservation land. With more than 17 miles of hiking trails, there are multiple opportunities to explore the mountain, which is covered with extensive areas of old-growth forests. In fact, some trees on Wachusett Mountain's sweeping slopes are as old as 350 years, having germinated from seeds cast down as the Pilgrims were establishing their roots in Plymouth. A great destination for hikers of all ages, the mountain today provides four seasons of exploration with summit views stretching from Boston's skyscrapers to the Berkshires.

Begin the journey on the Bolton Pond Trail. The route veers right twice before reaching the banks of the pond's small outlet stream. Remain near the rushing water and quickly reach the base of a small dam and the quiet, wooded pond. From here, the trail swings left, begins a moderate climb, and soon arrives at Balance Rock, a fascinating remnant of the last ice age. Arriving on the left is the Balance Rock Trail, a section of the 92-mile Midstate Trail. Nearly half of this described hike follows the Midstate Trail. Marked with yellow triangle blazes, the route bisects Massachusetts from Mount Watatic (see Hike 24) to the town of Douglas.

Leaving Balance Rock, ascend the Old Indian Trail. Across a dirt road, head up the steeper slope and in 0.2 mile turn right onto the Semuhenna Trail. Winding through cool, shady forests, the path makes its way around the mountain's ski

Closed to the public, Wachusett's tower rises high above the summit.

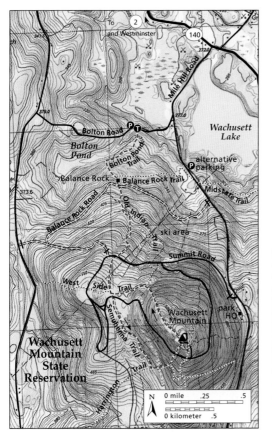

slopes and across the paved summit road, eventually intersecting the West Side Trail. Continue straight through a picnic area and over the paved summit road a second time. Upon circling a small pond, quickly emerge into a stand of towering trees, where you will find yellow birch and red oaks that are hundreds of years old. Continuing below the rocky summit slopes and near a small brook, the Semuhenna Trail ends at a junction with the Harrington Trail.

Turn left to begin the final 0.3-mile ascent up the Harrington Trail. This toughest climb of the day leads over rock, past a viewpoint spur, and across the paved road before ending at the base of a tall fire tower. The busy summit offers splen-

did views, particularly during autumn's peak foliage. For a quieter experience, venture here in winter when more people seek the groomed trails below.

Start the descent along the Old Indian Trail. Leaving the north side of the parking area, descend past a chairlift station. The trail leads away from the slopes, gradually across ledges and through stunted forests. After a more pronounced drop, turn left onto the West Side Trail (the Old Indian Trail continues straight and provides an alternative route when the ski area is closed). Follow this path 0.3 mile back to the Semuhenna Trail. From here, turn right and retrace your steps to the beginning.

24 MOUNT WATATIC

Distance: 2.9-mile loop
Hiking time: 2 hours
Difficulty: Moderate
Low point: 1250 feet
High point: 1832 feet
Season: Year-round
USGS map: Ashburnham, MA
Information: Massachusetts Department of Conservation and Recreation

Getting there: The trailhead and parking area are located on the north side of Route 119 in Ashburnham, 1.7 miles east of the New Hampshire border and 1.4 miles west of the junction of Routes 101 and 119.

The southern terminus of the 21-mile Wapack Trail and the northern terminus of the 92-mile Midstate Trail, Mount Watatic's domed summit provides extensive views of eastern Massachusetts and southern New Hampshire. With the mountain destined to be yet another telecommunications facility in early 2000, members of the Ashby and Ashburnham Land Trusts organized the "Campaign for Watatic" to protect its unique natural and scenic qualities. In 2002, the campaign succeeded in the permanent protection of the summit, which today forms the heart of a nearly 1000-acre collection of conserved lands. Thanks to

these efforts, outdoor enthusiasts can forever enjoy this scenic mountain named for an Algonquin word meaning "wigwam place." Watatic makes visitors feel at home throughout the year.

The 1.1-mile ascent begins on Old Nutting Hill Road. Past a small wetland, reach a trail junction in 0.2 mile. Remain on the Wapack and Midstate Trails by veering right off the old road. Over a small ridge and around a bend, descend briefly to a stream crossing. Beyond, the path carves through a large rock split in two and then begins a steadier climb up a hemlock-covered ridge. At the base of a small ledge, the trail briefly leads left, then circles to the top of the rock face and views of Mount Monadnock. Continue to a scenic vista south toward Wachusett Mountain before reentering the evergreen forest. Up the shady slope, the route passes a dilapidated shelter and soon rises to the mostly open summit ending on the Granite State's Pack Monadnock Mountain. Established in 1923, the Wapack Trail provides many day-hiking opportunities, thanks to the volunteer efforts of the Friends of the Wapack.

To reach the parking area, turn left by rejoining Old Nutting Hill Road. After passing through an intersection where the State Line Trail leads right to the New Hampshire border, stay left for the final 0.7-mile journey. While the road is eroded in places, the corridor is wide and easy to follow.

Hemlocks shade much of Watatic's lower slopes.

with its extensive views. On a clear day, the Boston skyline is visible on the eastern horizon. To the southeast a short spur leads to a slightly lower summit outlook.

The loop resumes along the Wapack and Midstate Trails, which descend briefly northwest on an old service road but in a few dozen feet head left near state wildlife sanctuary signs. Winding down through the mixed hardwood forest, the trail parallels a long stone wall. After leveling off, scale and traverse Nutting Hill's rocky but mostly viewless summit. Reach a trail junction, following a brief descent. Ahead, the Midstate Trail concludes in 0.5 mile at the New Hampshire border, while the Wapack Trail continues for nearly 20 miles over a number of scenic peaks,

25 MOUNT MONADNOCK

Distance: 4.8 miles round-trip
Hiking time: 4 hours
Difficulty: Strenuous
Low point: 1470 feet
High point: 3165 feet
Season: April–November
USGS maps: Monadnock Mountain, NH; Dublin, NH
Information: New Hampshire Division of Parks and Recreation

Getting there: From Dublin, follow Route 101 west 0.4 mile and turn left onto East Lake Road (just before Dublin Pond). Drive 2.1 miles (East Lake Road becomes Marlborough Road) and then turn left onto Old Troy Road. Continue 1.8 miles to parking area on right. The final 0.9 mile is rougher and not maintained in the winter.

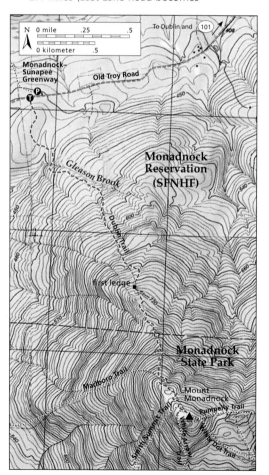

Behind Japan's Mount Fuji, Monadnock is considered the second most climbed mountain in the world. Its name is derived from Native American words that are now used to describe any mountain with a unique geologic formation that stands high above its neighbors. Mount Monadnock's size, relative solitude, and barren summit, most recently torched by overzealous wolf hunters in the nineteenth century, provide some of the finest views in New England. A vast trail network scales the many rocky ridges that emanate from the high point, with most visitors conquering the peak from the Monadnock State Park entrance on the east. The 2.4-mile Dublin Trail that rises from the northwest is a scenic, quieter alternative that also serves as the southern terminus of the Monadnock–Sunapee Greenway, a nearly 50-mile trail that offers countless day-hiking excursions.

The start of the Dublin Trail, like much of Mount Monadnock, has been protected with the help of the Society for the Protection of New Hampshire Forests (SPNHF). In 1915, SPNHF protected the first 600 acres of what is now more than 4000 acres of conserved land around the mountain. Much of the Dublin Trail is still owned by the statewide land trust, but New Hampshire manages it as if it were part of the state park.

Leaving the west corner of the lot, the trail crosses the dirt road and meanders over a low

A small pool reflects barren summit rocks.

ridge. Swing right on an old woods road and cross Gleason Brook. Veering left, wind up the narrower footway, briefly along the bubbling stream. The route climbs steadily up the ridge. As the incline increases, so too does the amount of rock and ledge. Bear right after a long, straight pitch and enter a darkening evergreen forest. The shade will soon be interrupted by the first of many openings along the ridge, roughly 1.5 miles from the start. Catch your breath and enjoy the western views of Vermont.

The final 0.9-mile climb to the summit becomes progressively more scenic with each step. From one open ledge to the next, each vista becomes grander and more expansive. At the same time, the sections of intervening forest grow thinner and shorter until the path emerges once and for all onto open rock. Watch your footing throughout. The hike requires minor scrambling. Kids of all ages should find it challenging but fun. Above tree line, follow the "D" painted on the rocks below. Marking the Dublin Trail, the letter will be joined by other letters as the Marlboro and White Arrow Trails enter from the right.

While you most certainly will not be alone at the summit, there are many places to spread out and enjoy the seemingly endless views in all directions. Be sure to follow the Dublin Trail on the way down—the other paths lead to distant parking areas. Take your time and, as many before you have done, savor a rewarding day on this spectacular mountain.

26 MOUNT CARDIGAN

Distance: 5.2-mile loop
Hiking time: 4 hours
Difficulty: Strenuous
Low point: 1380 feet
High point: 3121 feet
Season: Year-round
USGS map: Mount Cardigan, NH
Information: New Hampshire Division of Parks and Recreation

Getting there: From Bristol, take Route 3A north to the southern tip of Newfound Lake. Turn left near a stone church and follow West Shore Road 1.8 miles. Continue straight onto Fowler River Road. Turn left at an intersection in 1.2 miles. Drive 1 mile and turn right in Alexandria. In 0.2 mile veer right and continue 3.8 miles on Shem Valley Road. After crossing a brook, bear right on a dirt road that leads 1.4 miles to the Appalachian Mountain Club's (AMC) Cardigan Lodge. Parking is available on the left.

Mount Cardigan's bald granite dome towers over the western side of New Hampshire's Newfound Lake. From its summit, views abound—from Mount Monadnock on the Massachusetts border to the Presidential Range in the heart of the White Mountains. Don't let Mount Cardigan's relatively low elevation fool you; the trails

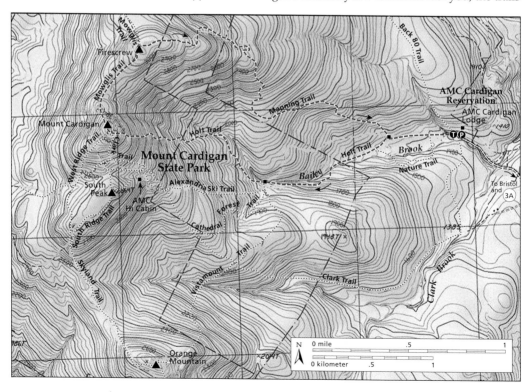

Tricky when wet or icy, Cardigan's exposed granite is an ideal hiking surface when dry.

ascending the summit are as steep and challenging as many that scale New England's highest peaks. The mountain also provides a tremendous variety of options. Many visitors choose the shorter, state park hikes beginning in the west; however, the more interesting trails ascend from the AMC lodge in the east. This hike attacks the mountain's steepest face and concludes by traversing its most scenic ridge.

Begin up the wide, well-traveled path near the lodge. Surrounded by 1200 acres of conservation land owned and managed by the AMC, the lodge and nearby campsites, as well as a rustic cabin high on the mountain, are available for overnight stays. Contact AMC for more information or to make reservations. The loop begins in 0.3 mile where the Holt and Manning Trails diverge. Stay left and continue paralleling Bailey Brook. In 0.5 mile a bridge leads to the other side and soon ascends to Grand Junction.

To the left, you can follow more gradual routes to the top, including the Clark Trail via the Cathedral Forest Trail. For a more vigorous and challenging journey, continue straight on the Holt Trail. At first relatively level near the shrinking stream, the trail abruptly changes and wastes little time scaling the extremely steep, rocky slopes. Through the thinning forest, the path makes its way up smooth ledges—Cardigan is a mountain to avoid in rain or ice. Watch your footing, be prepared to use your hands, and enjoy the expanding views. A final scramble ends atop the polished, barren summit. From the base of the fire tower there are 360-degree views of the surrounding terrain, which appear endless on the clearest of days.

In addition to abundant beauty, the oft-breezy summit is frequently teeming with fellow hikers. When you have had your fill of either, or the constraints of time have set in, begin the descent north along the Mowglis Trail. After an initial steep drop, follow the ridgeline trail 0.6 mile through a saddle and up to the start of the Manning Trail. Stay right and quickly reach the Firescrew. This flat, barren ridge offers continual vistas over generally relaxing terrain; its name describes the shape of the smoke that emanated from the 1855 fire that burned much of the mountain. Following a few short descents, pass over a final open ledge and across a small stream. Steeply descending a narrow pine-covered spine, the trail swings left and meanders back to the Holt Trail. Turn left and return 0.3 mile to the trailhead.

BERKSHIRES–TACONICS

Summit pines frame a Taconic view from Monument Mountain.

With the highest elevations in Massachusetts and Connecticut, the Berkshire–Taconic region forms a western barrier between New England and New York's Hudson River Valley. Running in a north–south direction, the region includes some of the oldest mountain ridges in New England. The region is also home to an abundance of quintessential New England villages and inns.

While largely forested, the Berkshire–Taconic area is noteworthy for its steep slopes, scenic cascades, and a scattering of prominent rock outcroppings. Many of these dramatic features occur along or near the Appalachian Trail as it leads north toward Vermont. This excellent year-round destination is the perfect location to warm up for more challenging excursions in northern New England.

27 MACEDONIA RIDGE TRAIL

Distance: 6.7-mile loop
Hiking time: 5 hours
Difficulty: Moderate–Strenuous
Low point: 700 feet
High point: 1357 feet
Season: Year-round
USGS maps: Ellsworth, CT; Amenia, NY
Information: Connecticut Department of Environmental Protection

Getting there: From Route 7 in Kent, follow Route 341 west 1.8 miles. Turn right onto Macedonia Brook Road. In 0.8 mile stay left at the fork. Drive 0.7 mile more and park in the small picnic area beyond the bridge crossing Macedonia Brook.

Macedonia Brook snakes through a scenic valley in western Connecticut. Bordered by steep ridges, the brook forms the core of a 2300-acre park that began with a 1552-acre donation to the state in 1918. While most hikers who venture here opt for the less-than-1-mile ascent of scenic Cobble

The final climb to Cobble Mountain on a beautiful summer day

Mountain, this 6.7-mile loop provides greater variety, solitude, and more numerous wildlife viewing opportunities. With camping sites in the park and lodging nearby, a trip to this beautiful corner of Connecticut can easily be extended with other adventures to nearby Kent Falls and pleasant treks along the Appalachian Trail.

From the trailhead, follow the Blue Trail west up a steep slope. Passing the first of many blue blazes marking the entire loop, it is hard to imagine the more industrial activities that once took place here, including cider, grist, and sawmills as well as an iron forge. A couple of switchbacks lead to a small brook crossing. Bear right and emerge upon an ever-increasingly open series of outcrops. As you continue climbing, each step offers wider views of the forested valley sprawling below. Return to the shady forest canopy and proceed over minor ups and downs. At 1.6 miles from the start, near an intersection with the White Trail, ascend a rocky slope that leads to the top of Cobble Mountain and 180-degree views encompassing the Catskill Mountains of New York and the southern Taconic Range.

The loop descends rapidly; watch your footing around a steep, forested ledge. Soon, the path arrives at a small saddle and a junction with the Green Trail. Staying left, follow the blue blazes up to another pleasant view of the Macedonia Brook Valley. Once over the ridge, the trail winds gradually down to a woods road. Turn left and in about 100 yards go straight across another road onto a grassy lane. In 0.4 mile briefly turn left onto a paved road. Near Hilltop Pond, the trail veers east, up a steep, hemlock-covered slope. Descending past stone walls and through dense ferns, make your way to the banks of Macedonia Brook.

Go left on a dirt road, cross a bridge, and then immediately swing right, back into the forest. The gradual terrain of the loop's eastern section begins to dominate. After heading east up a woods road, the blue-blazed route swings south and pleasantly leads over an undulating ridgeline for nearly 2 miles, with other paths joining from left and right. The final descent begins through semi-open oak forests, but as the trail falls northwest a last time, the canopy closes. A few more steps, and the gurgling sounds of Macedonia Brook can once again be heard.

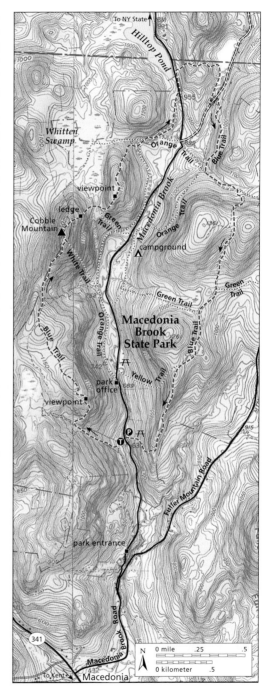

28 MOHAWK MOUNTAIN

Distance: 6.2 miles round-trip
Hiking time: 4 hours
Difficulty: Moderate
Low point: 1400 feet
High point: 1683 feet
Season: Year-round
USGS map: Cornwall, CT
Information: Connecticut Department of Environmental Protection

Getting there: The parking area is located on the south side of Route 4 in Cornwall, 1.3 miles east of the junction of Routes 4, 43, and 128, and 4.1 miles west of the junction of Routes 4 and 63 in Goshen.

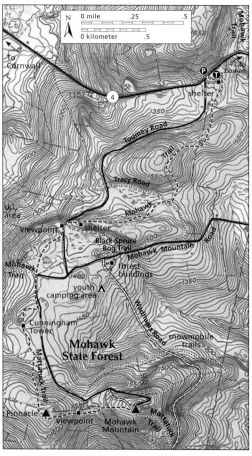

More noteworthy for its alpine skiing, Mohawk Mountain is also a pleasant hiking destination in the center of a 3700-acre state forest established in 1921. The peak's gentle slopes are covered with thick forests occasionally interrupted by openings offering delightful snapshots of the region's rolling terrain. The day's journey passes numerous historical features and provides an optional visit to a black spruce bog—very rare for Connecticut, but more common farther north. From the 1683-foot summit an expansive view north to Bear Mountain and the Berkshires awaits.

From the parking area, veer left on a dirt road near a plaque commemorating the Civilian Conservation Corps work here in the 1930s. Turn right, before reaching the picnic area, onto the blue-blazed Mohawk Trail, a former section of the Appalachian Trail. Today, the Mohawk Trail can be combined with the rerouted Appalachian Trail to complete a multi-day 35-mile backpack loop. Past a shelter, the trail reaches an interesting rock formation shrouded in mountain laurel. Swing right and begin a modest climb up a low ridge. Down the other side, the route crosses the overgrown Tracy Road, used in the winter by cross-country skiers. Continue west over relaxing terrain, and in 0.5 mile you'll reach a second shelter and Toumey Road beyond—1.3 miles from the start. Cross the road to a striking western viewpoint of the Catskills.

Ascend the road briefly, then turn right as the path winds across ski slopes and around a chairlift, to a trail junction. Bear south on the blue-blazed Mattatuck Trail (the blue-blazed Mohawk Trail continues west). Through the parking area, follow Toumey Road straight for 0.2 mile before veering right, back into the

The Civilian Conservation Corps left a significant mark on Mohawk State Forest.

forest. The remaining 1-mile section passes a number of interesting features, including Cunningham Tower. Built in 1915, the stone tower once provided excellent views of the area, before the trees grew taller around it. After passing an old well, the trail meanders over the wooded Pinnacle and through a fern-carpeted meadow with limited views. The final climb to the high point ends along a dirt road. Despite the communications towers (not open to the public) and worn-down buildings, the grassy summit is an excellent place to lounge and enjoy the scenery,

particularly on a crisp autumn day.

Retrace your steps to the parking area. For an interesting diversion, just before reaching the Mattatuck–Mohawk Trail junction, follow the paved road right 0.3 mile to several Forest Service buildings. Here a short, well-marked trail leads left into a black spruce bog where a boardwalk winds over sphagnum moss and through the dark evergreen forest. The Black Spruce Bog Trail can also be reached from the summit by heading east on a snowmobile trail and then north along Wadhams Road.

29 RANDS VIEW

Distance: 6.6 miles round-trip
Hiking time: 4 hours
Difficulty: Moderate
Low point: 685 feet
High point: 1250 feet
Season: Year-round
USGS map: Sharon, CT
Information: Appalachian National Scenic Trail

Getting there: From the junction of Routes 41 and 44 in Salisbury, follow Route 44 northeast toward Canaan. Drive 0.6 mile and park on the east side of the road near the Appalachian Trail sign (do not block any driveways). During the winter, parking may be limited near the trailhead because of snowbanks.

Some consider Rands View to be the finest vista on the Connecticut section of the Appalachian Trail. It is hard to argue with them. This pleasant half-day hike also includes bucolic scenes from the more forested Billys View, an interesting geologic protrusion, towering white pine and hemlock trees, and a seemingly endless carpet of jack-in-the-pulpits.

A hiker surveys the landscape from Bear Mountain to Mount Everett (l–r).

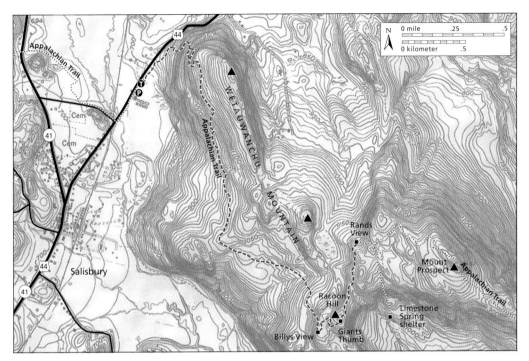

With the exception of the first half-mile, this quiet hike in western Connecticut takes advantage of gradual inclines and a soft pathway. For a slightly longer excursion, include an additional 1.5-mile round-trip extension to the partially open summit of 1461-foot Mount Prospect.

The hike begins along the west edge of a large field. In 0.1 mile enter the shady forest and begin a short, but aggressive climb up the steep side of Wetauwanchu Mountain. The large trees help distract from the difficult climb, and before long the path plateaus. What ensues is a gently rolling route that gradually descends to a low point on the ridge, where a transcontinental cable lies buried beneath the ground.

Rising slowly, the trail crosses a small stream where high concentrations of jack-in-the-pulpits can be found. These interestingly shaped flowers showcase small red berries in the fall. In addition to this welcome native plant, the area is also covered with Japanese barberry, a prolific invasive species that chokes out competition in the understory.

After joining a woods road, rise slowly to a mostly wooded rock outcrop, Billys View, and scenes of the Salmon Creek valley. Continuing along the ridge, the trail swings under a long ledge to the top of Raccoon Hill. Just below the summit, the Giants Thumb, an 8-foot-tall cobble, stands curiously above the eroded ground that surrounds it.

Leaving the oft-rubbed rock behind, hike down a ridge covered in stately pines and hemlocks. In a small boulder-filled notch, the path veers left and meanders to the edge of a large field—the site of Rands View. Enter the meadow and bear right to its high point where the views of the Taconic Ridge and the Housatonic Valley are spectacular. With the abundance of maple and birch in the area, this spot is especially enticing during peak fall foliage.

Take your time and enjoy the scenery—Rands View is a perfect place to picnic or soak in the sun's warm rays. If you want additional exercise, continue south along the Appalachian Trail 0.8 mile as it slowly ascends Mount Prospect. Otherwise, simply retrace the 3.3-mile journey to Route 44 and spend time exploring the town of Salisbury, one of the prettiest villages along the Appalachian Trail's 2000-mile trek from Georgia to Maine.

30 MOUNT FRISSELL

Distance: 5.2 miles round-trip
Hiking time: 4 hours
Difficulty: Moderate–Strenuous
Low point: 1830 feet
High point: 2453 feet
Season: Year-round
USGS map: Bash Bish Falls, MA
Information: Massachusetts Department of Conservation and Recreation

Getting there: From Route 41 in South Egremont, Massachusetts, follow Mount Washington Road west 4.5 miles. Stay left (becomes East Street) and continue south. In 4.5 miles, pass the Mount Washington Forest Headquarters on the right. Remain on East Street 2.7 miles to the Connecticut border. Parking is available on the right at the trailhead and on the left, just across the border.

Three scenic summits in three separate states showcase this sojourn that starts in southwestern Massachusetts. As an added bonus, the journey passes over the highest point in Connecticut, one of the few states whose high point is not the top of a hill or mountain. Tunneling through mazes of mountain laurel, this 2.6-mile trek that ends at New York State's Brace Mountain includes a

handful of short, steep sections; however, the hike is more noteworthy for its expansive views enjoyed throughout.

Pick up the Mount Frissell Trail as it begins just north of the state border. After a sharp left turn, the path swings south into the Nutmeg State and enters private property (please remain on the trail). In 0.4 mile reach the base of Round Mountain. Here, a 0.3-mile climb ensues up the vertical, rocky slope. Carefully negotiate your steps and soon arrive atop the appropriately named mountain. At 2296 feet and sparsely forested, Round Mountain is an excellent vantage point to gaze out to surroundings that include Mount Everett, Bear Mountain, and distant Mount Greylock.

The 0.5-mile trek to Mount Frissell's forested 2453-foot crest leads north by descending into a

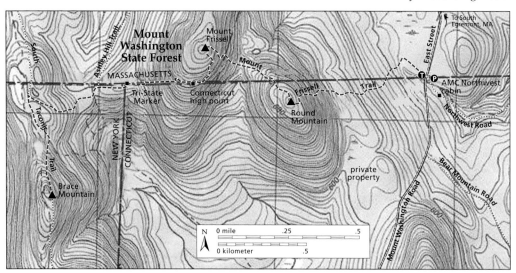

Brace Mountain's patriotic summit offers extensive 360-degree views.

narrow gap. Reentering Massachusetts' Mount Washington State Forest, the route rises abruptly past a number of impressive vistas. Swing south at the summit register and descend along a prominent outcrop offering pleasant scenes of Riga Lake. A sharp right turn leads quickly to a pile of rocks marking the top of Conneticut. While 73 feet below the mountain's apex in Massachusetts, this border location is 64 feet higher than nearby Bear Mountain, the state's highest summit.

The well-trodden path follows the state border west to a wide-open ledge with views of Brace Mountain and the towering Catskills beyond. Drop steeply down the granite face. Soon the terrain eases. Follow the straight path 0.3 mile to a stone post that marks the boundary of Connecticut, Massachusetts, and New York. A border disagreement resulted in Connecticut's omission from the post. Beyond, follow the route 0.4 mile as it weaves along the flat ridge before ending at the South Taconic Trail. Standing at the western edge of the Taconic

Ridge, this spot looks impressively out toward the Hudson River Valley. Turn left and hike 0.4 mile up a final, gentle pitch that leads to 2311-foot Brace Mountain. From the grassy pinnacle, enjoy the day's most extensive views and most relaxing resting spot.

Return to East Street via the same trails. It can feel grueling rescaling Frissell and Round once again. Take your time and enjoy the abundant natural beauty. If you want a less challenging trip, skip Brace Mountain and turn back at the Connecticut high point instead. This 2.6-mile round-trip hike still offers many rewards. For an alternative hike leaving the same parking area, consider following the 0.8-mile Northwest Road. It leads east at a gate just south of the border. While unmarked, it is easy to follow. After passing an Appalachian Mountain Club cabin on the right, it proceeds east to the Appalachian Trail. Turn left to reach the head of Sages Ravine in 0.3 mile. See Hike 31 for more information on this unique natural area.

31 BEAR MOUNTAIN

Distance: 8.1 miles round-trip
Hiking time: 6 hours
Difficulty: Strenuous
Low point: 750 feet
High point: 2316 feet
Season: Year-round
USGS map: Bash Bish Falls, MA
Information: Connecticut Department of Environmental Protection

Getting there: From the junction of Routes 41 and 44 in Salisbury, take Route 41 north 3.3 miles to the parking area on the left.

A challenging daylong journey to Connecticut's most celebrated mountain summit and one of Massachusetts' most alluring natural treasures, this popular 8.1-mile tour is a must-visit Berkshire adventure. Journey here throughout the year to experience the ever-changing scenery, from snow-draped quiet to bursting mountain laurel, from vibrant foliage to rushing water. Under the canopy of towering trees, the beaten-

down paths lead to campsites and spectacular vistas. Amid the diverse habitats you can enjoy the melodious tunes of colorful songbirds, the hammering rhythm of resident woodpeckers, and the graceful flight of circling raptors.

Begin on the Undermountain Trail as it leads west under a stately forest canopy. Weaving moderately up the slope, the path reaches Brassie Brook in 0.9 mile. Swing to the right and climb 0.2 mile to an intersection. Turn right here onto the 2.1-mile-long Paradise Lane Trail. After a quick climb, pass a spur leading right to a group camping area. Beyond, the incline eases. Over undulating terrain, proceed past numerous small wetlands as the trail leads beneath the mountain's summit area. After cutting through a dark hemlock grove and entering Massachusetts, descend quickly to a junction with the Appalachian Trail (AT).

The loop continues left; however, for now, veer right and descend into Sages Ravine. Reaching the banks of Sawmill Brook in 0.1 mile, bend right and follow the tumbling water downstream. A bridge leads left to an inviting campsite. Continue into the narrowing chasm where the brook falls over increasingly higher drops. Flush with vegetation, the moist ravine receives cascading streams from each side. Make your way down to a series of stone steps that lead to the other side. Here the river drops out of view to the east and the AT continues north to scenic Mount Race. Turn back here and retrace your steps through the ravine.

At the Paradise Lane junction, remain south on the AT and hike across a small saddle, where unmarked Northwest Road departs west (see Hike 30). Rising to the left, the white-blazed

Flowering hobblebush and cascades adorn Sages Ravine.

path soon reaches the base of a long, steep pitch—by far the most difficult section of the hike. Catch your breath before embarking up the punishing 0.4-mile climb; watch your step and take your time. Before long, you'll reach a well-deserved reward—the sweeping 180-degree views from atop Bear Mountain's immense summit rock pile.

The hike continues along the AT. Dropping 0.9 mile, the ledge-covered trail passes numerous vistas, sinks into dense mountain laurel, and arrives at Riga Junction. Ahead, the AT reaches the Brassie Brook lean-to in 0.5 mile, for those interested in spending a night on the mountain. To return to the parking area, turn left, rejoining the Undermountain Trail. Dropping off the ridge, the path soon crosses Brassie Brook and in 0.8 mile reaches the Paradise Lane intersection. Remain on the Undermountain Trail for the final 1.1 miles of the day's exhilarating travels.

32 ALANDER MOUNTAIN

Distance: 7.6 miles round-trip
Hiking time: 6 hours
Difficulty: Moderate–Strenuous
Low point: 715 feet
High point: 2239 feet
Season: Year-round
USGS maps: Copake, NY; Bash Bish Falls, MA
Information: Massachusetts Department of Conservation and Recreation

Fall colors brighten a view of Mount Everett.

Getting there: From Copake Falls, New York, follow Route 344 east (becomes Falls Road in Massachusetts) for 2 miles to a large parking area on the right. From Route 41 in South Egremont, drive west on Mount Washington Road for 4.5 miles. Stay left on East Street, continue 3.3 miles, and then turn right onto Cross Road. In 0.6 mile, turn right onto West Street. Continue 1 mile and pick up Falls Road on the left. Drive 1.4 miles to the parking area on the left.

Hidden in the southwest corner of Massachusetts and surrounded by more than 10,000 acres of publicly owned conservation land, this hike to the state's highest single-drop waterfall and one of its most scenic mountains is a must-visit destination. Bash Bish Falls lies at the base of a deep chasm of rock cliffs. Hidden from the nearby roadway, the falls' rugged beauty contrasts with and delightfully complements the gentler, open ridges of nearby Alander Mountain. Together these two picturesque natural features can be tied together on a rewarding 7.6-mile journey that includes a trek through nearby New York State.

From the large parking area, pick up the 0.6-mile-long Bash Bish Gorge Trail as it leaves south at a small gate. Descending quickly along a woods road, the path soon reaches the flat valley floor. Swing right toward Bash Bish Brook and carefully make your way across (may be difficult during high water). Remaining level for a few hundred feet, the trail leads to the upper end of the gorge, as the brook seemingly disappears into a rocky abyss. The steepest climb of the day ensues. In the beginning, a metal fence marks the edge between safe travel and a deadly tumble below, but quickly the route leads away from the gorge. The heart-pounding ends at a junction with the South Taconic Trail.

Catch your breath and then proceed south. While briefly ascending, pass a northern viewpoint just below the wooded summit of Bash Bish Mountain. For 1.2 miles the trail leads over moderately rolling terrain with an occasional glimpse west into the Empire State. Meandering along the quiet ridge, a short drop is followed by an aggressive climb that ends on a series of open ledges. With the Albany skyline and Mount

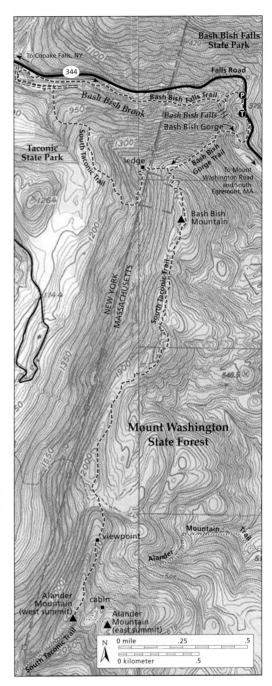

Greylock looming north, Mount Everett to the east, and the Catskills in the west, complete the final 0.4 mile that leads to scenic Alander

Mountain's mostly open western summit to enjoy equally stunning views south. From here, trails lead to a nearby rustic cabin and semi-open ledges on the eastern summit.

Retrace your steps north along the South Taconic Trail. At the Gorge Trail intersection, veer left. A 1.4-mile descent quickly enters New York State. After a short spur leads right to a delightful ledge, the route briefly enters private land. Be sure to remain on the trail as it winds into Taconic State Park and down to a park road. Follow the road left and across a bridge to a large parking area. Pick up the Bash Bish Falls Trail that leads to the falls from the eastern side of the lot. Paralleling the running water for 0.8 mile, the wide path moderately ascends back into the Bay State to the base of the twin falls, which drop hundreds of feet down the slope before tumbling 60 feet more into a small pool below. The hike concludes with a final 0.3-mile steep climb back to Falls Road—a somewhat cruel end to a glorious day.

Bash Bish Falls, the highest in Massachusetts

33 MOUNT EVERETT

Distance: 7.6 miles round-trip
Hiking time: 6 hours
Difficulty: Strenuous
Low point: 750 feet
High point: 2602 feet
Season: Year-round
USGS map: Bash Bish Falls, MA
Information: Massachusetts Department of Conservation and Recreation

Getting there: The small parking area is located on Route 41's west side in Sheffield, 2.8 miles north of the Connecticut border and 5.2 miles south of the junctions of Routes 41 and 23 in South Egremont.

The highest peak in the southern Berkshires, Mount Everett prominently stands out among a sea of lower 2000-foot summits. Rising sharply

from the east, the mountain's steep slopes are carved by Race Brook as it flows down a series of long cascades. To the north, picturesque Guilder Pond's blue waters and laurel-filled forests lie in a serene basin atop Everett's high ridgeline. From the summit, rocky outcrops amid a dwarf pitch pine–scrub oak forest offer those who venture to its heights numerous views of the surrounding countryside. Mount Everett's great variety provides plentiful year-round enjoyment.

The 1.9-mile Race Brook Trail begins at a large kiosk. Past a field, continue west under a dark evergreen canopy to a small sign. To the right a path leads gently to Lower Race Falls before climbing steeply to the main trail in 0.4 mile. Stay left and continue to a river crossing. While difficult during high water, the crossing can be a mixed blessing, because the falls shrink to a trickle during significant dry periods. Once across, begin a very steady ascent. Beyond the Lower Falls Trail's western junction, the main path swings north and climbs to the base of the Upper Falls, where water careens down a large rock face.

Cross the brook and make your way under, then up the ledge-covered slope. Beyond a small viewpoint, the trail returns to Race Brook and begins a pleasant 0.5-mile journey, paralleling its course through a moss-covered grove. Upstream, pass a tent-site area, available on a first-come,

first-served basis, and quickly arrive at the Appalachian Trail. To the south, Mount Race can be reached in 1.1 miles. Join the white-blazed route as it leads north; the terrain begins level, but before long becomes more rugged. With each step, the rocky surface is surrounded by fewer and shorter trees—the reward being ever-increasing views, including a 180-degree summit vista showcasing Bear Mountain, Mount Frissell, and Alander Mountain to the south and west.

At the base of the former fire tower (removed in 2003), remain on the Appalachian Trail. Descend east and in a few hundred feet arrive at a spur left to a ledge with extensive views north and east. Past the viewpoint, the route leads north and drops to a dirt road (closed to vehicles). Stay straight on the footpath. After losing

Mount Everett rises more than 600 feet above Guilder Pond.

nearly 600 feet in a little more than a half-mile, cross the dirt road to a small picnic area near the shore of Guilder Pond. Accessible by cars, this popular spot is a shorter alternative access point to climb Mount Everett from the town of Mount Washington.

To complete the enjoyable circuit of the pond, follow the Appalachian Trail north another 0.1 mile. Here a loop trail veers left and soon reaches the shore, a perfect spot for viewing mountain laurels blooming in June. The well-marked path slowly winds around the pond and, although scenic, often stays distant from the water. Upon arriving at the dirt road near the pond's outlet, follow it left for 0.1 mile back to the Appalachian Trail. Retrace your steps to Route 41, and for variety use the Lower Falls Trail on the descent. Ambitious hikers should consider extending the day by 2.2 miles round-trip by adding a side trek to the scenic summit of Mount Race.

34 MONUMENT MOUNTAIN

Distance: 2.8-mile loop
Hiking time: 2 hours
Difficulty: Moderate
Low point: 930 feet
High point: 1642 feet
Season: Year-round
USGS map: Great Barrington, MA
Information: The Trustees of Reservations

Getting there: From the junction of Routes 183 and 7 in Great Barrington, follow Route 7 north 1.6 miles to the large parking area on the left. From downtown Stockbridge, follow Route 7 south 3.1 miles to the parking area on the right.

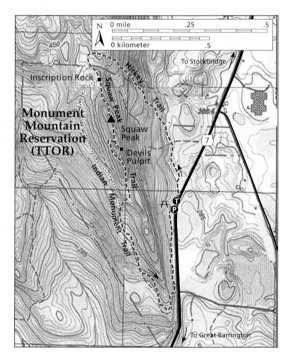

Since 1891, The Trustees of Reservations (TTOR)—a more than 100,000-member-strong land conservation organization—has helped to preserve nearly 25,000 acres of Massachusetts' most special places. In their quest to help each of us to "find our place," they offer nearly 100 locations for public exploration. One of TTOR's most popular reserves is the 503-acre parcel that surrounds Monument Mountain's Squaw Peak. Visited by more than 20,000 people each year, the uniquely shaped monolith is steeped in Native American lore. Tradition speaks of a young maiden, her forbidden love, and a tragic last leap over the sheer white cliff face. In the 1850s, the peak lured Nathaniel Hawthorne and Herman Melville,

Monument Mountain's lichen-covered ledges provide stunning views.

whose travels here helped inspire the writing of *Moby-Dick*. While most others enjoy less noteworthy memories of their Monument Mountain experiences, hiking to the top of Squaw Peak is a welcome addition to any Berkshire vacation.

Begin north along the Hickey Trail. The relatively level path soon begins a steady ascent. After passing a large boulder on the left, continue along a seasonal stream to a small wooden bridge. Once across, the route swings around a large cave on the left and quickly reaches Inscription Rock. Commemorating the original land transfer that protected the mountain in 1899, the smooth rock sits near a three-way junction.

Join the Squaw Peak Trail, which leads south along the narrowing ridgeline. Up a series of rock steps, the scenic path skirts a number of viewpoints to the east and quickly reaches the 1642-foot summit. Perched high atop the lichen-covered, white-rocked peak, you can take in tremendous views of the surrounding hillsides—Mount Everett and its Taconic neighbors to the southwest, and the towering saddle-shaped Mount Greylock to the north. Explore the summit environs and the many different cliff-side vantage points, but watch your step (and those of small children).

Descending south along the ridge, the path reaches a spur left to a scenic vista. Follow this short trail to a view of Devils Pulpit, an area of jagged quartzite cliff formations. Beyond, the route drops steadily and methodically down the ledge-covered slopes and soon ends at a junction with the Indian Monument Trail. Turn left onto more level terrain. The wide trail eventually approaches Route 7. Before reaching the busy highway, swing north onto a more rustic path. Parallel the road to the trailhead.

To plan future trips to TTOR's other natural treasures, visit the website at www.thetrustees.org.

35 MOHAWK TRAIL

Distance: 5-mile loop
Hiking time: 4 hours
Difficulty: Moderate–Strenuous
Low point: 630 feet
High point: 1711 feet
Season: Year-round
USGS map: Rowe, MA
Information: Massachusetts Department of Conservation and Recreation (fee)

Getting there: From the town of Charlemont, follow Route 2 west. After crossing the Deerfield River, drive 2 miles and turn right at a sign for Mohawk Trail State Forest. Cross a small bridge, stay left, and continue 0.1 mile to the park entrance. Parking is available on the left near the forest headquarters.

The 6457-acre Mohawk Trail State Forest is frequented by bears, campers, swimmers, and anglers. However, those who venture on its handful of challenging hiking trails discover a different world. Stepping beyond the pavement and the campfire-filled valley, you find some of New England's tallest and oldest trees. Additional

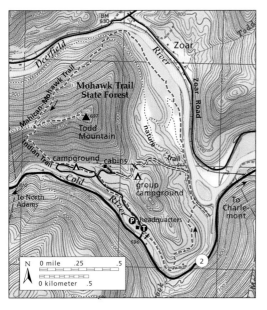

strides lead down the Mahican–Mohawk Trail, the remnants of an ancient Native American trading route once connecting the Connecticut and Hudson River Valleys. This scenic loop traverses picturesque forests, provides pleasing views, and offers a journey through early-American history.

Begin eastward on the dirt road that hugs the north banks of the Cold River. In 0.3 mile, turn left on a lightly used trail that weaves over a low ridge before descending to the Deerfield River. Hike north along the wide lane as it parallels the fast-flowing river for a little more than 1 mile. At first the route leads through a large field, east of the park's famous tall pines. Continue north into the forest to a bend in the river. Veer left, up the hill, and quickly join the Mahican–Mohawk Trail. With the sounds of white-water enthusiasts echoing through the valley, plod up the increasingly steep slope. The historic path wastes little time, carving a beeline under a dense stand of old trees.

As the incline eases, reach the narrow ridgeline and a four-way intersection. Pick up the spur to Todd Mountain that leads 0.3 mile east. After cresting a lower summit, drop briefly before climbing to the high point. There are a number of viewpoints along the way, including one from the summit. Each provides limited but nice snapshots of the rolling hillsides south and east.

Back at the four-way intersection, the quickest way down is south along the Indian Trail. If you want to extend the hike by 2 miles round-trip, follow the Mahican–Mohawk Trail west toward Clark Mountain. (See the USGS map.) The trail swings north of the wooded summit;

Tall trees and old growth forests line the historic Mahican-Mohawk Trail.

however, after winding up a serene forested ridge it descends a few dozen feet to a large field with distant views. The Indian Trail provides a no-nonsense route to the state forest's campground. Watch your footing in places where the soil is loose and brace your knees for the aggressive 0.4-mile drop back to the Cold River Valley. After a final pitch, the path swings left and ends at a large sign. Follow the paved road east 0.7 mile to the parking area.

36 | SPRUCE HILL

Distance: 3.6-mile loop
Hiking time: 3 hours
Difficulty: Moderate
Low point: 1880 feet
High point: 2566 feet
Season: Year-round
USGS map: North Adams, MA
Information: Massachusetts Department of Conservation and Recreation

Getting there: From the junction of Routes 8 and 2 in North Adams, take Route 2 east. Drive 4.3 miles and turn right onto Central Shaft Road (0.4 mile beyond the Florida town line). Follow Central Shaft Road 2.1 miles and veer right at the intersection. Continue another 0.9 mile on Central Shaft Road to the forest headquarters. Drive 0.1 mile beyond the building and park near the start of Old Florida Road.

Showcasing a small part of the Hoosac Mountain Range, the 11,118-acre Savoy Mountain State Forest offers hikers diverse opportunities throughout the year on more than 50 miles of trails. Its signature hike, Spruce Hill, provides some of the finest views in western Massachusetts and does so with much less effort than other hikes in the region. The 1.3-mile journey to the summit is frequented by bird-watchers in search of migrating hawks, but rewards all with

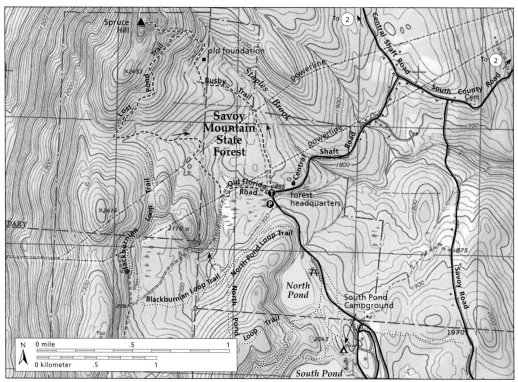

Two hikers enjoy views of Mount Greylock.

scenery that includes Mount Greylock's steep eastern flank, the rolling mountains of southern Vermont, and the rocky pinnacle of distant Mount Monadnock.

Start along Old Florida Road, a rutted dirt way hardly passable by vehicles, and quickly join the Busby Trail on the right. Passing under powerlines in 0.1 mile and again 0.3 mile farther, the wide path's gentle grades continue 0.6 mile. Abruptly, after passing the remains of a stone foundation on the right, swing steeply left to a trail junction and long rock wall.

Continue straight toward the summit, located 0.2 mile ahead. As the path nears the high point, a number of official and unofficial paths diverge. The main trail bends right and ascends a stone staircase. Winding across a small plateau, a final pitch leads to a north-facing ledge with excellent views. From here, a narrow path cuts west to a

second ledge with views of Mount Greylock and North Adams.

Return 0.2 mile down the mountain and turn right onto the Lost Pond Trail. After climbing a low ridge, the path gently descends 0.8 mile along shady, boulder-filled slopes to a small forested pond. Bear sharply left and parallel a small stream 0.2 mile to a junction with the Blackburnian Loop Trail. Follow the flat route left 0.8 mile across a small cascading stream and under the previously crossed powerlines. While under the second set, drop left to Old Florida Road.

Stay on the old road and hike east 0.3 mile back to the car. While flat, the road is susceptible to puddles, so watch your step. If you have time, check out nearby North Pond, a nice picnic area and swimming location. The forest also provides overnight camping at South Pond and offers a short hike to 50-foot-high Tannery Falls.

37 MONROE STATE FOREST

Distance: 10.3-mile loop
Hiking time: 7 hours
Difficulty: Strenuous
Low point: 1015 feet
High point: 2730 feet
Season: Year-round
USGS maps: North Adams, MA; Rowe, MA
Information: Massachusetts Department of Conservation and Recreation

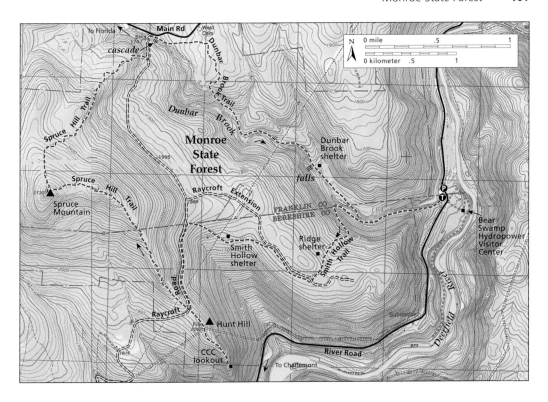

Getting there: From Charlemont, follow Route 2 west 2.1 miles. Turn right onto Zoar Road (before Route 2 crosses the Deerfield River). Drive 2.4 miles and then turn left onto River Road. Follow this road 8.5 miles to a parking area on the left (just beyond the Bear Swamp Hydropower Visitor Center).

Nestled in a corner of Massachusetts more famous for its former nuclear plant, the 4000-acre Monroe State Forest offers a quieter setting than other Berkshire natural areas. With more than 10 miles of trails weaving through old-growth hemlock, paralleling cascading brooks, scaling picturesque hardwood ridges, and passing three overnight lean-tos, Monroe is the perfect place for half-day, all-day, or multi-day adventures. This challenging circuit uses the forest's entire trail network, including a spur to a perch high above the Deerfield River. Since some of the routes are lightly used and not well blazed, less-experienced hikers should remain on the clearly marked Dunbar Brook Trail—the loop's most scenic section.

From the parking area, briefly climb under powerlines. The Dunbar Brook Trail quickly diverges right into the woods and begins a 0.7-mile journey above the banks of the flowing brook. At an intersection, where the main route crosses a bridge and continues upstream, veer left onto the Smith Hollow Trail as it ascends rapidly from the brook. The climb levels near the Ridge shelter, a small lean-to located aside a tiny stream. Like the other two campsites on the loop, this structure is available on a first-come basis.

Beyond the shelter, the trail reaches Raycroft Extension, a lightly used dirt road. Turn right and follow the road 0.5 mile to where the Smith Hollow Trail leaves left. Veering left again in 0.1 mile, descend abruptly to the Smith Hollow shelter. While a nice spot, it lacks convenient water. Beyond the lean-to, the path bends sharply right, cuts under powerlines, and rises to Raycroft Road near the town boundary (the less

Opposite: *A cascade tumbles along the upper reaches of Dunbar Brook.*

adventurous can skip Smith Hollow by staying on Raycroft Extension and then turning left onto Raycroft Road to reach this same point).

Follow Raycroft Road south 0.6 mile to a junction. Turn left to reach the top of Hunt Hill. Here powerlines allow for views of Mount Greylock. To the southeast, pick up the narrow path that descends 0.3 mile to Raycroft Lookout. Built by the Civilian Conservation Corps, this stone structure provides stunning views of the Deerfield River and the nearby Bear Swamp Hydropower Reservoir.

Return to Raycroft Road and join the Spruce Hill Trail, which enters the forest at the intersection. The lightly used Spruce Hill Trail can be difficult to follow in places, so take your time and watch for the sporadic blue blazes. After climbing gradually 1.6 miles, reach the mostly wooded summit, where very few spruces still grow. Dropping north, the path leads 1.5 miles down an occasional steep slope, past wetlands, and around large boulders. Bear left on Raycroft Road and quickly reach Dunbar Brook.

Cross the bridge and rejoin the Dunbar Brook Trail on the right. Past a small cascade and large stone foundation, the trail begins a 2.8-mile trek back. At first rising away from the brook, the path soon descends past massive rocks and under towering trees back to the water's edge. Pleasantly leading along the tumbling brook, the trail meanders to the Dunbar Brook shelter, the nicest overnight spot on the hike. Here an unmarked path leads 0.1 mile to the brook and a nice waterfall. From the shelter, continue east, while enjoying the soothing sound of the bubbling water and the abundant shade from the impressive canopy. After crossing to the brook's south side, stay left for the final 0.7 mile.

38 MOUNT GREYLOCK

Distance: 11.2-mile loop
Hiking time: 8 hours
Difficulty: Strenuous
Low point: 1100 feet
High point: 3491 feet
Season: Year-round
USGS map: Williamstown, MA
Information: Massachusetts Department of Conservation and Recreation

Getting there: From Route 2 in Williamstown, follow Route 43 south 2.5 miles, then turn left onto Hopper Road. Drive 1.3 miles and stay left on Hopper Road. Continue 0.7 mile to the Haley Farm parking area.

Towering nearly 1000 feet over the rest of southern New England, Mount Greylock's 3491-foot summit shines in the heart of the Berkshires. Traversed by a popular road and frequented by many visitors, the mountain can feel overwhelming to hikers seeking tranquillity. Fortunately, Mount Greylock is blessed with a network of trails that leads adventurers to quieter vistas, roaring streams, forested ridgelines, tumbling waterfalls, and wildlife-filled hollows. This daylong excursion, with overnight opportunities, will invigorate and invite you to partake in future treks to its heights. Choose midweek or off-season to avoid crowds; otherwise, smile and add people-watching to your day's entertainment.

Begin on a shady farm road. In 0.2 mile reach the start of the day's loop, just beyond the Haley Farm Trail. Turn right onto the Hopper Trail. At first over level terrain, the route slowly enters The Hopper, a large, steep-walled ravine forming Greylock's western side. Swing right and continue up an increasingly difficult but straightforward climb. Slicing up the mountain slope, the trail levels, then intersects Sperry Road at a

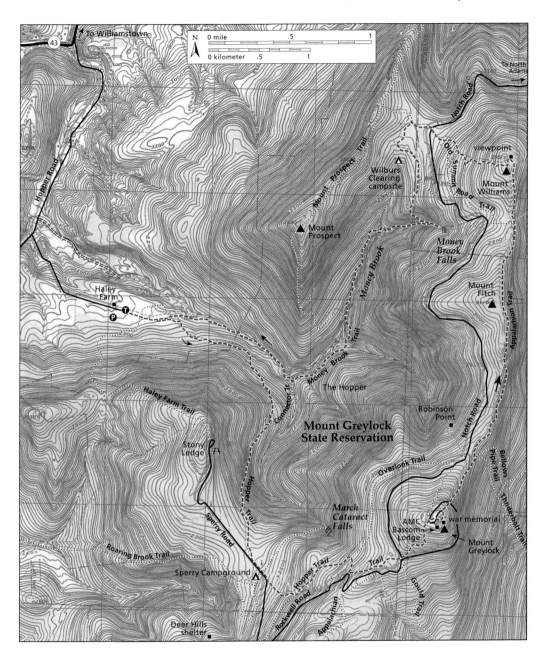

state reservation campground, 2.4 miles from the start. To the right, the road leads 0.8 mile to scenic Stony Ledge. Turn left and follow the road 0.2 mile past the campground entrance and a path leading 0.8 mile to March Cataract Falls, to where the Hopper Trail reenters the woods on the left.

Up the slope, bend northeast at a T intersection and follow the level path to a junction with the Overlook Trail—a scenic but longer alternative to the summit. Veering sharply right, remain on the Hopper Trail as it heads toward and then parallels Rockwell Road before ending at a junction

Greylock's war memorial provides panoramic views when open.

with the Appalachian Trail (AT). Hike north on the white-blazed path and follow it 0.6 mile past a quaint pond, across the paved road, and up to the busy summit. Surrounded by pavement and buildings, including the Appalachian Mountain Club's Bascom Lodge (available by reservation), the grassy high point is punctuated with a stone-tower war memorial. When open, the tower provides excellent 360-degree views of five states; otherwise, there are unobstructed scenes east and partial views in other directions.

The descent north follows the AT 3.2 miles. Drop past the Thunderbolt ski shelter and across the summit road. In 0.5 mile the Thunderbolt Ski Trail leads right. Just beyond here, stay left on the AT (the Bellows Pipe Trail descends straight). For 1.6 miles, enjoy a leisurely ridge walk over the wooded summit of Mount Fitch and then down to a four-way intersection. Remain on the AT and climb 0.2 mile to Mount Williams and a rock perch with fine views of southern Vermont. After traversing the high point, descend to Notch Road. Cross the pavement and in 0.1 mile turn left on the Money Brook Trail.

The 3.5-mile route leads past the Wilburs Clearing campsite, before dropping rapidly to a 0.1-mile spur left to secluded Money Brook Falls. Follow the rushing stream down a narrowing ridge. After descending to, then crossing, a small tributary, the route rises away from the water. Thankfully, the ascent is short and followed by a more moderate grade that leads past the start of the Mount Prospect Trail to a crossing of Money Brook. Over the final stretch, the trail eases as it follows the running water most of the way, crossing it twice more on bridges. Emerging into pastureland, make your way past the Hopper Trail and back to Haley Farm.

GREEN MOUNTAIN STATE

A boardwalk leads toward the top of Vermont.

The hiking centerpiece of Vermont is the 270-mile Long Trail. Dubbed the "Footpath in the Wilderness," the Long Trail was developed between 1910 and 1930. Running the length of the state from Massachusetts to Québec, it is the nation's oldest long-distance trail and the inspiration for the much longer Appalachian Trail (the two coincide for 100 miles). Famous as a backpacking destination, it joins with more than 175 miles of connecting trails offering countless day hikes as well.

Vermont, New England's least-populated state, is also home to the 385,000-acre Green Mountain National Forest and numerous state-owned lands. A wonderful year-round destination for hikers of all skill levels, the Green Mountain State's topography is most alluring in autumn when its prolific maple forests are aglow in bright reds and oranges.

39 GLASTENBURY MOUNTAIN

Distance: 22.2-mile loop; 20.4 miles one-way with shuttle
Hiking time: 2–3 days
Difficulty: Moderate–Strenuous
Low point: 1260 feet
High point: 3748 feet
Season: Year-round
USGS maps: Bennington, VT; Woodford, VT
Information: Green Mountain National Forest

Getting there: From the junction of Routes 7 and 9 in Bennington, follow Route 9 east 5 miles to the parking area on the left. Alternatively (or if using two cars), drive 4 miles east of Bennington, turn left onto Harbour Road, and continue 0.8 mile. Park near the water tank on the left—do not block any roads.

Established in 2006, the 22,425-acre Glastenbury Wilderness highlights one of Vermont's remotest areas. Its namesake mountain, while not in the wilderness, provides sweeping 360-degree views from its 1927-built fire tower. Located more than 10 miles from the nearest road via modestly inclined trails, Glastenbury Mountain is an ideal backpacking destination. This circuit includes the well-trodden Long/Appalachian Trail corridor, as well as a far more rustic path over the mountain's West Ridge. While lacking dramatic scenery, the hike lures those seeking a quietness most likely interrupted by an unsuspecting wild creature around the next bend.

Starting at the eastern trailhead, join the Long Trail north as it quickly crosses the MacArthur Memorial Bridge and briefly heads downstream.

A hiker follows the Long Trail north on a sunny spring day.

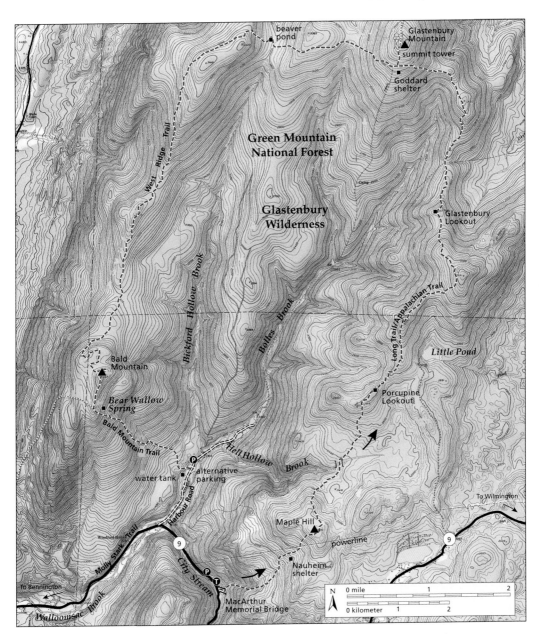

Veer right and ascend the most demanding section of the hike, a 1.3-mile and 1000-foot climb. After passing a curiously shaped split rock near the midpoint, the white-blazed path levels near a spur to the Nauheim shelter. This Green Mountain Club–maintained lean-to is the first of two along the journey, both available on a first-come basis.

Continue straight to a powerline corridor with limited views. On the far side, the route enters the wilderness before scaling Maple Hill.

Over the next 6 miles, enjoy the gently rolling terrain through a pleasant northern hardwood forest. The path crosses Hell Hollow Brook (camping is prohibited in this area to protect

Bennington's water supply), arrives at a handful of partially overgrown lookouts, and traverses terrain bursting with colorful wildflowers.

Upon descending to an old road, the final 2-mile trek to the Goddard shelter begins. Departing the wilderness, enter the day's first extensive evergreen forest and plod up a series of stone steps. Before long, you arrive at the lean-to, just beyond its water supply. Located 0.3 mile from the summit and roughly halfway along the journey, the Goddard shelter is a perfect place to overnight. Keep in mind, this can be a popular destination, so be prepared to tent nearby. From here, the 0.3-mile jaunt to the summit is straightforward. At the top, seven staircases lead above the forest canopy up the recently renovated tower. While the structure's height and see-through steps can be unnerving, the seemingly endless views enjoyed are well worth the nail-biting effort.

Begin the hike back on the West Ridge Trail. Departing the shelter, the path reenters the wilderness and drops gradually 2.4 miles to a sprawling beaver pond complex. Beyond, rise up a short but steep pitch. Level off for a nearly 5-mile trek south along the lightly traveled route. Skirting below the ridgeline at first, the trail eventually proceeds down the crest. Nearing Bald Mountain, the tread improves significantly. Weave steeply up and over the mountain's two peaks (both are no longer bald), and descend to an intersection with southern views of Mount Greylock.

To the right, the Bald Mountain Trail leads to Bennington. To return to your car, descend left 1.9 miles to Harbour Road. The rapid descent concludes on private land—be sure to remain on the trail. If you have not set up two cars, turn right on Harbour Road and hike 0.8 mile to Route 9. The trailhead parking area is located 1 mile to the east, extending the journey to 22.2 miles.

40 STRATTON POND AND MOUNTAIN

Distance: 13.1-mile loop
Hiking time: 9 hours/2 days
Difficulty: Moderate–Strenuous
Low point: 2230 feet
High point: 3936 feet
Season: Year-round
USGS maps: Stratton Mountain, VT; Sunderland, VT
Information: Green Mountain National Forest

Getting there: From the town of Stratton, follow Kelly Stand Road west 3.4 miles to a parking area on the right. Beginning in East Arlington, pick up Kelly Stand Road in the village of East Kansas. Drive east 10.5 miles to the trailhead on the left. Access in the winter is only from the east. (Winter parking is 0.7 mile east of the trailhead.)

This classic hike includes the largest lake on the Long Trail and the summit where James P. Taylor first visualized its creation. In 1917, his dream came true and today Stratton Pond and Mountain are a key link along the trail's 270-mile journey from Massachusetts to Canada. The

highest mountain in Vermont south of Killington, Stratton offers hikers 360-degree views of four states from its summit tower, while the pond's blue waters provide an idyllic resting spot for camping, picnicking, and wildlife observation.

The 3.8-mile trek to the mountaintop begins gradually. With little elevation change, follow the pathway 1.4 miles to International Paper (IP) Road. Once across the multi-use road (not open to cars), the trail climbs more steadily. Winding around Little Stratton Mountain, reach a saddle at 2.7 miles. Continue up modest grades to the forested high point and summit tower. To enjoy the extensive views, ascend the first couple flights of stairs. Once atop the tower, countless mountains

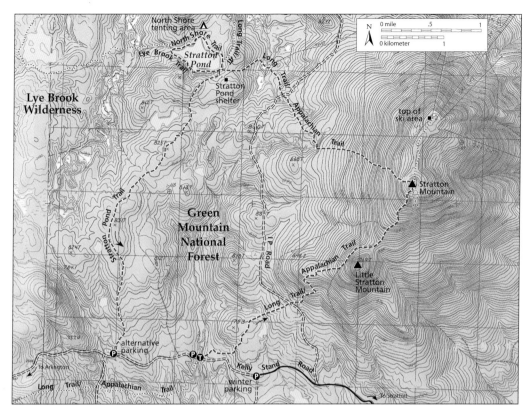

are visible in all directions: Greylock to Killington, Equinox to Monadnock. To the north an unmarked swath leads 0.7 mile to the ski area.

The 3.2-mile hike to the pond descends rapidly to the west through spruce-fir forests. As the terrain eases and the forest brightens, scamper over a bubbling brook and cross IP Road. The path drops to a wooden bridge, and then leads over a low hill to the Stratton Pond Trail junction. Bear right to reach the pond's grassy shore. To fully enjoy the peaceful surroundings, take advantage of the 1.4-mile loop around its perimeter. Start on the Lye Brook Trail and wind 0.7 mile along the south shore to boardwalks near the pond's outlet. Here, enjoy excellent views of the mountain. Back in the forest, pick up the scenic North Shore Trail, a 0.6-mile path that passes a tenting area. This facility and the nearby Stratton Pond shelter, both managed by the Green Mountain Club, are

A few yellow leaves add color to Stratton Pond in late October.

A hiker enjoys the view of Stratton Mountain from Stratton Pond.

available for a small fee on a first-come basis.

To complete the circuit, hike south along the Long Trail to pick up the Stratton Pond Trail. The route soon passes a spur leading left to the shelter. Veer right and follow the 3.7-mile trail over gentle, rolling terrain. While the landscape is often wet, the trail is lined with boardwalks to ease the way. A final descent leads to Kelly Stand Road. Follow the road east 1 mile to the parking area.

The pond and the mountain make excellent, shorter day hikes on their own. Also, this area, which includes the 17,718-acre Lye Brook Wilderness, is a backpacking paradise. You could complete an invigorating 25-mile three- or four-day excursion by following the Long Trail north of Stratton Pond to the Branch Pond Trail. (See the USGS map.) Here the William B. Douglas shelter is ideally located only 1.4 miles from scenic Prospect Rock. Continue south along the lightly used Branch Pond Trail, which follows pristine Bourn Brook. At Bourn Pond, follow the Lye Brook Trail east 1.8 miles to Stratton Pond. (Note: A microburst did significant damage to this trail in 2003. Check with the Forest Service to get current trail conditions.)

41 MOUNT ASCUTNEY

Distance: 6 miles round-trip
Hiking time: 4 hours
Difficulty: Moderate–Strenuous
Low point: 1100 feet
High point: 3150 feet
Season: Year-round
USGS map: Windsor, VT
Information: Vermont Department of Forests, Parks, and Recreation

Getting there: From Interstate 91, take Exit 8 and follow Route 131 west 3.2 miles. Turn right onto Cascade Falls Road and then in 0.1 mile left onto High Meadow Road. Follow the dirt surface 0.4 mile. The road swings right near a private residence and ends at parking area.

Rising above geologically unrelated surrounding hills, Ascutney is a classic monadnock-style mountain that towers over the Connecticut River Valley. The sprawling peak formed 100 million years ago when hot magma pushed toward the Earth's surface. Its name comes from a series of Algonquin words meaning "mountain of the rocky summit." Today, Ascutney is surrounded by more than 2000 acres of conserved land that includes a state park, four primary hiking trails, and a campground. This 6-mile round-trip journey along the Weathersfield Trail visits pleasant cascades and picturesque vistas en route to a summit observation tower that showcases exquisite 360-degree views of four states.

Beginning under a canopy of imposing maple trees, the path swings right and crosses the top of Little Cascade Falls in 0.4 mile. Here the water falls gently down a small ledge. Climbing more quickly up switchbacks, recross the stream at the base of a deep flume and ascend a small wooden ladder. Passing semi-open outcrops with views south across the pastoral landscape, the trail winds 0.5 mile over a small incline before descending abruptly to a large ledge. To the left, the bubbling brook forms Crystal Cascade Falls and plummets dozens of feet to the rocks below.

The route continues upstream along the east bank and then swings right. Up a hemlock-covered ridge, the path parallels the water from a more distant location before returning to its side. Hop across to where the path intersects an old woods road. At a sign marking the Halfway Brooks, 1.7 miles from the start, catch your breath—the difficulty is about to ratchet up. Scaling the steep slope, follow the turns and bends that eventually lead to the ridgeline and a viewpoint south toward Stratton Mountain.

Continue through the evergreen forest to a spur right to Gus's Lookout. Named for a

1967 charter member of the Ascutney Trails Association, this vantage point offers excellent views into western New Hampshire. Rejoin the main trail a few hundred feet beyond. Ahead, a large boulder sits perched on the left. Continue climbing to a small saddle where a path winds 0.1 mile left to the rocky top of West Peak and more views. This saddle also includes an intersection with a hang gliders' trail that leads east to a parking area and west to a launching pad.

Remain on the main trail 0.3 mile as it rises to the summit observation tower. Built in 1989, the sturdy structure provides expansive views of southern Vermont, the White Mountains, and

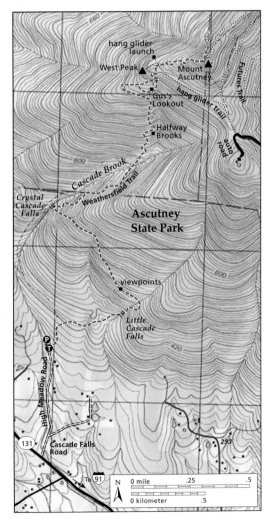

Pastoral views near Little Cascade Falls

west to New York State. Before returning to the parking area the same way you came, follow the wide path south that leads anticlimactically to the mountain's high point. The surrounding communications towers shield the scenery, but you cannot come this far without touching the top.

42 LUDLOW MOUNTAIN

Distance: 6 miles round-trip
Hiking time: 4 hours
Difficulty: Moderate
Low point: 1450 feet
High point: 3343 feet
Season: Year-round
USGS map: Mount Holly, VT
Information: Vermont Department of Forests, Parks, and Recreation

Getting there: At the junction of Routes 103 and 100 north of Ludlow, follow Route 103 west 2.7 miles and turn left onto Station Road. Drive 0.8 mile, cross a railroad track, and turn left onto a dirt driveway that ends at a small parking lot.

Much more noteworthy for its Okemo ski slopes, Ludlow Mountain rewards hikers as well. On a clear day, from the mountain's summit tower, you can gaze afar, taking in much of southern Vermont and peaks in three surrounding states. The gradual 3-mile Healdville Trail that meanders to the top provides an excellent passageway throughout the year for hikers of all ages. Tunneling through extensive hardwood forests, mostly along moderate grades, the hike's most difficult part is climbing the final few staircases to enjoy the splendid 360-degree vista.

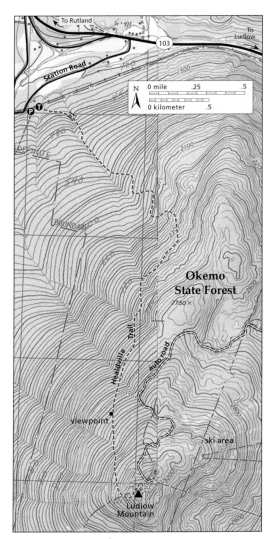

After a short descent, climb moderately 0.4 mile to a northern view of Killington Mountain and the surrounding agricultural landscape. Here the forest slowly transitions to evergreens. As the trail approaches the summit, swing past moist depressions and around small ledges. Arrive at a final trail junction (the path left leads to the top of the ski area and auto road). Follow the path right 0.1 mile to the summit and the base of the fire tower.

Surrounded by trees, the only option to obtain views is to ascend the tower. Once up a few flights of stairs, the views begin to emerge: Stratton Mountain, Mount Monadnock, the Adirondacks, and on a clear day, Mount Washington far to the northeast. Local lore recounts Native Americans referring to Ludlow Mountain with the name used by the ski area, Okemo, meaning "all come home." After making yourself sufficiently at home, descend using the same trail.

A moss-covered ledge just below the summit

At a large kiosk, the Healdville Trail enters the forest on an old road and soon crosses a wooden bridge. The level beginning becomes a bit steeper as the path parallels the tumbling brook. However, the route quickly eases along a series of sweeping switchbacks. Cutting beneath tall stands of maple and birch, gradually make your way up the rocky mountain slope. Near the trail's halfway point, the grade levels considerably. At 1.9 miles you reach a sign; to the left an unmarked path leads to an auto road and the ski slopes. Continue straight on the main trail.

43 BAKER PEAK AND GRIFFITH LAKE

Distance: 8.3-mile loop
Hiking time: 6 hours
Difficulty: Moderate–Strenuous
Low point: 720 feet
High point: 2600 feet
Season: Year-round
USGS map: Danby, VT
Information: Green Mountain National Forest

Getting there: Take Route 7 south of Danby. Turn left in 2.1 miles onto South End Road. Drive 0.5 mile to a small parking area on the left.

Located in the Big Branch Wilderness Area, Baker Peak is arguably the most scenic summit on the Long Trail south of Route 4. From its rocky high point there are excellent views of the Taconic Range and the Otter Creek Valley far below. While a journey to Baker Peak by itself is a worthy destination, you can extend the hike an additional 2.5 miles and visit the sparkling blue waters of Griffith Lake. Hidden high upon the Green Mountain Ridge, this elongated water body is the perfect place to enjoy the midday sun.

Begin on the Lake Trail as it climbs steadily 0.7 mile while following the banks of a small stream. Briefly entering private land, the trail swings left and soon enters the 6767-acre Big

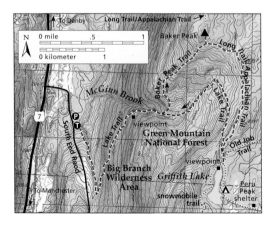

Branch Wilderness. The climb continues up the well-constructed former carriage road that once led to the Griffith Lake House, a private home of Vermont's first millionaire, lumber baron Silas Griffith. At 1.5 miles cross a metal bridge cut into the side of a ledge. A couple hundred yards farther, a small pile of rocks on the right marks a short spur that leads to a scenic perch and views of Dorset Mountain. Beyond, wind into the deep McGinn Brook Valley. After crossing the gurgling stream, reach the Baker Peak Trail.

Head north on the 0.9-mile path and begin an aggressive but straightforward 800-foot ascent. Through a thinning forest of rock and ledge, make your way up to a Long Trail (LT)/Appalachian Trail (AT) intersection, just 0.1 mile south of the summit. Turn left up the rugged white-blazed trail. With each step, ever-increasing views abound until reaching the exposed summit. The 270-degree vista is especially impressive south and west toward the Taconic Range.

The journey to Griffith Lake follows the LT/ AT south for 2 miles. With little overall elevation change, the trek rises up and over a number of small ridges. Under a thick green canopy, continue past the upper end of the Lake Trail and down to a junction with the Old Job Trail. Here the LT/AT leads straight for 0.2 mile over boardwalk to a Green Mountain Club tenting area (available for a small fee on first-come basis) and a small viewpoint on the lake. For a better place to enjoy the lake's beauty, turn right onto a snowmobile trail. It will soon lead you to side paths to the lake's western shore, including an area of fallen trees that provides excellent seating.

Dorset Mountain dominates the view from Baker Peak.

For the final leg of the day's trip, begin by retracing your steps 0.1 mile to the Lake Trail. Follow this route 1.4 miles as it descends gradu- ally at first, but then more quickly while nearing McGinn Brook. Hike past the Baker Peak Trail for the final 1.9 miles to the parking area.

44 DEER LEAP

Distance: 5.3 miles round-trip
Hiking time: 4 hours
Difficulty: Moderate
Low point: 1550 feet
High point: 2770 feet
Season: Year-round
USGS map: Pico Peak, VT
Information: Vermont Department of Forests, Parks, and Recreation (fee)

Getting there: From the junction of Routes 100 and 4 east of Sherburne Pass, follow Route 100 north 0.6 mile to Gifford Woods State Park. Turn left into the entrance and park near the contact station.

Deer Leap, a dramatic outcrop that rises above Sherburne Pass, is a popular destination for families. Most visitors opt for the shorter 2.2-mile round-trip that begins from Route 4. This longer, quieter, and more scenic trek includes an excursion through Gifford Woods State Park, a pleasant 2.2-mile section of the Appalachian Trail (AT), and an energizing ascent of Deer Leap Mountain.

Famous for its old-growth hardwoods, the state park includes a campground that provides an excellent base from which to explore the region. A fun excursion throughout the year, this hike is especially enticing in autumn when the abundant sugar maples are aglow in bright oranges.

Follow the campground road south to an AT sign. To the left, the white-blazed trail leads across Route 100 to Kent Pond and roughly 2 miles east to scenic Thundering Brook Falls. Remain on the pavement and head straight up a small incline. At the west end of the campground, turn right between sites 10 and 12. Entering the forest, the AT climbs gradually at first. Under a

Clouds break above the Deer Leap Overlook.

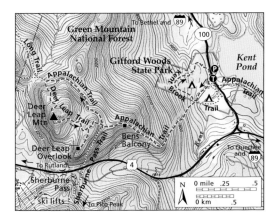

thick canopy of hardwood trees, the route intersects the Kent Brook Trail and then begins a more aggressive climb. Winding through the dense understory, the vegetation rings with a chorus of songbirds.

Eventually, the trail crests atop a low ridge and, 1.2 miles from the start, arrives atop Bens Balcony, a small ledge on the left that offers nice views of Killington Peak. Descending 0.2 mile, the path leads to an intersection with the Sherburne Pass Trail. Marked by blue blazes, this most popular option descends south 0.5 mile to Route 4. Veer right and reach the eastern junction of the Deer Leap Trail. For now, remain on the AT as it strolls peacefully over undulating terrain to the north side of the mountain. In 0.8 mile, turn left on the Deer Leap Trail's western terminus.

Rising swiftly, the straightforward route offers a few narrow views north toward the main spine of the Green Mountains. In 0.7 mile, skirt the 2782-foot summit and begin a steep descent to a saddle. After crossing a small brook, wind around and up a small but sheer ledge. Quickly, arrive at the Deer Leap Overlook spur. Dropping 0.2 mile south, the well-trodden path soon ends dramatically atop the impressive rock outcrop. Be sure to remain on the trail and keep a close eye on young children. The views of nearby Pico Peak and west toward New York are impressive.

Return to the main path and keep right. Hike 0.4 mile down to the AT, turn right, and remain on it for the 1.4-mile journey back to the campground. Or for variety, just before reaching the campground, turn left onto the Kent Brook Trail,

Gifford Woods is famous for its towering hardwoods.

which meanders 0.6 mile across interesting terrain before concluding at the parking area. Also, leading from the south side of the contact station, a well-manicured path leads 0.1 mile through an old-growth interpretive area.

45 RATTLESNAKE CLIFFS

Distance: 4.8-mile loop
Hiking time: 4 hours
Difficulty: Moderate–Strenuous
Low point: 600 feet
High point: 1720 feet
Season: Year-round
USGS map: East Middlebury, VT
Information: Green Mountain National Forest

Getting there: From the junction of Routes 73 and 53 in Forest Dale, follow Route 53 north 5.4 miles to a large parking area on the right. Alternatively, from Route 7 south of Middlebury, follow Route 53 east 3.8 miles toward Branbury State Park. Drive 0.3 mile past the park entrance to the parking area on the left.

Rattlesnake Cliffs and the Falls of Lana comprise two dramatic destinations in the Green Mountain National Forest's 20,000-acre Moosalamoo Scenic Recreation Area. Located in west-central Vermont, the Moosalamoo area lies in the shadows of higher summits to the east; however, in many ways, the region's natural features are more stunning and picturesque. In fact, the breathtaking views of the Champlain Valley and the distant Adirondack Mountains enjoyed from atop Rattlesnake Cliffs' precipitous perch are among the finest in the Green Mountain State.

Begin on the Silver Lake Trail, a wide path that swings north, passes under a large water pipe, and reaches the top of the falls in 0.5 mile. Here unofficial routes lead left to aerial views of the cascading water. Bear left onto the Falls of Lana Trail. After a bridge leads over Sucker Brook, stay right at an intersection and continue a few hundred yards to the 1.2-mile Aunt Jennie Trail. Follow this straightforward but demanding path north until it ends at the Rattlesnake Cliffs Trail. Turn left and slither around and over small ledges to a sign pointing straight to the cliffs; to

The path to South Rattlesnake Cliff leads to great views of Silver Lake.

the right the Oak Ridge Trail ventures to Mount Moosalamoo.

After briefly descending, the Rattlesnake Cliffs Trail splinters. To the right stands a slightly wooded but precipitous perch with tremendous views to New York's distant peaks. Left, a route winds to a more open and less tenuous spot offering southern views of Silver Lake and surrounding hills. (Note: Sometimes from late spring to midsummer portions of the cliffs are closed to protect nesting peregrine falcons.)

Back at the upper junction of the Aunt Jennie Trail, continue straight on the Rattlesnake Cliffs Trail. Descending 1.2 miles into a large, deeply forested bowl, the trail eventually crosses a tiny stream and reaches the North Branch Trail in a small field. Hike west and in 0.3 mile pick up the Falls of Lana Trail on the right.

Past a picnic area, the footpath winds left, as another route leaves north. Ascend a narrow gap in the ridge. To the right, a spur leads to open ledges and excellent views of Lake Dunmore. The trail soon drops steeply and nears the impressive falls. Named in honor of General Wool, a Mexican-American War veteran nicknamed Lana (the Spanish word for wool), the falls carve a deepening seam in the bedrock. The trail quickly drops 0.3 mile and ends in a small camping area. Across the street, Branbury State Park offers excellent swimming for a modest fee. To the left, follow Route 53 0.3 mile to the parking area.

For a longer journey, extend the described hike by 2.4 miles round-trip and climb Mount Moosalamoo. It is a pleasant walk with some occasional views of the Green Mountains. In addition, an 11-mile loop can be completed by continuing past the summit of Moosalamoo to its namesake campground. Then return following the North Branch Trail. While the trails to the falls and the cliffs are popular, these longer trails are much quieter.

On future adventures in this region, consider exploring south to Silver Lake and its surrounding ridges. The terrain is gradual while offering pleasant views and abundant wildlife.

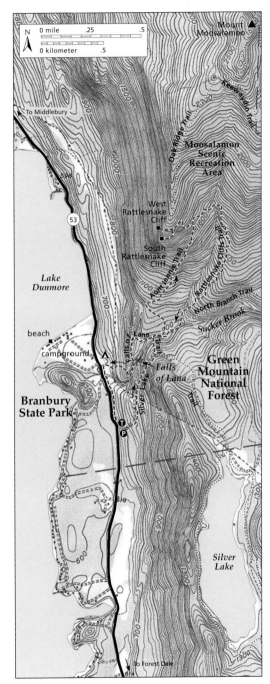

46 MOUNT INDEPENDENCE

Distance: 3.6-mile loop
Hiking time: 2 hours
Difficulty: Easy
Low point: 95 feet
High point: 306 feet
Season: Year-round
USGS map: Ticonderoga, NY
Information: Vermont Division of Historic Preservation (fee)

Getting there: From the junction of Routes 22A and 73 in Orwell, follow Route 73 west 0.3 mile and then bear left. Follow Mount Independence Road (becomes gravel) 4.8 miles to the visitor center parking area.

The site of a strategic American Revolutionary War fort, Mount Independence was named after news arrived from Philadelphia regarding the signing of Thomas Jefferson's now-famous Declaration. Located on the opposite shore of Lake Champlain from the more recognized Fort Ticonderoga, this lesser-known encampment played

Mount Independence's monument can be found near the bridge site.

Fort Ticonderoga lies across Lake Champlain from Horseshoe Battery.

a critical part in the ultimate demise of British General Burgoyne's failed attempt to divide the American colonies in half. Today, visitors can experience this historic site on more than 3 miles of mostly level trails, learn about the early struggles of the American Revolution while touring an informative museum, and enjoy many natural wonders surrounding Lake Champlain.

Begin at the park visitor center. Depending on your preference, you can tour the center's museum before or after your journey. The displays and artifacts paint a vivid picture of the difficulties experienced by soldiers on both sides of the battle. Once you are ready to venture outdoors, begin on the west branch of the handicapped-accessible Green Trail. This well-marked path, like each of the trails in the park, includes numbered spots along the way. The park provides a brochure that describes each location in greater detail.

The Green Trail soon leads to a spur left that arrives at a viewpoint across the lake to Mount Defiance and distant Fort Ticonderoga. In 1777, British artillery shelled Mount Independence from high atop Mount Defiance, helping to hasten the speedy evacuation of the site by American colonial forces. Back to the main branch of the Green Trail, continue east past the former site of a hospital to the start of the Blue Trail. Turn left

on the less-manicured Blue Trail and descend quickly toward the shore of the lake. Pass a number of archaeological remains, including a ramp where a crane once lifted supplies to the top of the peninsula. After swinging through a field, the path ends at a junction with the Orange Trail.

Turn left and descend to the northern tip of the point. Here, the trail visits two spots on the shore of Lake Champlain, the first from a small outcropping and the second near a former floating bridge site. Continue south past a stone obelisk and slowly climb to the Horseshoe Battery site and nice views of Fort Ticonderoga. Follow the west branch of the Orange Trail as it wanders across the center of the peninsula. Rising up gentle terrain, the path weaves in and out of open fields and soon reaches a spur right that leads to a scenic point near the old crane site.

Hike south over the area's 306-foot high point; scan the remains of the former fort's barracks. Level terrain follows and spurs your imagination. How difficult it must have been, being stationed here more than two centuries ago, with waves of redcoats marching south. As the Orange Trail ends at a junction with the Green Trail, turn left on the well-groomed path as it passes seven additional archaeological markers en route to the visitor center.

A long boardwalk leads across the boggy upper regions of Bread Loaf Mountain.

47 BREAD LOAF MOUNTAIN

Distance: 8 miles round-trip
Hiking time: 6 hours
Difficulty: Moderate–Strenuous
Low point: 1960 feet
High point: 3835 feet
Season: May–October
USGS maps: Bread Loaf, Lincoln
Information: Green Mountain National Forest

Getting there: From Route 125, 0.2 mile west of the Bread Loaf School in Ripton, turn northeast onto United States Forest Service (USFS) Road 59. Follow USFS 59 3.6 miles and then turn right into the small parking area on the field's edge.

Through nicely forested landscapes, this pleasant hike into the 25,237-acre Breadloaf Wilderness showcases the best of what central Vermont hiking has to offer. In addition to scaling a New England Hundred Highest Peak, the day's journey offers nice views of the Champlain Valley and the distant Adirondacks and visits a serene, high-elevation pond tucked away in a secluded basin. As an added bonus, unlike many treks to similar-sized mountains in New England, this 8-mile journey by and large traverses gradual terrain. Take this hike in early summer for wildflowers and abundant songbirds, or in midautumn for vibrant foliage.

From the parking area, the Skylight Pond Trail quickly enters the recently expanded wilderness, Vermont's largest. After crossing a small stream at 0.4 mile, the trail veers left and begins to climb more moderately. Over the next 2.1 miles the trail ascends a series of gradual switchbacks. Wind up the slope through the ever-changing forest canopy. Past small ledges the final climb ends at a four-way junction.

Turn south onto the Long Trail and ascend no more than 0.1 mile to a short spur right. Marked with double blue blazes, the path leads a few hundred feet to dramatic Sunset Rock. This narrow ledge provides an impressive view west toward Middlebury and Lake Champlain. Returning to the Skylight Pond Trail, stay right and follow the path 0.1 mile to its end at the picturesque pond. Perched above the small water body is Skyline Lodge. A rustic overnight facility maintained by the Green Mountain Club, the lodge is available for a small fee on a first-come basis. A short path leads from the lodge to the water's edge.

For the day's final excursion, take the Long Trail north to Bread Loaf Mountain. The initial 0.5 mile is fairly steep, the most difficult section of the hike, but soon the path crests atop the flat ridge. Hike 0.7 mile over the smaller west peak, through a shallow saddle, and then up toward the mountain's high point. At a spot where the Long Trail swings abruptly right, follow the spur left to the summit and beyond to a small viewpoint with nice western views.

Now 3.8 miles from the start, retrace your steps south along the Long Trail and return west on the Skylight Pond Trail. Enjoy the relaxing descent to the parking area. For a shorter alternative, omit the journey to Bread Loaf Mountain. A hike to Skylight Pond and Sunset Rock is 5.4 miles and can be completed in about three hours.

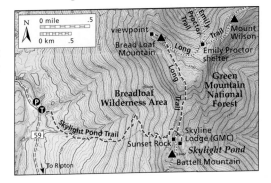

48 MOUNT ABRAHAM

Distance: 5.2 miles round-trip
Hiking time: 4 hours
Difficulty: Moderate–Strenuous
Low point: 2424 feet
High point: 4006 feet
Season: May–October
USGS map: Lincoln, VT
Information: Green Mountain National Forest

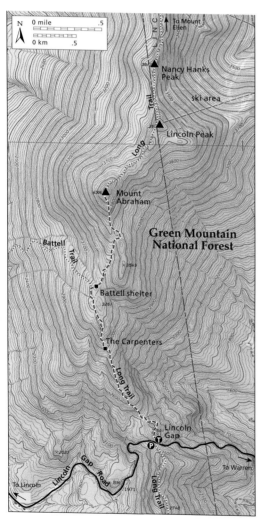

Getting there: From Warren, pick up Lincoln Gap Road off Route 100. Follow it 4.2 miles west to the height-of-land and parking on both sides of the road. From Lincoln, drive southeast 1.1 miles on East River Road. Stay left at an intersection and continue 3.7 miles to Lincoln Gap's height-of-land.

Mount Abraham provides one of the finest views along Vermont's scenic Long Trail. From just over 4000 feet in elevation, the small summit area is just above tree line and is surrounded by a 360-degree view that encompasses much of the state, as well as the high peaks in New York and the rugged mountains of New Hampshire. Beginning from the highest public road crossing of the Long Trail, this 5.2-mile round-trip hike is an enjoyable trek to one of the state's highest mountains.

The path enters the woods on the road's north side and winds around a small, rocky knoll. After a brief descent, follow the route as it steadily climbs up the ridge with occasional glimpses west through the evergreen canopy. At 1.2 miles from the trailhead, reach The Carpenters, a pair of large rocks on either side of the trail named for two former trail workers. Beyond, the trail levels slightly and in 0.5 mile reaches an intersection with the Battell Trail.

Ascending 2 miles from the west, the Battell Trail is an excellent, less-popular option for climbing Abraham that also provides winter access. It is one of many features in Vermont named in honor of Colonel Joseph Battell, a philanthropist, conservationist, and horse breeder

The Long Trail splits the Carpenters en route to Abraham.

from Ripton. In 1911, the colonel donated more than 1000 acres of Camels Hump's (Hike 49) summit to the state. Upon his death in 1915, Battell bequeathed 30,000-plus additional acres of mountainous terrain to Vermont, the federal government, and Middlebury College. Today, much of this donation is part of the Green Mountain National Forest and includes land on Mount Abraham and Bread Loaf Mountain to the south (Hike 47). Turn right and in 0.1 mile arrive at the Battell shelter, a small lean-to available on a first-come basis.

Continuing north, the final 0.8 mile ascends 900 feet. At first, the trail climbs easily along a wide pathway, but soon becomes steeper and rockier. Scrambling up and over small ledges, carefully make your way up the granite slope. There are plenty of places to grab onto and, with

ever-increasing views, numerous spots to pause and catch your breath. The shrinking vegetation gives way to wider and wider views, eventually ending atop the wide-open 4006-foot summit. Here there are a number of areas roped off to protect the fragile alpine plants that have been slowly reclaiming the summit environs. Despite these protected spots, there is still ample room to take in the abounding beauty.

To complete the hike, retrace your steps to Lincoln Gap. However, if you are looking for a lengthy adventure, continue north on the Long Trail 3.7 miles to the top of Mount Ellen. (See the USGS map.) This scenic ridge walk has a number of small ups and downs, but provides many views and access to another of Vermont's five 4000-foot mountains. The hike from Lincoln Gap to Mount Ellen is 12.6 miles round-trip.

49 CAMELS HUMP

Distance: 7.4 miles round-trip
Hiking time: 6 hours
Difficulty: Strenuous
Low point: 1500 feet
High point: 4083 feet
Season: Year-round (not April–May)
USGS maps: Waterbury, VT; Huntington, VT
Information: Vermont Department of Forest, Parks, and Recreation

Getting there: Take Exit 10 from Interstate 89 in Waterbury and head south to the junction of Routes 2 and 100. Turn left, drive 0.1 mile, and then veer right on Winooski Street. After crossing a bridge in 0.4 mile, bear right onto River Road and drive 4 miles. Turn left onto Hump Road and follow the state park signs. At 3.1 miles, pass parking on the left for Camels Hump View (this is a winter parking area). The road bends right and climbs steeply 0.5 mile to a large parking lot.

Among a sea of rounded summits, the distinctive shape of Camels Hump stands out like no other in Vermont. While picturesque from afar, the peak is even more impressive up close

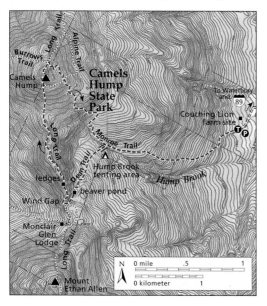

from any one of a half-dozen trails that ascend its rocky summit. This recommended loop is a popular choice that showcases successive views from the mountain's rugged southern ridge, a traverse across a fragile alpine zone, and extended miles through thick forests teeming with wildlife. Choose this hike off-season or midweek to avoid crowds, but no matter when you choose it, you will not go home disappointed.

The journey begins from Professor Monroe's former Couching Lion farm site. Named for French explorer Samuel de Champlain's description of the mountain, the farmland was donated to Vermont years ago and added to the existing park, now comprising nearly 24,000 acres. The aptly titled Monroe Trail steadily climbs under hardwood forests and in 1.3 miles reaches an intersection. Veer left onto the Dean Trail and follow the level terrain to a bridge leading across Hump Brook. After a spur leaves left to a tenting area, the ascent resumes and soon reaches a small beaver pond on the right with views of the peak and the rocky ridge ahead. The Dean Trail ends 0.3 mile farther at a four-way junction in Wind Gap.

Heading north on the Long Trail, wind up a more precipitous, rocky slope. The route emerges atop open ledges offering spectacular views. In and out of the trees, the climb eases past additional vistas. About a mile from the gap, the trail begins a more aggressive ascent up a steep incline to the base of the mountain's sheer southern face. To the right, the Alpine Trail offers a bad-weather option to the day's trek. Follow the Long Trail left as it rises above tree line and in 0.2 mile reaches the summit. Covered in rock

Camel Hump's distinctive summit rises to the north.

and vegetation-protected areas, Camels Hump provides 360-degree views encompassing the Champlain Valley and Adirondacks to the west, the White Mountains to the east, as well as the main ridge of the Green Mountains from Killington in the south to Jay Peak up north.

The loop descends 0.3 mile on the Long Trail. At a four-way intersection, the former site of a hotel that burned in 1875, turn right rejoining the Monroe Trail. The route pleasantly leads 1 mile through shady evergreen trees to a small cross-

ing of Hump Brook. The straightforward descent continues another 0.8 mile to the start of the Dean Trail. Stay straight for the final 1.3 miles.

If interested in a less-crowded alternative to Camels Hump, follow the Monroe and Dean Trails into Wind Gap. Pick up the Long Trail south and hike 1.2 miles to 3680-foot-high Mount Ethan Allen. Named for a Revolutionary War hero and Vermont's most famous historic figure, this destination offers a quieter 7-mile alternative to a peak with more limited views.

50 BIG DEER MOUNTAIN

Distance: 5.2-mile loop
Hiking time: 3.5 hours
Difficulty: Moderate
Low point: 1460 feet
High point: 1992 feet
Season: Year-round
USGS map: Marshfield, VT
Information: Vermont Department of Forests, Parks, and Recreation (fee)

Getting there: Follow Route 232 south from Route 2 in Marshfield. Drive 4.4 miles to the entrance of the New Discovery Campground on the left. After entering the park, drive 0.2 mile and turn right. Follow the dirt road 1 mile to the Osmore Pond picnic area.

Located in the 25,000-acre Groton State Forest, Big Deer Mountain and its surroundings provide

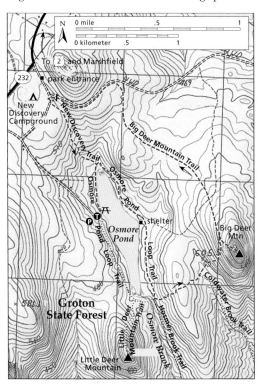

quiet, scenic hiking on moderate trails. With a number of interesting natural features and ample opportunity to enjoy wildlife, this public land area is a great location to explore throughout the year and is also home to five state park campgrounds. This recommended loop is an excellent introduction to a forest you will want to visit again and again.

Begin at the large picnic pavilion and follow the short path north to the shore of Osmore Pond. Draped in conifers, this large body of water often echoes with haunting loon calls. Take the trail left and wind around the northern tip of the pond, where a route leads left toward the campground. Stay right and continue circling the pond.

While flat, the terrain is a bit uneven and rocky. Take your time and enjoy the sights, sounds, and smells. The 1-mile section along the pond's eastern side remains a short distance from the water, but occasionally spurs lead to the shore, including one path near a small lean-to. Soon the flat trail ends at a four-way intersection. To the right, you can climb scenic Little Deer Mountain—1.2 miles round-trip—or return to the picnic pavilion, completing a shorter loop in 0.5 mile. Straight ahead, the Hosmer Brook Trail travels 1.3 miles to Big Deer Campground on Groton Lake. (See the USGS map for this alternative access site for the hike.)

Turn left and continue the trek to Big Deer Mountain by beginning a brief but steady climb up a low ridge. After a short descent, reach another intersection. Stay left and climb 0.3 mile to the Big Deer Mountain Trail. Follow the trail southeast 0.3 mile. After a steep climb, the path leads across a flat summit ridge. Continue past a

Opposite: *Autumn colors can arrive on Big Deer Mountain in August.*

large boulder to an open ledge with views south over Groton Lake. Additional scenic ledges can also be found a few dozen feet east of the boulder where the mountainside ends more abruptly.

Return to the main trail and stay straight. Over moderately undulating terrain, the path leads 1.1 miles to a gated dirt road. Turn left and follow the road 0.3 mile through the gate into the New Discovery Campground. Stay on the camp road, pass the bathhouse, and reach a small field on the left. On the southeastern edge of the field, pick up the New Discovery Trail which leads 0.5 mile down to Osmore Pond. En route, be sure to scan for signs of moose, a common inhabitant of the area. Turn right for the final 0.3-mile jaunt to the picnic pavilion.

51 WORCESTER RANGE

Distance: 8 miles one-way with shuttle; 11-mile loop
Hiking time: 6 hours
Difficulty: Strenuous
Low point: 1120 feet
High point: 3642 feet
Season: Year-round (except April–May)
USGS map: Stowe, VT
Information: Vermont Department of Forests, Parks, and Recreation

Two hikers perch atop Stowe Pinnacle with Mount Mansfield in the distance.
(Photo by Maria Fuentes)

Getting there: To reach the southern trailhead and start of this shuttle hike, take Exit 10 off Interstate 89, travel 2.9 miles north on Route 100, and turn right onto Howard Avenue. Head 0.3 mile into Waterbury Center and take the second left (Maple Street). In 0.1 mile turn right and follow Loomis Hill Road east 1.9 miles. As the pavement ends, stay left on Sweet Road and travel 1.4 miles to the Waterbury Trail parking area on the right.

For the northern trailhead, take Exit 10 off Interstate 89, travel 8.1 miles north on Route 100, and turn right onto Gold Brook Road (1.8 miles south of Routes 100 and 108 junction in Stowe). Follow the road left in 0.3 mile. Stay straight at 0.9 mile. Reach Upper Hollow Road in 0.7 mile. Bear right and drive 0.6 mile to the Stowe Pinnacle Trail parking area on the left.

To reach the southern trailhead from the northern one, drive 1 mile south on Upper Hollow Road. Turn left and continue 1 mile south. Bear left on a narrow and rough dirt road (passable by most vehicles in the summer) and reach the Waterbury trailhead in 1 mile on the left.

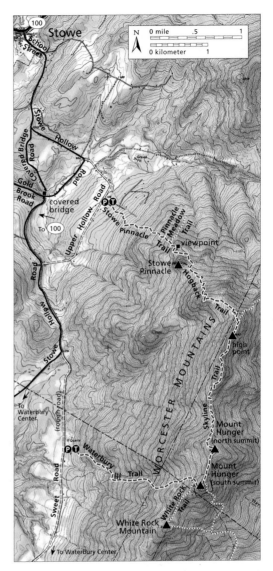

One of Vermont's most scenic ridges, the 15-mile-long Worcester Range includes over 20 miles of trails, which lead through lush forests to bald summits, small cascades, and secluded outcrops. Much of the range is managed by Vermont as part of Putnam State Forest and Elmore State Park. This 8-mile hike visits two of the most picturesque spots on the range, Stowe Pinnacle and Mount Hunger, by way of a ridge walk along the Skyline Trail. Beginning and ending at parking areas 3 miles apart, the hike is best completed using two cars. Alternatively, either summit makes for an enjoyable journey by itself.

Begin on the Waterbury Trail and head into the dark forest. Swinging through a field of boulders, the path climbs steadily for nearly a mile to the base of a long, tumbling cascade. Catch your breath and prepare for a relentless 1.2-mile ascent that rises more than 1500 feet. After crossing the stream to the south side, the route swings out of the valley and up the steep

mountain slope. Watch your footing, as the trail is very rocky and uneven. At the base of the final climb, a trail descends right 0.7 mile to scenic White Rock Mountain. Rising past this junction, emerge onto open ledges with tremendous western views of Vermont's highest elevations. A few more steps leads to Mount Hunger's open south summit, where 360-degree views include New Hampshire's White Mountains.

The trek continues north 3 miles along the Skyline Trail. Through fern-draped forests, weave between narrow rock clefts while occasionally emerging atop scenic perches. The lightly used trail initially makes its way around the wooded north summit of Mount Hunger before descending into a narrow saddle. Rising out of the depression, the route leads across a narrowing ridgeline. After reaching the unnamed high point of the range, drop to a junction.

To the right, the Skyline Trail proceeds 6 miles along the ridge to Worcester Mountain's open summit. (See the USGS map.) There a trail leads east 2.5 miles toward Route 12. Instead, turn left onto the 1-mile-long Hogback Trail. After an abrupt descent, briefly level off. Over a small bump on the ridge, the path drops 0.5 mile and ends at the Stowe Pinnacle Trail. Continue straight 0.1 mile to this rocky promontory that offers breathtaking views across the valley to Mount Mansfield's towering heights.

To complete the day's travels, follow the well-used Stowe Pinnacle Trail 1.6 miles down the steep mountain slope. The trek begins easily while wrapping around the peak's north side. Through a low sag and past a spur right to a viewpoint, the incline increases significantly. While steep, the path generally provides decent footing. Stay left at a junction with the Pinnacle Meadow Trail. Carefully make your way down the many switchbacks to a grassy field and the parking area that follows.

If you are unable to spot cars, follow Upper Hollow Road 1 mile to the left. Up a steep incline, bear left and continue another mile over the hillside. Turn left a third time. Follow this narrow road 1 mile to the Waterbury trailhead to complete an 11-mile loop. If only one trail interests you, consider the 4.4-mile round-trip hike to Mount Hunger's south summit or the 3.3-mile round-trip trek to Stowe Pinnacle—both hikes offer tremendous rewards on their own.

52 MOUNT MANSFIELD

Distance: 6.5-mile loop
Hiking time: 5 hours
Difficulty: Strenuous
Low point: 1800 feet
High point: 4393 feet
Season: Year-round (not April–May)
USGS map: Mount Mansfield, VT
Information: Vermont Department of Forests, Parks, and Recreation

Getting there: From Route 15 west of the Underhill–Jericho town line, follow River Road east 2.8 miles into Underhill Center. Continue straight an additional mile and turn right onto Mountain Road. This road dead-ends in 2.7 miles at Underhill State Park's campground and day-use parking area. The park is accessible in the winter, but the road is not plowed the entire 2.7 miles.

The Green Mountain State's highest peak boasts Vermont's longest and most scenic high-elevation ridge. For nearly 2 miles the Long Trail meanders above tree line with 360-degree views throughout. The rocky footpath scales a number of interesting summits, which from a distance—and with imagination—resemble parts of a human head. From The Chin, the mountain's high point, the expansive scenery attracts many hikers, as well as visitors from the auto road and gondola. A great hike whenever you choose it (assuming the weather cooperates), hike Mansfield early morning, midweek, or off-season to avoid crowds.

Traditionally, the hike from Underhill State Park began on CCC Road. The recently constructed Eagles Cut Trail offers a shorter, straighter alternative. Beyond a gate and kiosk, pick up this

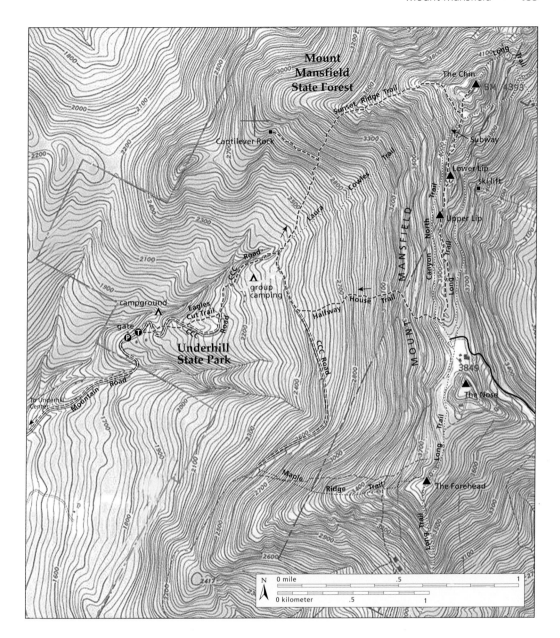

new route in a parking area on the right. The path climbs steadily 0.3 mile. Turn left and take CCC Road an additional 0.3 mile to the Sunset Ridge Trail. Heading northeast, this narrower footway soon passes the start of the Laura Cowles Trail, then climbs an increasingly steep slope. In 0.7 mile a spur leads left 0.2 mile to Cantilever Rock,

an interesting geologic formation jutting from the adjoining ledge. The main route continues to rise, soon emerging onto wide-open Sunset Ridge. While the climb is no less difficult, the abundant views are a welcome distraction. Carefully continue up the rocky slope. Nearing the summit, the 2.2-mile path turns abruptly right and passes the upper end of the Laura Cowles Trail. Ahead, reach the ridgeline and the white-blazed Long Trail.

Head left 0.2 mile to Vermont's highest elevation and views from Québec to Killington, Mount Marcy to Mount Washington. While enjoying the splendor, watch your step—a carpet of fragile alpine plants is trying to expand across the summit area.

From the high point, head south down the Long Trail and follow it 1 mile over the Lower and Upper Lips toward The Nose. Above tree line throughout, the footing is occasionally rough, but the scenery is spectacular. Keep in mind that the exposed ridge is not recommended during lightning storms or other severe weather. For the more adventurous, the Subway and Canyon North Trails drop west off the main ridge, allowing for the exploration of caves and ledges before returning to the main trail.

Beyond a glacial erratic and large cairn, pick up the Halfway House Trail on the right. Leading 1.1 miles down the mountain, this route quickly drops below tree line, past interesting rock formations and occasional vistas. Use extra care early on; the footing soon improves. Upon reaching CCC Road, turn right. Pass the Sunset Ridge Trail in 0.2 mile and reach the parking area 0.6 mile farther.

This trailhead's added advantage is its many options. A longer choice would be to continue south on the Long Trail to The Forehead. Here the Maple Ridge Trail drops west to CCC Road, allowing for an 8.6-mile loop. For a shorter 5.8-mile hike, use the Sunset Ridge and Laura Cowles Trails.

A cairn marks the way along Mount Mansfield's scenic summit ridge.

53 SMUGGLERS NOTCH

Distance: 5.7 miles round-trip
Hiking time: 4 hours
Difficulty: Moderate
Low point: 2160 feet
High point: 3320 feet
Season: June–October
USGS map: Mount Mansfield, VT
Information: Vermont Department of Forests, Parks, and Recreation

Getting there: From the junction of Routes 100 and 108 in Stowe, follow Route 108 north 9.8 miles. Just beyond the height-of-land in Smugglers Notch, find parking on both sides of the road and the trailhead on the right. Alternatively, from the north, pick up Route 108 at its junction with Route 15 in Jeffersonville. Drive 8 miles south to the trailhead on the left.

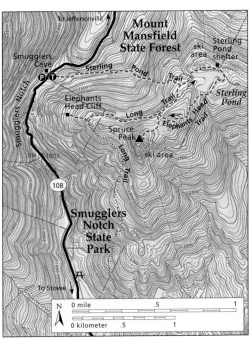

Arguably the most scenic body of water in the Green Mountains, Sterling Pond's long, picturesque shoreline provides many views of Mount Mansfield and other nearby peaks. Although surrounded by ski areas, the frequently visited pond lies nestled in a secluded basin, seemingly far removed from civilization. Most visitors stop at the pond's western shore. For a fuller, quieter, and more enjoyable hike, take the loop around the pond and add side trips to Spruce Peak and Elephants Head Cliff.

The Sterling Pond Trail departs Smugglers Notch, soon climbing a rock staircase. Weaving through birch forests, around ledges, and over small streams, continue the steady ascent. Watch your step along the final section of the 1.1-mile path; then turn left onto the Long Trail. Coinciding with a ski area connector route, the Long Trail quickly leads to Sterling Pond. This sandy, scenic spot is where most hikers stop. For additional beauty, continue trekking along the north rim of the pond. The Long Trail climbs past a chairlift and in 0.2 mile reaches the Sterling Pond shelter. Maintained by the Green Mountain Club, this lean-to is available for a small fee on a first-come basis.

At the shelter, turn right onto the 0.7-mile Elephants Head Trail. The blue-blazed path immediately leads to the water and an excellent viewpoint. From here the trail weaves around the uneven eastern shore, passing small caves, large rocks, and an occasional vista before rising steeply out of the basin. Crest the evergreen-covered ridge to a four-way intersection. Here, follow the wide path left 0.2 mile to the Spruce Peak ski area. Veer right up the slope and quickly enjoy views north to Québec. As the swath swings left and levels, head west into the woods.

A young hiker enjoys solitude at Sterling Pond.

Spruce Peak summit and excellent views of Mount Mansfield soon emerge.

Return to the four-way intersection and turn left onto the Long Trail. Follow the footpath 0.7 mile and down a few hundred feet. Bear right on a spur that descends quickly to the top of Elephants Head Cliff (may be closed from late spring to summer to protect peregrine falcons). The small cliff perch provides a spectacular bird's-eye view of Smugglers Notch. Head back to the four-way intersection a third time and once again turn left. Follow the Long Trail 0.3 mile, then take the Sterling Pond Trail west to your car.

The recommended 5.7-mile hike can be adjusted for shorter excursions, including the most popular 2.4-mile trip to the pond and back. For a longer, more difficult hike, begin at the Smugglers Notch picnic area (on Route 108, 1.4 miles south of the Sterling Pond Trail). Here, follow the Long Trail 2.3 miles to the Elephants Head Cliff. Continue to Spruce Peak and Sterling Pond. Take the Sterling Pond Trail back to Route 108 and descend winding Route 108 to the picnic area. This 7.5-mile hike is a good winter option when the road through the notch is closed.

54 DEVILS GULCH

Distance: 5-mile loop
Hiking time: 3.5 hours
Difficulty: Moderate
Low point: 1100 feet
High point: 1580 feet
Season: Year-round
USGS maps: Hazens Notch, VT; Eden, VT
Information: Vermont Department of Forests, Parks, and Recreation

Getting there: From the junction of Routes 100 and 118 in Eden, follow Route 118 west 4.8 miles. Turn right and follow a short dirt road a few hundred feet to the parking area.

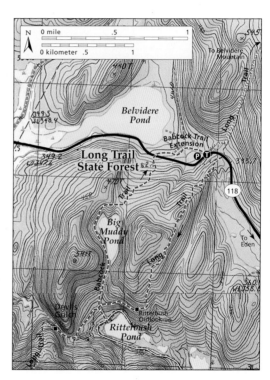

A maze of boulders, caves, and rock outcrops, Devils Gulch is short but also one of the most difficult sections of the Long Trail. It is also one of the trail's most fascinating geologic areas as well. Only 0.2 mile in length, the damp moss- and fern-covered gulch is alive with amphibians, shadows, and hidden crevices. The gulch, yet another satanically named New England location, is a must-see feature of the Vermont landscape. Along the way, enjoy enchanting, hardwood forests and two delightful ponds.

Near a gate and small kiosk, head toward Route 118. Cross the road (traffic can move quickly here) and veer left a few hundred feet. Entering the lush woods near a small sign, the trail traverses a flat, wooded ridge and soon crosses beneath a powerline. Beyond, the path enters the Long Trail State Forest, steadily climbs up a low ridge, and reaches the journey's high point in 1.1 miles, then begins a gradual 0.6-mile descent to Ritterbush Outlook. This mostly wooded viewpoint provides partial views of the similarly named pond below, as well as nearby hillsides.

A short but steep drop down a series of rock steps ensues. Upon leveling, pass some interesting boulders and cross a small stream to a junction with the Babcock Trail. Here an unmarked old road leads left 0.1 mile to Ritterbush Pond and a rustic building near its shore. Remain straight on the Long Trail for now and gradually climb 0.4 mile to the eastern entrance of Devils

Gulch. Follow the trail as it turns sharply right and leads up a wooden ladder. Through a tight passageway, the route ascends a low hill and then enters the heart of the narrow gap. Carefully make your way over slippery logs, under a small cave, and around an obstacle course of fallen rocks. Reach the head of the gulch in 0.2 mile before returning to the Babcock Trail.

Left on the Babcock Trail, a short but steady climb leads 0.3 mile to the southern end of Big Muddy Pond. Remaining high above the narrow pond, the path winds through young

Hikers of all sizes feel small within Devils Gulch.

forests while following an old road. A brief climb around the northern end of the pond is followed by a 0.6-mile, modest descent to Route 118. Carefully cross the paved road and pick up the Babcock Trail Extension directly on the other side. After a brief stint in the woods, the trail veers right onto a dirt road. In a few hundred yards, reenter the woods east for the final 0.2-mile stretch to the parking area.

To extend the hike or for a scenic trek on a different day, follow the Long Trail north from the parking lot. (See the USGS map.) It leads 2.6 miles up the slopes of Belvidere Mountain. Here the Forester's Trail leads 0.2 mile to the summit fire tower and extensive views of northern Vermont and southern Québec.

55 MOUNT PISGAH

Distance: 4 miles round-trip
Hiking time: 3 hours
Difficulty: Moderate–Strenuous
Low point: 1300 feet
High point: 2751 feet
Season: Year-round
USGS map: Sutton, VT
Information: Vermont Department of Forests, Parks, and Recreation

A safe distance back from the west overlook's precipitous drop

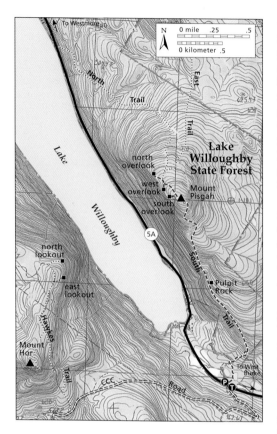

Getting there: From the junction of Routes 5 and 5A in West Burke, follow Route 5A north 5.8 miles to a parking area and trailhead on the right.

Rising 1500 feet, almost vertically, above the long, narrow expanse of Lake Willoughby, Mount Pisgah showcases one of New England's most stunning backdrops. This 4-mile round-trip journey includes stops at four precarious perches, each more spectacular than the last. At heights appreciated mostly by resident peregrine falcons, a trek to the top of Mount Pisgah offers the most rewards to those able to withstand the fear of standing on the brink.

Follow the South Trail as it descends briefly to a large wetland. Crossing wooden bridges, the route reenters the hardwood forest and winds gradually around a field of boulders. You soon arrive at the base of a steep mountain slope. Switchbacks moderate the incline, and 0.5 mile from the start the trail heads northwest along a level ridge. The gentle trail continues to skirt the side of an increasingly sheer edge and in 0.4 mile arrives at the first jaw-dropping vista, tiny Pulpit Rock. Watch your step while enjoying the incredible scenes of the deep blue waters as they reflect the rising cliffs of Mount Hor.

Leaving Pulpit Rock, the South Trail swings inland and begins an 0.8-mile steady climb to the summit. Methodically make your way up the moderately steep slope. As the deciduous forest transitions to conifers, the path swings east and then west before ascending across a semi-open granite slab with excellent views of the White Mountains.

Ahead, the South Trail ends at the wooded 2751-foot summit. To reach the mountain's most breathtaking spots, continue on the North Trail for 0.3 mile. Along the way, three spurs lead left to viewpoints, each offering differing angles and sensations. The northernmost spur is the longest, a few hundred feet, and arrives at the least perilous location. It also offers the best views north into Québec. In contrast, the southernmost spur falls rapidly to the edge of a precipitous drop, highlighted by a mesmerizing view. The middle spur leads to the west overlook, which is a combination of the other two.

Take your time and enjoy the scenery. When sufficiently awed, retrace your steps over the summit and down to the parking area. As an alternative 6.9-mile loop, if you do not mind walking south along a busy paved road for 3 miles, continue along the North Trail for 1.9 miles to its beginning on Route 5A.

For a more thorough appreciation of the area, consider visiting nearby Mount Hor as well. Shorter and less steep, Hor's 3.6-mile hike via the Hawkes Trail provides an excellent perspective of Mount's Pisgah's impressive rock face from several lookouts.

WHITE MOUNTAINS

In January, snow and ice abound on Franconia Ridge (seen from Mount Liberty).

The premier hiking destination of New England, the White Mountain National Forest extends more than 780,000 acres, encompassing a large portion of northern New Hampshire and a small corner of western Maine. Augmented with state parks in Franconia and Crawford Notches, as well as the summit of Mount Washington, the region contains more than 1200 miles of diverse hiking trails and countless overnight backpacking opportunities.

Located within three hours of downtown Boston and other population centers, the White Mountains are a popular destination twelve months a year, offering the widest variety of hiking opportunities in New England—from short nature walks, to challenging ascents of the region's highest peaks, to everything in between. The White Mountains are a must-visit destination for any New England hiking itinerary.

56 MOUNT ISRAEL

Distance: 4.2 miles round-trip
Hiking time: 3 hours
Difficulty: Moderate
Low point: 930 feet
High point: 2630 feet
Season: Year-round
USGS map: Center Sandwich, NH
Information: White Mountain National Forest

Getting there: From the junction of Routes 113 and 109 in Center Sandwich, follow Route 113 west. As Route 113 swings left, stay straight. Follow Grove Street (becomes Sandwich Notch Road) for 2.5 miles (it changes from pavement to dirt). At the bottom of a hill, turn right and follow the narrow road 0.4 mile to Mead Base and a grassy parking area on the right.

Delightfully located between New Hampshire's sparkling, azure Lakes Region and the verdant, southern flank of the White Mountains, Mount Israel is a perfect half-day adventure for the whole family. The Wentworth Trail provides the most direct access to the open summit ledges. Meandering up the mountain's slopes, the route combines steady climbs with more relaxing grades. Through ever-changing forest canopies and around oddly shaped rocks, the journey to the top is only surpassed by the impressive panorama enjoyed while there.

Begin on the grassy path that enters the woods behind the old farmhouse. Do not be discouraged; the initial 0.3-mile climb is aggressive but short. Leading right and across a stone wall, the path takes a more leisurely course to a small brook. Hop over the running water and follow the trail as it leads upstream. After the route swings away from the stream, begin a 0.7-mile climb, on switchbacks. Rising steadily, you reach an outcrop on the left with excellent southern

Approaching the summit, the Wentworth Trail weaves in and out of the forest.

Mounts Whiteface and Chocorua (l–r) dominate the views from Mount Israel.

views of Squam Lake, the setting for the movie *On Golden Pond*.

Push up one last short climb and arrive atop the summit ridge. Pleasantly zigzagging through the evergreen canopy, the path rises more gently 0.3 mile to a granite ledge that showcases a wall of impressive mountains from Sandwich Dome to Mount Chocorua. Continue east along the ridge. After descending briefly, the trail rises over additional ledges. Looking behind, catch a glimpse south of Lake Winnipesaukee and the Belknap Range. Through a final tunnel of trees, pass the Mead Trail and ascend the last pitch to the large summit cairn. Enjoy the picturesque scenery before retracing your steps.

For an 8.5-mile loop, consider descending the 1.7-mile Mead Trail. Upon reaching the Guinea Pond Trail, turn left onto the flat pathway that leads past moose-filled wetlands. At the trail's end, turn left onto the lightly used Sandwich Notch Road. A small climb is followed by a longer descent. In 2.5 miles, pick up the Bearcamp River Trail on the left. This path leads 0.6 mile past Beede Falls to Mead Base.

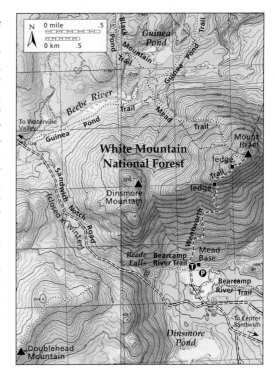

Winter hiking on Whiteface can be tricky, but beautiful.

57 MOUNT WHITEFACE

Distance: 8.2-mile loop
Hiking time: 7 hours
Difficulty: Strenuous
Low point: 1140
High point: 4020 feet
Season: Year-round
USGS maps: Mount Tripyramid, NH; Mount Chocorua, NH
Information: White Mountain National Forest

Getting there: Follow Route 113A to Wonalancet Village, 6.6 miles west from Route 113 in the center of Tamworth or 6.7 miles east from Route 113 in North Sandwich. Turn north onto Ferncroft Road. Follow this dirt road 0.5 mile and turn right. Parking is a few hundred feet farther on the left.

For more than a century, the Wonalancet Out Door Club (WODC) has maintained a collection of scenic and challenging trails that explore the White Mountain National Forest's most southern range. Within this region's sweeping ridgelines and steep mountain slopes lie an abundance of gems: quiet vistas, fern-draped forests, and gnarled rock outcrops. Perhaps the most spectacular of these features is the prominently visible Mount Whiteface, the area's signature summit. While accessible from a number of directions, this circuit beginning from the Ferncroft trailhead provides the most options with varying lengths and degrees of difficulty.

Follow the driveway back to Ferncroft Road and turn right. Past some private residences, turn left across Squirrel Bridge. Here the Blueberry Ledge Trail begins a 3.9-mile climb to Mount Whiteface's south summit. As the road dead-ends, the trail leads right. Beyond a junction with the Blueberry Ledge Cutoff, enter the White Mountain National Forest and, soon after, the 35,800-acre Sandwich Range Wilderness. The gradually rising path eventually emerges onto exposed rock and traverses an open area with limited southern views. Return to the woods beyond the upper junction of the Cutoff trail, 2 miles from the start, and begin a more aggressive climb.

After hiking through a small saddle where the Tom Wiggin Trail enters, ascend to an open ledge with views of the south peak and the white face that inspired the mountain's name. From here, scale a series of short, steep rock faces that are not ideal when wet or icy. Each scramble brings increasing views, culminating with a 180-degree vista from the south summit, where New Hampshire's Lakes Region stretches out far below. A short drop north along the Rollins Trail, followed by a slightly longer climb, ends at Mount Whiteface's wooded 4020-foot high point.

For the return trip, hike back over the south peak to the start of the 1.1-mile Tom Wiggin Trail. Turn left and descend rapidly down the steep but unexposed slope to the valley floor and a reprieve for burning knees. Carefully cross the Wonalancet River, which may be tricky during high water. The path ends at the Diceys Mill Trail. Veer right for an enjoyable 1.9-mile finish to the day's journey, as the path drops relaxingly

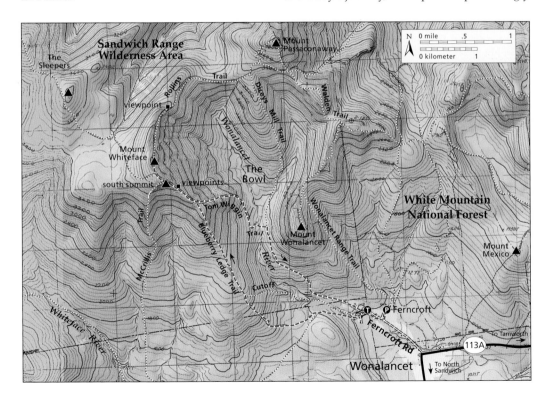

through an idyllic hardwood forest. At a private residence, stay right and follow the roadway back to the Ferncroft parking area.

For a less-steep, but 2-mile-longer descent, follow the Rollins Trail north from the Mount Whiteface summit. This quieter option traverses a ridge high above the steep slopes of The Bowl, a natural area of old-growth forests, before concluding on the Diceys Mill Trail, only 0.9 mile below the summit of Mount Passaconaway. Turn right to reach the parking area in 3.7 miles. Adding the steady climb to the top of Mount Passaconaway to this hike will result in an 11.9-mile loop and two 4000-foot mountains.

58 WELCH AND DICKEY

Distance: 4.4-mile loop
Hiking time: 4 hours
Difficulty: Moderate–Strenuous
Low point: 1060 feet
High point: 2734 feet
Season: Year-round
USGS map: Waterville Valley, NH
Information: White Mountain National Forest (fee)

Getting there: Take Exit 28 from Interstate 93 in Campton. Drive 5.6 miles northeast on Route 49 and turn left. Cross the bridge, continue 0.6 mile, and turn right. Follow the road 0.6 mile to the parking area on the right.

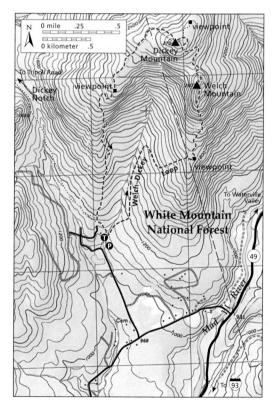

Ravaged by fires in the 1880s, today Welch and Dickey's smooth granite domes provide some of the finest views in the White Mountain National Forest. This popular loop scales both summits and offers great dividends for the effort; however, do not underestimate the challenge. Steep in sections, the trail scrambles up exposed rocks from one dramatic perch to another. While accessible year-round, it is to be avoided when icy or when thunderstorms threaten. The mountains and their scenic ridges are especially enticing on crisp autumn days when the Mad River Valley is aglow in a potpourri of colors.

Begin the loop in a counterclockwise direction by heading northeast toward Welch Mountain. Across a small stream, the route meanders easily for 0.7 mile through the shady valley. Abruptly swinging right near a large boulder, begin a steadier climb toward the ridgeline. Slowly the forest thins and the footing hardens. Pass a kiosk explaining the fragility of

Mount Tripyramid's distinctive three-peak summit, from Welch Mountain

the summit's plant life, and heed the advice to remain on the marked trail. Ahead lies the first of many panoramas.

With the mountaintop in view, veer left and carefully make your way up the increasingly steep slope. Each step brings broader vistas as the path winds methodically up rock, around ledges, and through patches of forest, including dwindling groves of jack pine (a fire-dependent species found in few White Mountain locations). Take your time, enjoy the scenery, and you'll soon reach Welch Mountain's barren summit. With incredible views in all directions, the scenes of Mount Tripyramid's distinctive three-peaked ridge and the south slide that scars its slopes are particularly noteworthy.

The loop drops 0.2 mile into a saddle buried under a large cairn. Proceed quickly up the rocky path to open ledges on Dickey Mountain's east side. Just before reaching the wooded summit, an unmarked trail branches right 0.2 mile to an impressive northern outlook. Over the high point, the route descends into evergreen forest, but gradually reemerges onto an exceptional open ridge that offers stunning near and distant views. Bearing right, the trail reenters the forest for good, passes a small cliff face, and then steadily leads down the slope. At a wooden bench the incline eases. Continue along relaxing grades to a signed junction. Turn left onto the old road, and in a few hundred feet arrive back at the parking area.

Mount Kancamagus casts its reflection onto Lower Greeley Pond.

59 GREELEY PONDS

Distance: 4.8 miles round-trip
Hiking time: 3 hours
Difficulty: Moderate
Low point: 1940 feet
High point: 2300 feet
Season: Year-round
USGS map: Mount Osceola, NH
Information: White Mountain National Forest (fee)

Getting there: From Interstate 93 in Lincoln, take Exit 32 and head east on Route 112 (Kancamagus Highway). Drive 10.1 miles to a parking area on the right, just before the road swings sharply left.

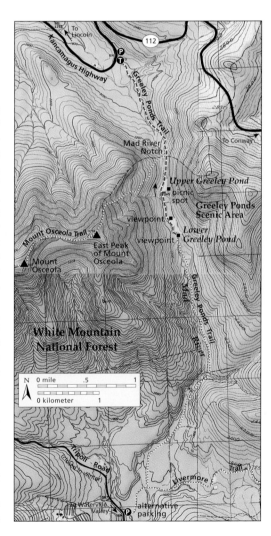

Located in an 800-acre scenic area of the White Mountain National Forest, the Upper and Lower Greeley Ponds are serene reflectors of surrounding ledge-draped mountain slopes. The frequently visited water bodies teeming with brook trout nestle snugly high within Mad River Notch. Accessible from Waterville Valley on an easier, but 3-mile-longer route, this moderate hike from the north offers an optional, challenging diversion to nearby Mount Osceola and its East Peak. From either direction, a journey to Greeley Ponds is an excellent family adventure throughout the year. Choose the hike midweek or off-season if searching for added tranquillity.

The 1.3-mile start to the day's hike is a gradual climb to Mad River Notch's height-of-land. After crossing a small stream, the path winds over boardwalk and across moist ground. Watch the footing early; the tread will quickly improve as the incline increases. Scale the slope and approach a small stream just before the final climb that ends at a junction with the Mount Osceola Trail. To the right the footway leads steeply 1.5 miles to the wooded East Peak of Mount Osceola. It then proceeds 1 mile across the ridge and through a saddle to the top of 4340-foot Mount Osceola. This demanding 5-mile (four-hour) round-trip option offers extensive views near the East Peak slide and from the cliff-side site of the former Mount Osceola fire tower.

To continue to the ponds, stay left. Past a large boulder, the path descends near a small brook and rapidly approaches the north shore of the Upper Pond. Remaining a few dozen feet above the shore, the trail swings around the west side before dropping to the pond's outlet. Enjoy the serenity of the placid water and the scarred slopes of Mount Kancamagus to the east. An unmarked path leads east across the outlet to a small beach on the far side—a perfect picnic location.

The main trail continues south, descending 0.3 mile to a spur that veers left to the north shore of the Lower Pond. This wider, more expansive pond provides increased visibility of the ledges on the adjoining mountainside. In addition, the more diverse plant life attracts a greater variety of bird and animal visitors. Walk softly and keep alert for resident wildlife as you hike across the final 0.2-mile stretch to the Lower Pond's south shore, a popular place for anglers. The 2.3-mile return follows the same course and includes a 120-foot climb over the height-of-land.

60 PEMIGEWASSET WILDERNESS

Distance: 25.2-mile loop
Hiking time: 2–3 days
Difficulty: Strenuous
Low point: 1160 feet
High point: 4902 feet
Season: May through October
USGS maps: Mount Osceola, NH; South Twin Mountain, NH
Information: White Mountain National Forest (fee)

Getting there: Follow Interstate 93 to Lincoln and take Exit 32. Travel 5.4 miles east on Route 112 (Kancamagus Highway) and turn left into the large parking area.

While beautiful, there are few places in the White Mountains where modern civilization appears distant. The heart of the 45,000-acre Pemigewasset Wilderness is such a place, but has not always been. Until the 1940s much of the region was heavily logged and burned. Thanks to the foresight of many conservationists, today it is a land more noteworthy for its roaring rivers, cascading falls, rugged landscapes, scenic peaks, and backpacking potential. This loop scales five New Hampshire 4000-foot mountains, traverses breathtaking scenery, and passes through forests teeming with wildlife.

After crossing the large suspension bridge spanning the Pemigewasset River's east branch, turn right onto the Lincoln Woods Trail. Follow the abandoned railbed 2.9 flat miles as it parallels the rushing water. After a bridge leads over Franconia Brook, the Lincoln Woods Trail reaches a three-way intersection and the Pemigewasset Wilderness boundary. Turn left onto the Franconia Brook Trail to join another abandoned railroad bed. The route ascends slowly while passing a number of wetlands and beaver ponds that occasionally flood portions of the trail. While large rodents and a growing forest continue to erase signs of the area's logging history, abandoned camps and artifacts remain—all protected by federal law. At 8.1 miles from the start, reach the Appalachian Mountain Club's (AMC) Thirteen Falls tent site (the first of two AMC campsites available for a small fee on a first-come basis). Located near a series of scenic cascades, Thirteen Falls exudes tranquillity.

The journey continues up the Twin Brook Trail, which climbs gradually northeast and in 2.7 miles reaches the Frost Trail. To the left, the mostly wooded summit of 4024-foot Galehead Mountain can be scaled in 0.4 mile. Veer right, and you soon arrive at the AMC's Galehead Hut, which provides bunks and meals (reservations

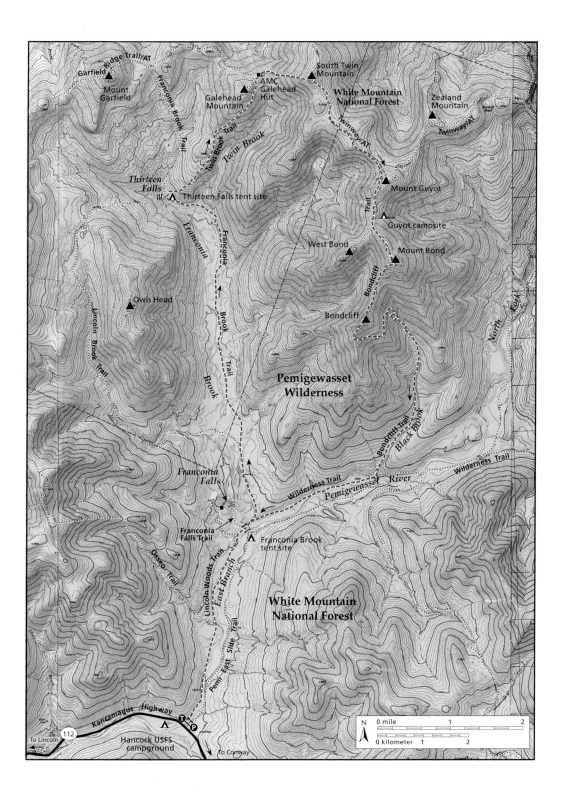

Garfield Ridge Trail/AT

Garfield

Mount
Garfield

Galehead
Mountain

AMC
Galehead
Hut

South Twin
Mountain

White Mountain
National Forest

Zealand
Mountain

Twinway/AT

Francoonia Brook Trail

Twin Brook Trail

Twin Brook

Twinway/AT

Thirteen
Falls

Thirteen Falls tent site

Mount Guyot

Guyot campsite

Trail

Franconia Brook Trail

Franconia

West Bond

Mount Bond

Owls Head

Bondcliff

Lincoln Brook Trail

Bondcliff

Brook

Pemigewasset
Wilderness

Brook Trail

Bondcliff Trail

Black Brook

North Fork

Franconia
Falls

Wilderness Trail

Pemigewasset River

Wilderness Trail

Franconia
Falls Trail

Wilderness Trail

Franconia Brook
tent site

Osseo Trail

Lincoln Woods Trail

East Branch

White Mountain
National Forest

Pemi East Side Trail

Kancamagus Highway

112

To Lincoln

Hancock USFS
campground

To Conway

N

0 mile   1   2

0 kilometer   1   2

The dramatic slide-scarred slopes of West Bond

required). From here, the hike's most difficult section ensues—an 0.8-mile climb, rising 1100 feet up the boulder-covered Twinway. Fortunately, the hard work pays off atop 4902-foot South Twin Mountain. The highest peak between the Franconia Ridge and the Presidential Range, South Twin provides a dazzling 360-degree panorama that includes views of both.

Pleasantly descend the gently rolling ridge along the Twinway as it leads 2 miles to the Bondcliff Trail, 0.1 mile below Mount Guyot's rounded summit. Follow the Bondcliff Trail right 0.8 mile over Guyot's more scenic west peak and into a saddle where a 0.2-mile spur leads left to the AMC's Guyot campsite. Only 6.3 miles from Thirteen Falls, this popular spot includes a shelter, tent sites, and overflow camping areas. If you are able to set up camp early, consider a 1.8-mile round-trip excursion to New England's most isolated 4000-footer, West Bond—this spectacular peak is reached via a 0.5-mile branch off the Bondcliff Trail.

The trek's 11-mile conclusion leads south, climbing above tree line to 4698-foot Mount Bond. With views in all directions, this picturesque location, named for a nineteenth-century White Mountain surveyor, is a fine place to start the day. Descending rapidly to the southwest, the trail falls through a thinning forest, but not for long. Near the col, a nearly 1-mile section across wide-open landscape begins. The trail slowly rises above the dramatic edge of Bondcliff and its incredible views of the West Bond slides. While not an ideal place in bad weather, there are few places in the White Mountains more awe-inspiring. After cresting the high point, take time to savor the incredible beauty.

Reenter the forest over a tricky rock face and begin a slow and steady 4.4-mile descent, eventually following and crossing Black Brook on four occasions. The relaxing hike ends at the Wilderness Trail. Turn right and follow the level pathway 1.8 miles to the Lincoln Woods Trail, 2.9 miles north of the parking area.

61 MOUNT CHOCORUA

Distance: 7.8 miles round-trip
Hiking time: 6 hours
Difficulty: Moderate–Strenuous
Low point: 1480 feet
High point: 3500 feet
Season: Year-round
USGS map: Mount Chocorua, NH
Information: White Mountain National Forest (fee)

Getting there: Beginning from Route 16 south of Conway, follow the Kancamagus Highway (Route 112) west 10.6 miles to a large parking area on the left.

One of the most popular and frequently photographed peaks in the White Mountains, Mount Chocorua offers many options to ascend its rocky summit. While you cannot go wrong regardless of your choice, this trek from the north provides the most moderate ascent and offers a number of intriguing diversions, including scenic Champney and Pitcher Falls and the serene, summit of Middle Sister Mountain. Believed to be the final chapter of an all-too-common struggle between European settlers and Native Americans, the mountain may hold the remains of a courageous young Chocorua who plunged to his untimely death hundreds of years ago. Choose this hike today for a more pleasant and enjoyable excursion to this unique pinnacle.

The path crosses a small stream, passes a junction with the Bolles Trail, and arrives on the banks of Champney Brook. Remaining on the west side of the bubbling stream, the Champney Falls Trail alternates from ridges high above the water to more intimate locations. At 1.4 miles reach the start of the Champney Falls Loop Trail. Turn left and descend gradually. In 0.2 mile reach the base of the scenic falls, a series of cascades that culminates at the foot of a large boulder. To the east, the much thinner Pitcher Falls plunge into a deep, shady chasm. This cool location is a great spot to refresh before continuing the journey to loftier heights. The loop ascends a rock staircase along the west side of Champney

Falls. At the top bear right and soon return to the main trail.

A steady but gradual 1.5-mile climb ensues. Roughly halfway up, the rocky trail reaches a viewpoint of Mount Washington and then begins to ascend a series of switchbacks. As the

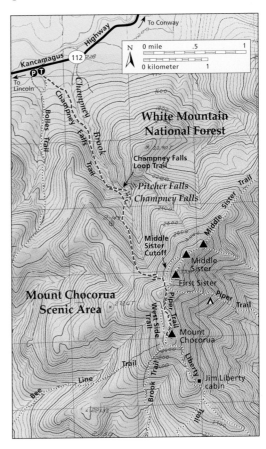

Champney Falls, a popular and pleasant stop on the way to Chocorua

hardwood forest transitions to spruce and fir, pass the Middle Sister Cutoff on the left. Soon after, the trail reaches a small ledge with limited views at a junction with the Middle Sister Trail. Continue straight 0.1 mile to the Piper Trail and turn right.

The remaining 0.7-mile stretch becomes increasingly striking beyond an intersection with the West Side Trail (bad-weather route). Here, the path emerges onto open rock. With each step views increase as you wind up, over, around, and through the granite summit ledges. While spectacular during nice weather, this location is not ideal if it is icy or if thunderstorms are threatening. Look closely for yellow blazes; the route is not always obvious. As you approach the top, the trail stays right of the summit and reaches a junction with the Brook Trail. Turn left and scramble up the final few hundred feet to the high point, where a 360-degree panorama awaits. Mount Chocorua's height and location make an ideal spot to plan future hikes of the many White Mountain summits in view.

For the descent, retrace your steps down the Piper and Champney Falls Trails. If the crowds on Mount Chocorua become too much, or for added enjoyment, consider extending your hike 0.7 mile by journeying over the First Sister to the summit of Middle Sister Mountain. Both peaks have great views and are often quiet. To complete this added circuit, use the Middle Sister Trail and the Middle Sister Cutoff.

62 MOUNT MOOSILAUKE

Distance: 8.2 miles round-trip
Hiking time: 7 hours
Difficulty: Strenuous
Low point: 1480 feet
High point: 4802 feet
Season: Year-round
USGS maps: Mount Kineo, NH; Mount Moosilauke, NH
Information: White Mountain National Forest

Getting there: From Interstate 93, take Exit 26 in Plymouth and follow Route 25 northwest 24.5 miles to the village of Glencliff. Turn right onto High Street and continue 1.3 miles up the hill to a small parking area on the right (just beyond the trailhead).

At 4802 feet, Mount Moosilauke's massive figure commands most views from the western half of New Hampshire's White Mountains. A legend of Abenaki Chief Waternomee talks of a 1685 ascent of this glorious mountain, nearly a hundred years before the Declaration of Independence. Today, the mountain continues to spiritually lure visitors to its expansive ridges, deep ravines, forested slopes, and exquisite alpine meadows. Dartmouth College faithful visit the peak as a rite of passage (the school owns 5000 acres on the mountain's southeast side). With many routes leading to the peak, which Native Americans

Snow can linger on Mount Moosilauke well into May.

The rose-breasted grosbeak's melodious song is as beautiful as its plumage.

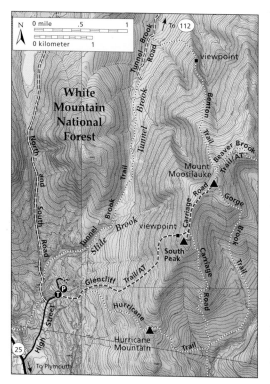

referred to as the "bald place," Mount Moosilauke is a place to visit again and again.

This scenic route follows the southern approach of the Appalachian Trail (AT). Pick up the Glencliff Trail from High Street and head through open fields, veering slightly left. As you enter the forest, stay left at a junction and begin the nearly 3-mile climb northeast to the summit ridge. Steady but not steep, the ascent wastes little time gaining elevation. Slowly, tall yellow birches give way to shorter spruce and fir. Before you know it, the trail reaches the base of a small scree slope on the right. A short spur leads up the rock to a tremendous view of Tunnel Brook valley far below. Just beyond this vista, the Glencliff Trail ends at Carriage Road. Before continuing on, make a hard right onto a 0.2-mile path that leads to South Peak. This destination offers great views, with many fewer fellow hikers than you will likely encounter on the main summit.

Back to the AT, turn left on Carriage Road for the final 0.9-mile climb to the top. This gradual conclusion to the hike's ascent begins in a stunted evergreen forest, but quickly emerges onto a barren alpine meadow. Please stay on the rock-bordered trail to help the fragile vegetation slowly recover from years of trampling. Today, the small plants provide splashes of color in early summer and reddish foliage as frost strikes in autumn. At nearly 5000 feet in elevation, the barren high point provides 360-degree views encompassing Franconia Notch, the Presidential Range, and much of the Green Mountains of Vermont. Often windy, the top offers some shelter beside the foundation remains of buildings that once stood there. Although this summit is often busy, there are ample places to enjoy the view.

Retrace your steps when sufficiently recharged—or for a more adventurous day, continue north on the Benton Trail. This 3.6-mile route descends to the northwest and passes a number of nice viewpoints. At its trailhead turn left on Tunnel Brook Road. In 0.8 mile pick up the Tunnel Brook Trail, which leads 4.4 miles through a scenic valley of small ponds, beaver dams, and bubbling brooks. Turning left on North and South Road and then left on High Street, the 13.7-mile loop concludes at the Glencliff trailhead.

63 CANNON MOUNTAIN

Distance: 8.2-mile loop
Hiking time: 7 hours
Difficulty: Strenuous
Low point: 1770 feet
High point: 4100 feet
Season: Year-round
USGS map: Franconia, NH
Information: New Hampshire Division of Parks and Recreation

Getting there: From Interstate 93 in Franconia Notch, take Exit 34B and head west 0.1 mile to the Cannon Tramway parking area. Hiker parking is available on the south side of the lot.

Spectacular views from multiple angles and diverse vantage points highlight this challenging but extremely rewarding loop in New Hampshire's Franconia Notch. The circuit scales Cannon Mountain's dome-shaped summit and rises to the top

Franconia Ridge provides an awesome backdrop to Lonesome Lake.

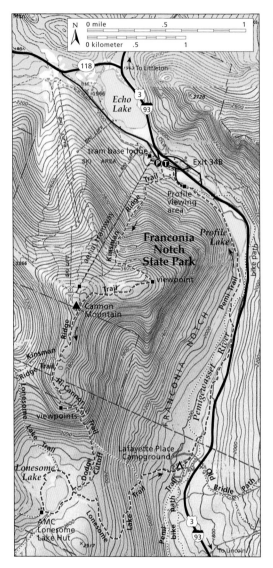

right to the trailhead. The route wastes little time scaling the steep and partially eroded mountainside. Past occasional glimpses of tramway towers, the route methodically ascends to and then briefly parallels a narrow alpine ski trail. Veering sharply left, the 1.5-mile start of the day's journey levels off near a spur branching east 0.1 mile to the top of Cannon Mountain's cliffs and mesmerizing views of Franconia Notch.

The main trail continues west 0.5 mile along the ridge. After a brief descent, scramble up and over rocks to reach a more manicured surface. Turn left on this gravel path and enjoy the many views, signs, and benches scattered along the 0.2-mile stretch that leads into a shady forest where a short side trail leaves right to the summit tower and extensive 360-degree views. During the summer and fall, especially on weekends, this can be a popular destination for visitors arriving at the nearby tramway station.

Return to the Kinsman Ridge Trail, then continue 0.3 mile south over level terrain. Picking up the Hi-Cannon Trail on the left, the journey soon becomes more difficult. Carefully make your way 0.6 mile to the first of many impressive, yet precarious, ledge outcrops, each offering aerial views of Lonesome Lake and Kinsman Mountain. Beyond the final perch, descend a steep wooden ladder and then wind through the boulder-filled landscape. The path eases near a junction with the Dodge Cutoff. Turn right and follow the 0.3-mile trail over rolling terrain to the shores of scenic Lonesome Lake.

To fully appreciate the area's beauty, embark on the 0.8-mile boardwalk-laden loop that circles the reflective blue waters. In a clockwise direction, head left through dense forests and across the pond's outlet to the Appalachian Mountain Club's Lonesome Lake Hut. Open year-round for overnight stays by reservation only (limited service in the winter), the popular hut's idyllic setting includes an incredible view of Franconia Ridge. The loop continues through marshes and past one vista after another as it winds around the pond's north shore. Turn right onto the Lonesome Lake Trail to complete the circuit.

Remain on the Lonesome Lake Trail and follow this gradual, well-used pathway 1.2 miles

of the immense cliffs that the majestic "Old Man of the Mountain" once called home. Descending ladders and wandering over scenic ledges, the route drops to the placid waters of Lonesome Lake and its famous mountain backdrops. Concluding along the banks of the Pemigewasset River, the full-day journey has much to offer to the hardiest of travelers.

To reach the Kinsman Ridge Trail, follow the service road exiting the southeast corner of the parking lot. Upon entering an open area, swing

Steep ledges on the Hi-Cannon Trail offer exquisite views of Lonesome Lake.

into the Lafayette Place Campground. Before reaching the river, turn left onto the Pemi Trail to begin the final 2-mile stretch. After crossing a paved bike path and the river, pass a beaver dam on the left and excellent views of Cannon Mountain. The undulating trail eventually crosses the river again, briefly follows the bike trail right, and then swings left to Profile Lake. Continue along the west shore and then ascend to a large parking area. Head straight and follow the driveway north to reach the tramway station.

64 FRANCONIA RIDGE

Distance: 13.9-mile loop
Hiking time: 10 hours/2 days
Difficulty: Very strenuous
Low point: 1400 feet
High point: 5260 feet
Season: Year-round
USGS map: Franconia, NH
Information: New Hampshire Division of Parks and Recreation

Getting there: From Lincoln, follow Interstate 93 north and drive 2.3 miles past Exit 34A. Turn right into the parking area. From the north, follow Interstate 93 into Franconia Notch. Turn right into Lafayette Place Campground's day-use parking area. A tunnel connects the two parking lots.

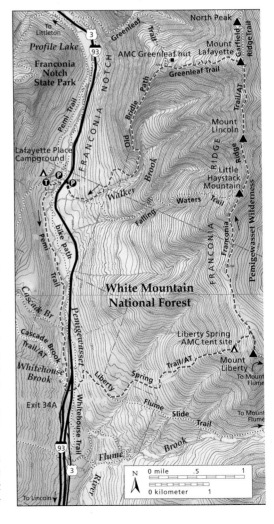

Perhaps the most popular high-elevation ridge in New England, the Franconia Range is not a place of solitude, especially on summer weekends. However, the alpine expanse between Little Haystack Mountain and Lafayette is as spectacular as any other location in the Granite State. This daylong or multi-day adventure is strenuous and demanding, but offers countless rewards, including cascading rivers, panoramic views, and the breathtaking summits of two 5000-foot mountains honoring men who left a lasting mark on American history.

Begin on the highway's west side and pick up the Pemi Trail as it leads south from the campground. Descending gently near the western banks of the rushing water, reach the popular Basin area in 1.9 miles. Here the river has carved a deep bowl in the granite. Continuing along the west bank of the river, the Pemi Trail passes a small cascade and becomes less traveled. Carefully cross Cascade and Whitehouse Brooks before turning left on the Cascade Brook Trail/ Appalachian Trail (AT).

Leading under the busy highway, the path soon leads to the Whitehouse Trail and a bike path. Bear left across the bridge, then turn right onto the Liberty Spring Trail/AT. Wind gradually

Fragile alpine flowers cling to life on Lafayette's summit.

up 0.6 mile to a junction with the Flume Slide Trail. Continue left to a stream crossing. Soon the path veers sharply left and begins a steady 1.2-mile ascent to the Liberty Spring tent site. Managed by the Appalachian Mountain Club (AMC), this overnight spot is available for a small fee on a first-come basis. In another 0.3 mile, arrive at the Franconia Ridge Trail.

Before heading north along the scenic ridge, follow the blue blazes south to Mount Liberty's rocky summit. Enjoy the excellent views of the notch and Mount Lincoln looming above. The 2.2-mile stretch north of Liberty is one of the ridge's quietest high-elevation areas. With the exception of AT thru-hikers, few others venture along this graceful ridgeline. After dropping and rising slowly, begin a steady ascent to a scenic ledge just below tree line. With the terrain flattening once again, emerge onto the open summit of Little Haystack Mountain at a junction with the ever-popular 3.2-mile-long Falling Waters Trail—an

option to consider for the descent if bad weather is threatening or muscles are tiring.

The next 1.6-mile trek to the summit of Mount Lafayette is a glorious stretch of alpine hiking. However, with no safe means of escape, it should only be attempted in good weather. With views in all directions, continue north along the ridge. While abundant beauty distracts, do your best to stay on rocky surfaces and avoid damaging fragile alpine plants. A short pitch ends atop the 5089-foot pinnacle of Mount Lincoln. Named in honor of the nation's sixteenth president, the scenic mountain is a fitting tribute to the nation's most famous former leader. A brief drop into a grove of stunted trees is followed by the final push to the seventh highest peak in New England. Named for a French national who aided America's battle for independence, Mount Lafayette stands nearly a mile high. Take your time and savor the 360-degree views and surrounding beauty; it is 4 miles and all downhill from here.

From the summit, follow the Greenleaf Trail west. The path meanders down the barren landscape, eventually reaching a thin forest and small pond. Ascend to the AMC's Greenleaf Hut (available by reservation only) before turning left onto the Old Bridle Path. Traversing Agony Ridge, the steep trail punishes the knees while thrilling the eyes. There are many exceptional vistas into Walker Ravine and the towering peaks above. After the last viewpoint, the trail drops quickly. Enter the shady forest, as the route moderates over the remaining 1.5 miles—a quiet end to a classic trek in the White Mountains.

If 13.9 miles is too long a journey, consider other possibilities. Most hikers opt for the 8.8-mile loop of Lincoln and Lafayette beginning on the Falling Waters Trail and ending on the Old Bridle Path. Similarly, to the south, the most popular route is to begin on the Whitehouse Trail and hike Mounts Liberty and Flume. Some ascend the steep Flume Slide Trail and form a loop, while others use the Liberty Spring Trail both ways. In either case, the hike is roughly 10 miles. However you choose to explore the ridge, pick a nice day for memories that will last a lifetime.

65 | MOUNT GARFIELD

Distance: 10 miles round-trip
Hiking time: 8 hours
Difficulty: Moderate–Strenuous
Low point: 1500 feet
High point: 4500 feet
Season: May through October
USGS maps: Franconia, NH; South Twin, NH
Information: White Mountain National Forest (fee)

Garfield's summit ledges showcase sweeping views of the Pemigewasset Wilderness.

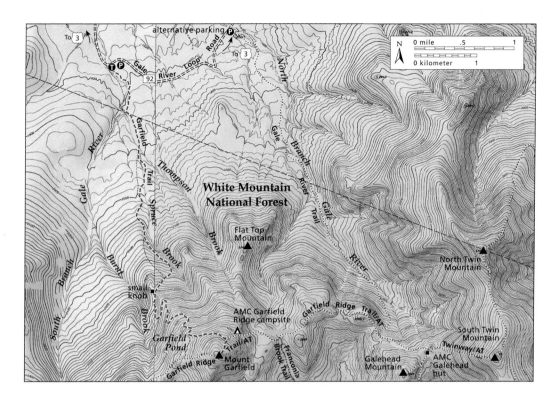

Getting there: From the intersection of US 3 and Interstate 93 north of Franconia Notch, follow US 3 east 4.7 miles and turn right onto Forest Road 92. Drive 1.2 miles to the parking area on the right.

Named for one of America's most heavily bearded and least-known presidents, Mount Garfield's ironically bald summit is appropriately situated between more well-known peaks. The nation's, twentieth leader, and a Civil War veteran, is most remembered for the assassination that ended his brief tenure in office (prompting the inauguration of Vermont-born Chester Arthur, the nation's fourth New England–born president). To the contrary, Garfield's namesake mountain is remembered more positively for its jaw-dropping views of the Pemigewasset Wilderness and the Franconia Range. A pleasant and gradual excursion through quaint forest slopes, the 5-mile trail to the top is a long day hike, as well as an excellent place to begin an overnight adventure.

The path begins above the banks of the South Branch of the Gale River. Leading over gently sloping terrain, follow the Garfield Trail as it crosses Thompson Brook and then Spruce Brook twice. Continue the moderate ascent. Straight over a snowmobile trail, the route begins to climb a bit more steadily. Enjoy the chorus of songbirds as you crest the top of a small knob, just beyond the climb's halfway point. Following a brief descent, enter a series of switchbacks that gradually wind up the ridge. Well after the birch and maple give way to evergreen, the trail straightens and plods ahead to a junction with the Garfield Ridge Trail (Appalachian Trail).

Turn right onto the Garfield Ridge Trail and rise steeply 0.2 mile—the hardest part of the hike. The aggressive but straightforward climb soon ends atop the open granite summit and the site of a former lookout tower. From this perspective, lower than many of the surrounding peaks, the views are indescribable. Below, the mountain's barren south slope falls over a series of cascading ledges. With many places to enjoy the scenery, Garfield is an excellent place to lounge on a summer afternoon. Return the way you came for one of the more knee-friendly, though long, descents from a New England 4000-foot mountain.

For a slightly longer hike, consider following the Garfield Ridge Trail west 0.5 mile. The 650-foot descent leads to a small, secluded high-elevation pond. If you are interested in an overnight trek, take advantage of the nearby Garfield Ridge campsite. Located east on the Garfield Ridge Trail, the site is managed by the Appalachian Mountain Club and is available for a modest fee on a first-come basis. For an alternative descent, follow the scenic Garfield Ridge Trail east and descend on the Gale River Trail. After dropping steeply, it winds pleasantly through the river valley. Upon reaching the parking area, follow the forest road 1.6 miles west back to the original trailhead to complete a 13.1-mile circuit.

66 ZEACLIFF

Distance: 9.2 miles round-trip
Hiking time: 7 hours
Difficulty: Moderate–Strenuous
Low point: 2000 feet
High point: 3740 feet
Season: May through October
USGS maps: South Twin Mountain, NH; Crawford Notch, NH
Information: White Mountain National Forest (fee)

Zeacliff's reflection from Zealand Pond

Getting there: From the junction of Routes 3 and 302 in Twin Mountain, follow Route 302 east 2.2 miles. Turn right onto Zealand Road and drive 3.4 miles to the parking area at the end.

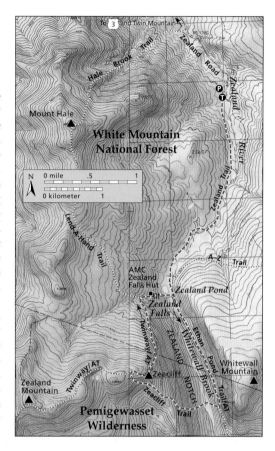

This delightful excursion into the heart of the White Mountains showcases many extraordinary natural features. With each step comes yet one more delectable treat, including roaring streams, tranquil forests, reflective ponds, tumbling cascades, gnarled boulders, and dramatic vistas. Although more than 9 miles in length, two-thirds of the hike traverses level terrain. The remaining one-third, while significantly steep, repays the effort with inspiring scenes within boulder-strewn Zealand Notch and breathtaking views atop the precipitous Zeacliff. As an added bonus, throughout the journey the changing habitat provides ample opportunity to encounter plentiful wildlife, from warbling songbirds to stomping moose.

For 2.5 miles the heavily used Zealand Trail leads gradually up the valley. While slightly uneven and eroded at first, upon reaching the banks of the Zealand River the footing improves substantially. Weave over small streams, through marshy wetlands, and past frequent viewpoints to a second three-way intersection. This marks the beginning of the 4.2-mile loop portion of the day's adventure.

Continue straight on the Ethan Pond Trail/Appalachian Trail (AT). Through peaceful birch forests, this former railbed proceeds 1.3 miles into the heart of Zealand Notch. The site of overzealous loggers a century ago, today the notch is an artist's paradise. With the rugged slopes of Whitewall Mountain and Zeacliff on the nearby edges, Mount Carrigain looms between in the distance. From the heart of the notch, pick up the Zeacliff Trail, which drops right into a field of boulders. Quickly entering the Pemigewasset Wilderness, the narrow path briefly swings north, then bends west and enters the forest. Descend abruptly to the banks of Whitewall Brook.

Hop over the stones to the other side and begin the 1.2-mile climb to Zeacliff. At first grueling and relentless, the heart-pounding ascent slowly plateaus into a fern-draped forest. Wrapping west around the cliff's face, the path scrambles up ledge and over rock, offering occasional glimpses of Mount Bond. A final rise leads to the Twinway/AT. Turn right and head 0.1 mile over granite and boardwalk to a spur that leads right to the top of Zeacliff and mesmerizing views that include the Presidential Range as well as much of the Pemigewasset Wilderness.

Follow the path as it parallels the cliff's side and rejoins the Twinway/AT. A steady 1.2-mile descent ensues, at first on a rocky pathway. Take your time; the trail leads to a small brook crossing and soon after the Appalachian Mountain Club's (AMC) Zealand Falls Hut. Open year-round for reservations (limited service off-season), this popular overnight facility is ideally located adjacent to the scenic falls. Cascading dozens of feet over smoothed rock, the falls are a popular place to enjoy the fresh mountain air. Follow the Twinway/AT 0.2 mile back to the Zealand Trail. Turn left for the 2.5-mile conclusion.

67 MOUNT WASHINGTON

Distance: 9.6-mile loop
Hiking time: 9 hours
Difficulty: Very strenuous
Low point: 2500 feet
High point: 6288 feet
Season: May–October
USGS map: Mount Washington, NH
Information: White Mountain National Forest (fee)

Getting there: From the junction of Routes 3 and 302 in Twin Mountain, follow Route 302 east 4.6 miles. Turn left onto Base Road (leads to cog railway station) and drive 5.6 miles to a parking area on the right.

Named in honor of a man who was "first in peace, first in war, and first in the hearts of his

countrymen," Mount Washington's 6288-foot summit is appropriately first on the list of the highest peaks in New England. Ascended by Darby Field in 1642, 147 years before George was inaugurated as the nation's president, today the mountain is a popular destination for hikers, auto road drivers, and cog railway riders. Covered by buildings and weather-tracking

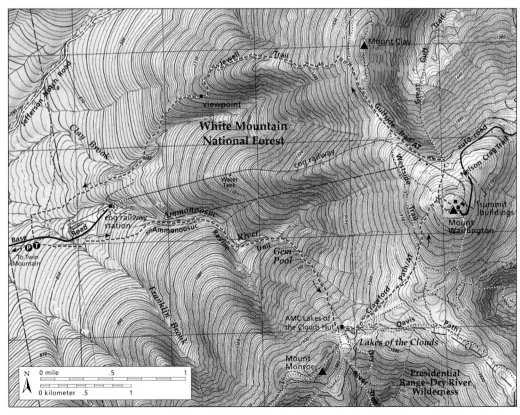

Mount Washington rises more than 1000 feet above the Lakes of the Clouds.

devices, the oft-swarmed summit can be chaotic; however, the challenging journey to the top of New Hampshire is also awash in raw natural scenery and limitless beauty. While some hikers before you have died from ill-preparedness and nasty storms, choose this hike with care for a glorious day in the White Mountains.

Begin on the Ammonoosuc Ravine Trail, which departs from the east side of the parking lot. Over gently rolling terrain, the path leads 1 mile to the banks of the Ammonoosuc River. To the left a trail leads quickly to the Mount Washington cog railway station. With the rushing water drowning out all but the loudest of noises, swing right and wind up the narrowing valley. In 1.1 miles arrive at serene Gem Pool at the base of a small cascade. This marks the start of a grueling 1-mile stretch.

Embarking up the unrelenting slope, pass a spur right that descends to a narrow perch with stunning views of the cascading river. Plod ahead, and your effort will soon be rewarded with increasing views through the shrinking forest canopy. Across a number of small streams, the trail eases slightly as it leads over rock and ledge (use extra care if wet or icy) to the Appalachian Mountain Club's (AMC) Lakes of the Clouds Hut. High above the tree line at 5012 feet above sea level, the ninety-bunk hut is available for overnight stays by reservation. It is also a good location to turn around if weather is threatening, because the final 1.4-mile climb is entirely exposed.

Turn left onto the Crawford Path, the oldest continuously used hiking trail in America, and wind between the hut's scenic namesake tarns. The cold water and footway are surrounded by lush alpine vegetation, so watch your step. At a three-way intersection, stay left on the white-blazed route. The steady climb up the Crawford Path slowly winds up the rock-strewn slope to the prolific summit buildings. While the congestion can be anticlimactic, enjoy the sweeping views that on a clear day encompass four states and the province of Québec. The summit buildings also offer food, restrooms, and temporary shelter from Memorial Day to Columbus Day.

The difficult 5.1-mile descent begins on the Gulfside Trail, which leaves northwest of the

167

summit between two buildings. Drop quickly to a junction and veer right. The route makes its way over the cog railway tracks. Completed in 1869, the active railway is a popular tourist attraction. Its coal-powered trains have historically sent numerous puffs of black smoke into the air, visible from miles away; however, this may begin to change, because in 2008 the railway added a diesel-powered train to its fleet. Swinging left past the Great Gulf Trail, the route parallels the tracks while hugging the edge of the deep ravine. With awesome views of the northern Presidential peaks to the right, drop into a small saddle.

Stay left along the western flank of Mount Clay and make your way to the Jewell Trail. Turn left onto the 3.7-mile path and begin an arduous, but attractive descent along the exposed ridgeline. With the aid of switchbacks, make your way back to the thick evergreen forests that carpet the lower slopes. While no longer exposed, the trek remains demanding. Past a final view of the mountain, drop rapidly to a crossing of Clay Brook. Rise past a path leading left to the train station. Stay right and hike 1 mile along the more moderate terrain. A bridge leads over Ammonoosuc River just before the trail reaches Base Road and the parking area.

Often in the clouds, Washington is inviting on a sunny August day (seen from Mount Monroe).

68 CRAWFORD NOTCH

Distance: 3.6 miles round-trip
Hiking time: 3 hours
Difficulty: Moderate
Low point: 1900 feet
High point: 2800 feet
Season: Year-round
USGS map: Crawford Notch, NH
Information: New Hampshire Division of Parks and Recreation

Getting there: From the junction of Routes 3 and 302 in Twin Mountain, follow Route 302 east 8.8 miles. A small parking area is available across from Saco Lake at the Crawford Notch Depot and along the side of the road (parking at the Appalachian Mountain Club's Highland Center is for overnight guests only).

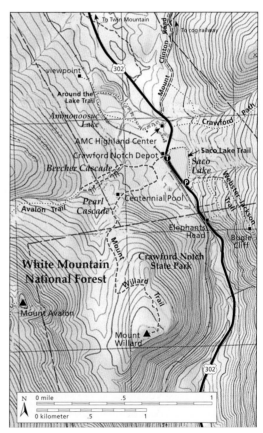

Like an altar surrounded by a towering cathedral, the low, open summit of Mount Willard's cliff face stands majestically amid the glacier-scoured higher peaks of Crawford Notch. The rockslides and steep ledges of Mounts Webster and Willey draw the eyes into the deep gulf beneath, where the Saco River, Route 302, and the Crawford Notch Railroad snake their way toward the Mount Washington Valley. As an added bonus, Mount Willard's bounty can be reached in a short half-day hike, a perfect choice for a family outing. Along with other nearby cascades, ledges, and wetlands, this trek is a great choice throughout the year.

The hike begins at the Crawford Notch Depot. Pick up the Avalon Trail on the other side of the tracks (note this is an active rail line). In a few hundred feet, turn left onto the Mount Willard Trail. This 1.6-mile path quickly crosses a shallow streambed and begins to climb moderately up the slope. Paralleling the running water, in 0.5 mile it reaches Centennial Pool, a small cascade on the right. After a steep climb, the path turns abruptly right onto the former carriage trail. The wide route winds steadily for nearly a mile before leveling. The final 0.2-mile stretch passes through pleasant spruce-fir forests to emerge onto the open summit. Here, perched high above a large sheer cliff, the view of Crawford Notch is tantalizing. On a clear day the summit of Mount Washington can be seen to the north. Mount Willard, visited by many, has a large open area from which to enjoy the views.

Willard provides exceptional shots of Mount Webster and Crawford Notch.

Continue the journey by retracing your steps back to the Avalon Trail and then turn left. In 0.1 mile reach a stream crossing. After making your way across the rocks, veer left onto a side trail. This quiet path leads to scenic Beecher and Pearl Cascades, especially pleasant in late spring. After passing the second cascade, the side trail swings back to the Avalon Trail. Turn right and return to Crawford Notch Depot.

Looking for additional hikes in the area? From behind the nearby Highland Center, a 1.8-mile loop leads around Ammonoosuc Lake and to a scenic view of the Presidential Range. Across the street a pleasant 0.3-mile path winds around Saco Lake. Farther east, the Webster–Jackson Trail leads 0.3 mile to Elephants Head's scenic ledge (via a short spur) and 0.6 mile to impressive views atop Bugle Cliff. The Webster–Jackson Trail can also be used to complete a more difficult 6.5-mile loop over two scenic mountains (see Hike 69). Lastly, follow the challenging Avalon Trail, beyond the cascades, 1.9 miles to Mount Avalon's summit ledges and expansive scenes of Crawford Notch. For a daylong adventure that includes two 4000-foot mountains, you can complete a mostly wooded 7.5-mile loop using the Avalon, Willey Range, Mount Tom Spur, and A–Z Trails. (See the USGS map for these additional hikes.)

69 WEBSTER CLIFF–DRY RIVER

Distance: 15.9-mile loop
Hiking time: 10 hours/2 days
Difficulty: Strenuous
Low point: 1275 feet
High point: 4052 feet
Season: May through October
USGS maps: Crawford Notch, NH; Stairs Mountain, NH
Information: White Mountain National Forest

Getting there: From Bartlett, follow Route 302 west toward Crawford Notch. In 10.9 miles reach the Webster Cliff trailhead. Parking is available on the south side of the road and along the driveway that leads left to the Ethan Pond Trail.

This challenging hike rises out of Crawford Notch's deep chasm to the dizzying heights of Webster Cliff. The trail leads to rock perches that lie in the shadows of soaring raptors. Choose this journey into a world of precipitous cliffs and marvel at its rugged beauty. Return on the same route to complete a rewarding 6.6-mile trek or, better yet, push on to the southern Presidentials and beyond to the remote Dry River Wilderness. In this region, there are endless opportunities to revel in a long-day or multi-day circuit. The described 15.9-mile loop will satisfy your senses and encourage you to return again and again to explore other corners of this wild landscape.

Begin on the Webster Cliff Trail, heading north along the Appalachian Trail (AT), and cross the bridge leading over the Saco River. The route rises slowly to a junction with the Saco River Trail. Stay left and follow the white blazes up an increasingly arduous slope. Watch your footing on the loose rock as you wind steeply up the ridge. Soon the path swings left and climbs to the first of countless vistas. From exposed rock to thick forest, pass a view north to Mount Washington and continue plodding up the scenic

The Webster Cliff Trail provides a bird's–eye view of Crawford Notch.

ridge. To the left, the scarred walls of Crawford Notch provide an amazing backdrop. Carefully ascend the series of inclines that eventually culminate atop 3950-foot Mount Webster amid spectacular scenery.

If you choose to turn back here, carefully descend the steep trail. For those seeking more adventure, follow the Webster Cliff Trail/AT north 1.4 miles over rolling terrain to the 4052-foot summit of Mount Jackson and 360-degree views, including spectacular snapshots of Mount Washington. Remaining on the Webster Cliff Trail/AT, drop quickly down the mountain's rocky north face. Once again, the route eases along a level ridgeline. Pass through a high-elevation bog and continue 1.5 miles to the Appalachian Mountain Club's (AMC) Mizpah Spring Hut and Nauman tent site. For a fee, both are available as overnight destinations—

the former by reservation, the latter on a first-come basis.

While the ridge continues with increasing splendor to Mounts Pierce, Eisenhower, Franklin, Monroe, and Washington, for this excursion descend into the 27,380-acre Presidential Range–Dry River Wilderness by turning right onto the Mount Clinton Trail. Hike 0.5 mile, then turn left, joining the 1.7-mile Dry River Cutoff. After traversing a plateau-like ridge, the path drops quickly while paralleling a small brook. Stay right on the Mount Eisenhower Trail and down to the Dry River. Carefully make your way across the rushing water (can be difficult in high water) and proceed uphill 0.1 mile to the Dry River Trail.

To the north, the trail leads 0.2 mile to an unmarked spur that drops left to the plummeting Dry River Falls, a quaint diversion. Turn right to begin the 4.7-mile trek out of the secluded valley.

A hiker captures a dramatic shot of Webster Cliff on a crisp September day.

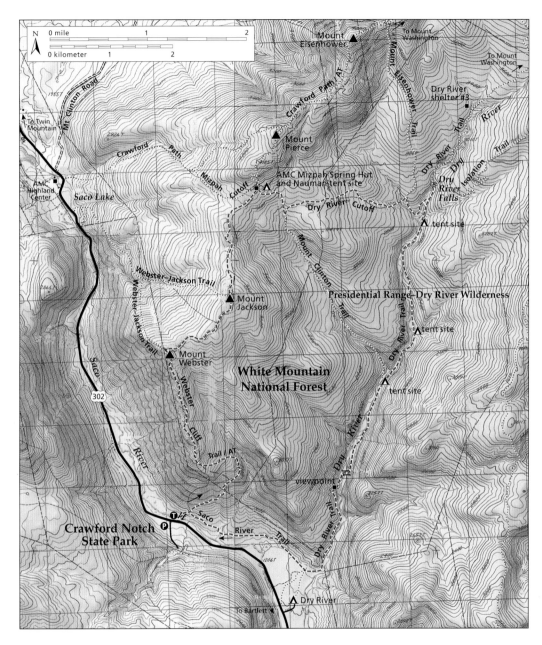

Past three designated campsites (flat areas ideal for tenting), the route mostly follows an old railbed that has washed out in a few places. To avoid these areas the trail occasionally scales the slope, only to drop back to the river. In 3.5 miles, reach a large suspension bridge (washed out in 2006, but replaced in 2009). After crossing the river, climb over a ridge with a view of Mount Washington. Depart the wilderness, and then turn right onto the Saco River Trail. Follow this path 1.7 miles back to the Webster Cliff Trail. Turn left to reach the end.

70 DAVIS PATH

Distance: 9 miles round-trip
Hiking time: 7 hours
Difficulty: Moderate–Strenuous
Low point: 1000 feet
High point: 3400 feet
Season: Year-round
USGS maps: Bartlett, NH; Stairs Mountain, NH
Information: White Mountain National Forest (fee)

Getting there: From Bartlett, follow Route 302 west 6.2 miles and turn right into the large parking area near the banks of the Saco River.

Constructed by Nathaniel Davis in 1845 as a 15-mile bridle path to Mount Washington, the Davis Path soon became too difficult to maintain. Fortunately, the route was resurrected in 1910 for hiking and for the past century has led many an adventurer on an enjoyable excursion. Passing just beneath the summit of five scenic peaks, the trail combines pleasant ridgeline

hiking with some of the White Mountains' most alluring vistas. This recommended daylong trek ventures along the path's first 3.7 miles and visits two incredibly picturesque mountaintops. In the process, you'll discover a trail that demands future exploration.

From the parking area, follow the dirt road that leads a few hundred feet upstream near the banks of the Saco River. Cross the large suspension bridge to a trail sign and plaque commemorating the recent conservation of the trailhead area, an effort aided by the Trust for Public Land. Proceed straight through a small wetland area, and then swing right into a pleasant hardwood forest. After crossing a small brook, the path enters the Presidential Range–Dry River Wilderness and begins to climb more aggressively. The straightforward 1.5-mile ascent provides an excellent workout and before long emerges onto a rock outcrop with splendid views of Mount Carrigain and the Saco River Valley. Continue 0.3 mile to the base of a large ledge, where a spur leads left up exposed granite to the barren top of Mount Crawford and an incredible panorama highlighted by Mount Washington's south face.

Upon returning to the Davis Path, veer left, entering a dark evergreen tunnel. For the next 1.5 miles the trail enjoys mostly moderate grades, emerging onto exposed ledges before skirting beneath Mount Resolution's scree-sloped west side. The oft-damp footway soon leads to a junction with the Mount Parker Trail. To the left, a steep 0.1-mile trail drops to the tiny Resolution shelter, available on a first-come basis. Make a hard right onto the Mount Parker Trail, which climbs rapidly to a large rock face. Carefully

November snow blankets Mount Washington (seen from Mount Resolution).

make your way up the open area (can be tricky when wet or icy) where views abound. Back in the woods, the route scales a wooded knoll, crosses a seasonal stream, and rises to the trail's high point. At 3400 feet, Mount Resolution's west summit offers breathtaking scenery including the southern Presidential Range and nearby Stairs Mountain's impressive cliff-covered face.

From here, retrace your steps to the trailhead. However, if time, energy, and enthusiasm abound, consider adding Stairs Mountain to the day's itinerary by hiking 0.7 mile north on the Davis Path. Up a steep pitch, the trail reaches a 0.2-mile spur to the summit's impressive outcrop. On future Davis Path trips, consider longer day or overnight hikes that venture farther north to Mounts Isolation and Davis. (See the USGS maps.) The latter peak is not frequently climbed, yet is one of the finest in the White Mountains.

The eastern newt's terrestrial phase, red efts are spotted throughout New England.

71 NANCY BROOK SCENIC AREA

Distance: 8.6 miles round-trip
Hiking time: 6 hours
Difficulty: Moderate–Strenuous
Low point: 940 feet
High point: 3140 feet
Season: Year-round
USGS maps: Bartlett, NH; Mount Carrigain, NH
Information: White Mountain National Forest (fee)

Getting there: From Bartlett, follow Route 302 west 5.3 miles to the Nancy Pond trailhead and parking spaces on the left.

Located in the heart of the White Mountain National Forest, this 8.6-mile round-trip excursion travels to a handful of the region's less visible treasures. Along the way, enjoy the sparkling cascades, roaring brook, and secluded pond named for a young, fleeing woman who perished centuries ago during a mountain storm. Weave through an old-growth spruce-fir forest—a dense canopy of trees, some more than 200 years old. Venture to the west end of Norcross Pond and stand atop an edge of the sprawling Pemigewasset Wilderness. Rarely crowded, the Nancy Brook Scenic Area is the ideal destination for the mind to wander and the body to energize.

Heading west on the Nancy Pond Trail, climb gradually up a series of old woods roads. After passing private residences on the right and crossing Halfway Brook, the trail approaches Nancy Brook 0.8 mile from the start. Swinging left,

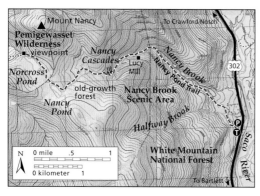

parallel the rushing water as the route leads up the valley. In less than a mile arrive at the banks of the brook. Carefully make your way to the other side—it can be tricky during high water—and continue heading upstream. In 0.2 mile pass the former Lucy Mill site on the left and enter the 460-acre Nancy Brook Scenic Area.

Over the next 0.5 mile the trail skirts along partially eroded slopes with the help of rock steps. After crossing Nancy Brook a second time, the trail climbs to the base of the stunning cascades. Here the clear water tumbles more than 300 feet down a large ledge before spraying into a large pool below. On a warm day, the falls provide a cool, refreshing mist. If you have had your fill, turn back here to complete a 4.8-mile round-trip hike. Otherwise, start up the most difficult part of the hike. Winding up switchbacks, the trail climbs 0.4 mile past nice views of the falls and Stairs Mountain before arriving at the top.

Continuing along the brook, enter the core of the scenic area and a world of mature trees. Inaccessible to loggers a century ago, this forest, while old, is not towering. Still, the diversity of ages and the complexity of vegetation are features rarely seen in the Northeast. Rising gradually from the cascades, the trail brings you to the quaint shore of Nancy Pond in 0.6 mile. Heavily trampled by moose, the 4-acre pond and adjacent swamp sit more than 3000 feet above sea level.

The final 0.9-mile stretch proceeds across a height-of-land that divides the watersheds of the Saco and Merrimack rivers. Here the trail enters the Pemigewasset Wilderness—the largest federally designated wilderness area in New England.

Nancy Cascades are among the tallest in the White Mountains.

Hike past Little Norcross Pond to the east shore of its larger neighbor. Wrapping around the north-shore the route offers pleasant scenes of the placid water, culminating with a magnificent viewpoint at the ledge-covered outlet. Recent beaver activity has raised the pond's level a few feet, so watch your footing near the shore. An ideal place to enjoy lunch and dream of future White Mountain adventures, Norcross Pond is the final stop on the day's trek. While it is a difficult place to leave, when necessary, follow the Nancy Pond Trail 4.3 miles back to the parking area.

72 SOUTH AND MIDDLE MOAT

Distance: 6.6 miles round-trip
Hiking time: 5 hours
Difficulty: Moderate–Strenuous
Low point: 650 feet
High point: 2800 feet
Season: Year-round
USGS maps: North Conway West, NH; Silver Lake, NH
Information: White Mountain National Forest (fee)

Getting there: At the junction of Routes 16 and 153 in Conway, drive 0.9 mile north on West Side Drive. Turn left onto Passaconaway Road (becomes Dugway Road) and drive 3.4 miles to the parking area on the right.

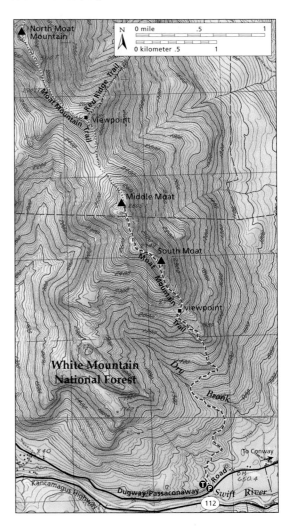

Standing guard on North Conway's western flank, Moat Mountain's long ridgeline provides some of the finest views in the White Mountains. Sometimes overlooked by hikers seeking one of New Hampshire's forty-eight 4000-foot summits, Moat Mountain rewards those whose primary quest is limitless natural beauty. The 3.3-mile excursion to the ridge's two most southern promontories begins gradually, becomes more challenging, and slowly emerges atop barren rocks. An excellent hike throughout the year, the mountain's southern exposure often allows exploration on snow-free spring terrain weeks before neighboring trails.

The hike begins on the recently relocated southern terminus of the Moat Mountain Trail. Rising gradually 1.3 miles, the route takes advantage of old woods roads. After descending to and then crossing a couple of small streams, the final one over a wooden bridge, you reach the base of the hike's major climb. Here, the terrain becomes more demanding, but also more fun. Up the rocky mountain slope, make your way through the increasingly open forest canopy. In the thin soils below, carpets of wildflowers blossom profusely, including the fragile pink lady's slipper.

Mount Chocorua from the first of many viewpoints en route to South Moat

Level off briefly and then begin a steadier ascent that leads dramatically to the first vista of the day—a snapshot of Mount Chocorua's pinnacle-shaped summit. Over the next 0.6 mile, scale a series of open ledges that can be tricky if wet or icy. For the most part, the route remains on the ledges' lower sides while occasionally weaving in and out of the pine-oak forest. Before long, the effort is paid off handsomely with 360-degree views atop South Moat. Towering to the north is Mount Washington's glistening summit; to the west, the heart of the White Mountains shadows the winding Kancamagus Highway; and looking east you see the vast expanse of the Mount Washington Valley.

South Moat is a popular turnaround point for many hikers, but to extend the thrill and find more secluded viewing areas, plod 0.6 mile north to the slightly higher, and equally exposed, Middle Moat summit. The scenic route there is relatively flat, with one minor descent, and well worth the added effort. Retrace your steps on the same trail to complete the journey.

If you are looking for a longer adventure, consider extending the hike 3.8 miles round-trip by taking the Moat Mountain Trail all the way to North Moat, the ridge's highest point. The journey there begins along Middle Moat's exposed northern ridgeline. After descending into a thickly forested saddle, the path rises to a junction with the Red Ridge Trail (and a nice viewpoint). The final 0.9-mile section climbs slowly over interesting rocky terrain before arriving at the spectacular, treeless summit.

73 CARTER DOME

Distance: 10.2-mile loop
Hiking time: 8 hours
Difficulty: Strenuous
Low point: 1487 feet
High point: 4832 feet
Season: Year-round
USGS map: Carter Dome, NH
Information: White Mountain National Forest (fee)

Carter Dome's views of the Presidential Range are particularly intriguing in winter.

Getting there: From the eastern junction of Routes 2 and 16 in Gorham, follow Route 16 south 6.9 miles to the parking area on the left. Beginning in Pinkham Notch, follow Route 16 north 3.7 miles to the parking area on the right.

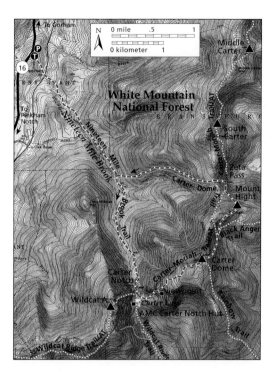

Located in close proximity to the imposing Presidential Range, Carter Ridge is one of the finest vantage points from which to gaze onto the rocky summits and deep chasms of its taller western neighbors. This challenging all-day hike combines soothing mountain streams, a rugged boulder-filled notch, and the ridge's most scenic location. In addition, the loop passes an Appalachian Mountain Club (AMC) hut offering overnight accommodations (by reservation only) and traverses the ninth highest peak in New Hampshire. These trails are accessible year-round, so choose a clear day any time of year to fully appreciate the tremendous beauty.

Start on the popular Nineteen Mile Brook Trail. One of the shorter and less-exposed paths to an AMC hut, this route is well trodden throughout the year (the hut remains open all year with limited service during the winter). The first 1.9 miles follow closely along the rushing mountain stream while rising gradually to an intersection with the Carter Dome Trail. Continue ascending moderately on the Nineteen Mile Brook Trail. Passing through pleasant forests, the trail reaches the Appalachian Trail (AT) at mile 3.6. To the right, the white-blazed path rises steeply to the top of Peak A of Wildcat Mountain. Stay left and in 0.2 mile arrive at Carter Lake and the start of the Carter–Moriah Trail/AT. Located in the heart of Carter Notch, this junction lies 0.2 mile north of the Carter Notch Hut complex.

Turning left, begin the toughest section of the day's hike—a 1.2-mile, 1500-foot climb to the top of Carter Dome. While not technically difficult, the incline is demanding, particularly in the beginning. After passing a scenic spur right that leads a few dozen feet up to a breathtaking view of the jagged notch below, the path moderates slightly. Cresting atop the flat summit, pass a large cairn and continue to a pleasant view of Mount Washington.

For a less-crowded and more spectacular vista, proceed gently 0.8 mile north to the less-visited Mount Hight. En route to Mount Hight, stay right on the Carter–Moriah Trail at its junction with the Carter Dome Trail (the Carter Dome Trail offers a bad-weather alternative). Less prestigious than its taller neighbor, Mount Hight's barren summit is the most inviting spot on the Carter Ridge, as it offers 360-degree views that include the newly designated Wild River Wilderness area to the east.

The 4.4-mile descent continues along the Carter–Moriah Trail as the path drops quickly into the spruce-fir forest. In 0.5 mile join the Carter Dome Trail, bear right, and soon arrive at Zeta Pass. Leaving the AT behind, follow the Carter Dome Trail left 1.9 miles as it steadily descends the mountain slope. Veer right onto the Nineteen Mile Brook Trail for the final 1.9-mile stretch to Route 16.

Cold Brook Fall is the last of many splendid natural features along this loop.

74 MOUNT ADAMS

Distance: 9.8-mile loop
Hiking time: 9 hours
Difficulty: Very strenuous
Low point: 1306 feet
High point: 5774 feet
Season: June through October
USGS map: Mount Washington, NH
Information: White Mountain National Forest

Getting there: The Mount Adams trailhead is located on Route 2 in Randolph, 5.4 miles west of the western junction of Routes 16 and 2 in Gorham, and 7.2 miles east of the junction of Routes 2 and 115 in Jefferson.

The highest undeveloped mountain in New England, Mount Adams is named for the nation's second president, John Adams of Massachusetts.

Positioned between Mount Jefferson and Mount Madison, together the three peaks form the impressive northern Presidential Range. With a large network of trails dissecting their slopes, the three summits offer a great variety of classic hiking opportunities. This challenging loop combines one of the area's stereotypical deep ravines with a long, exposed ridgeline. Be prepared and approach Mount Adams with caution; the weather can be dangerous, but under clear skies there are few places more awe-inspiring.

Begin at a large kiosk. After crossing a railbed, pick up the Air Line as it leads right. Gradually climb through thick hardwood forests, then veer right in 0.8 mile onto the Short Line. The Short Line continues a moderate ascent up the ridge for 1.9 miles, coinciding briefly with the Randolph Path. As you approach Cold Brook, the route ends at an intersection. Continue ahead on the King Ravine Trail. Here, the fun and difficulty increase dramatically.

Past scenic Mossy Fall, scramble over rocks for 0.7 mile to the foot of the amphitheater-shaped ravine. This is a good location to turn around if bad weather is threatening. Also, to the left, the Chemin des Dames Trail offers a steep but shorter alternative out of King Ravine to the exposed Durand Ridge. Ahead, the King Ravine Trail provides two options, the Elevated and the Subway. Choose the latter for caves and exploration, while the former is more straightforward. After the two reconnect, pass the imposing Great Gully Trail on the right and then a spur to the ice caves, a short loop that offers cool air on hot summer days. The final ascent out of the deep ravine is an invigorating, heart-pounding 1100-foot climb in 0.5 mile. Fortunately, the footing gradually improves with elevation and the scenes are spectacular.

Emerge through The Gateway, a narrow gap in the ridge, and turn right, rejoining the Air Line. After briefly intersecting the Gulfside Trail, veer left and up 0.6 rocky mile to Mount Adams's pointy summit. Enjoy the inspiring views of the Great Gulf bowl and imposing walls of its surrounding peaks.

Descending the mountain, while easier on the chest, is more difficult on the legs. Take your time and head 0.3 mile down the Lowes Path to Thunderstorm Junction. Continue straight at the large cairn and in 100 feet veer right onto the Spur Trail (not the more difficult Great Gully Trail that also departs more sharply right). Across open terrain, this scenic route traverses pleasant high alpine meadows. In less than a mile, the journey leads below tree line and soon reaches a spur right to a great location to gaze down upon King Ravine, the Knights Castle.

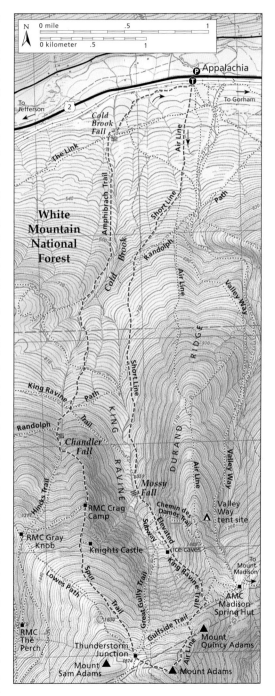

Remain on the Spur Trail and swing right past Crag Camp, a small overnight lodge operated by the Randolph Mountain Club (RMC). The path drops quickly over the next mile—watch your step—and after passing Chandler Fall ends at the Randolph Path. Stay right, cross Cold Brook, and quickly arrive at a five-way intersection. Turn slightly left onto the Amphibrach Trail and enjoy a relaxing 1.9-mile trek to scenic Cold Brook Fall. Veer right, cross the stone Memorial Bridge, and hike 0.7 mile to the Air Line, a few hundred feet south of the trailhead.

For a less difficult Mount Adams hike and one possible year-round, ascend the Air Line 4.3 miles to Mount Adams. Descend the Gulfside Trail to Madison Spring Hut and return 3.8 miles down the less-exposed Valley Way.

75 BALDFACES

Distance: 10.7-mile loop
Hiking time: 9 hours
Difficulty: Strenuous
Low point: 520 feet
High point: 3610 feet
Season: Year-round
USGS maps: Chatham, NH; Wild River, NH
Information: White Mountain National Forest (fee)

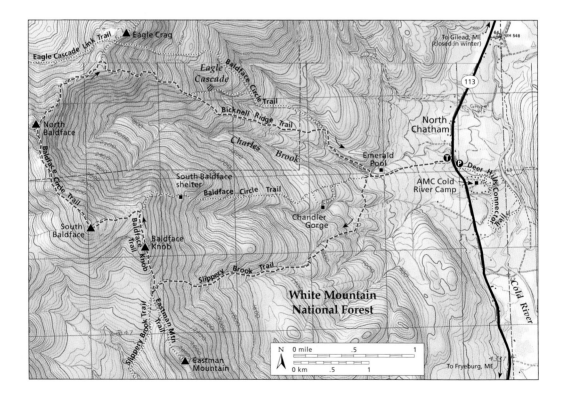

South Baldface's final ascent remains mostly in the open.

Getting there: From Fryeburg, follow Route 113 north 17.4 miles to North Chatham; or drive south on Route 113 from Route 2 in Gilead 12.7 miles (access in the winter is from the south only). The parking lot is on the east side of the road. (Note: Route 113 is winding, with unusual intersections, but clearly marked.)

At just over 3600 feet in elevation, North and South Baldface lie more than 1000 feet below many of their distant neighbors to the west. Yet, from afar, their barren summits stand apart among the more forested peaks surrounding them. Up close, the Baldfaces are even more breathtaking. Left bare in the wake of a 1903 fire, their exposed upper ridges provide innumerable scenic vistas in all directions. On their lower slopes, flowing streams form countless cascades and sustain the resident moose, deer, and bear populations. This increasingly popular hike offers numerous trail options and plenty of space. Regardless of which paths you choose, the Baldface circuit is a workout, exceeded only by its many rewards.

The Baldface Circle Trail begins easily on the west side of Route 113 (just north of the parking area) and in 0.7 mile reaches the start of the loop. To the right a 0.1-mile spur leads to Emerald Pool, a popular swimming hole beneath a small cascade. Turn left on the Baldface Circle Trail for 0.2 mile, then left again, heading south on the less heavily used Slippery Brook Trail. The more difficult and direct Baldface Circle Trail bears right and ascends gradually to a campsite before ascending a very steep, exposed ridge, whereas the Slippery Brook Trail makes a more moderate 2.6-mile ascent of the ridge.

Rise steadily to a saddle and a four-way intersection. To the left, the lightly trodden Eastman Mountain Trail leads 0.8 mile to an open summit. Swing north and join the 0.7-mile Baldface Knob Trail. After rising over the exposed knob and enjoying its excellent views, descend briefly before returning to the open granite at a junction with the Baldface Circle Trail. Bear left and proceed up the barren landscape. The final 0.5-mile climb ends atop South Baldface where 360-degree views include the towering summit of Mount Washington to the west and the blue waters of Kezar Lake east.

Follow the Baldface Circle Trail 1.2 miles to the summit of North Baldface. Meandering in and out of thin forests, the trail provides a scattering of incredible vistas. The final push to wide-open North Baldface leads once again to impressive views in all directions. In the trees and out onto open ledges, the path tumbles 0.9 mile down and occasionally up small inclines until reaching a small open bump on the ridge.

Pick up the Bicknell Ridge Trail on the right. (For a less-exposed but slightly longer option, stay straight on the Baldface Circle Trail.) The Bicknell Ridge Trail drops quickly down semi-exposed granite slabs where views of the large, glacially cut basin are stunning. Follow this path past the final open spot on the ridge, where the Eagle Cascade Link Trail diverges left, and for another 1.5 miles through scenic forests to the banks of a rushing stream. Carefully make your way across and rejoin the Baldface Circle Trail to the right. In 0.7 mile cross the stream a second time (difficult in high waters) and enjoy the final 0.7-mile stretch to the parking area.

76 EAST ROYCE MOUNTAIN

Distance: 7.2 miles round-trip
Hiking time: 5 hours
Difficulty: Moderate–Strenuous
Low point: 600 feet
High point: 3114 feet
Season: Year-round
USGS maps: Speckled Mountain, ME; Wild River, NH
Information: White Mountain National Forest (fee)

Getting there: From Fryeburg, follow Route 113 north 19.8 miles, or drive south on Route 113 from Route 2 in Gilead 10.3 miles (access in the winter is only from the south). The parking area is on the east side of the road (near the Brickett Place) 0.3 mile north of the Cold River Campground. The campground entrance is plowed for winter parking.

Tucked away in the Maine section of the White Mountain National Forest and just east of the New Hampshire border, East Royce's rugged slopes form the western wall of narrow Evans Notch. This scenic peak, nestled between two wilderness areas, offers splendid views of the Mahoosucs, the Presidential Range, and western Maine. East Royce is a popular destination from May to October when the road through Evans Notch provides access to the mountain's shortest and most frequently used trail. Available throughout the year, this longer excursion that begins at the Brickett Place provides a quieter and more interesting journey to the picturesque summit.

Pick up the Royce Trail on the west side of Route 113, across from the parking entrance.

Opposite: The Royce Trail passes numerous named and unnamed water features.

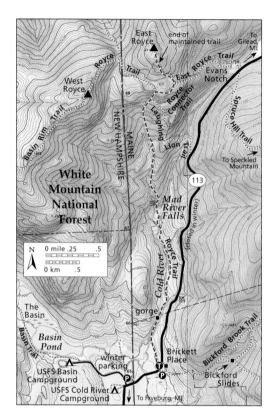

Tunneling through the wide swath, descend 0.3 mile past a field to the Cold River. Make your way across the small rocks to the other side. Swinging right, the trail hugs the riverbanks and over level ground soon passes a small gorge and cascades. In 0.4 mile cross the river once again. For 0.7 mile, the route climbs gently to a third crossing at the base of a pleasant cascade.

Climbing away from the Cold River, the trail begins a more aggressive climb and in 0.2 mile reaches a spur left that descends to a view of the charming Mad River Falls. Plodding onward, continue 1.1 miles up the increasingly steep and rocky terrain. Winding past interesting boulders and small cascades, the trail eventually skirts beneath impressive ledges before rising to a junction with the Laughing Lion Trail. Watch closely for the blazes in this area that mark the way. A final push leads 0.2 mile to the western end of the Royce Connector Trail. To the left, the Royce Trail continues 1.4 miles to nice ledges near the summit of West Royce—an optional extension for the day's hike.

Turning right on the Royce Connector Trail, meander over a flat ridge, then down to an intersection with the East Royce Trail, which descends steeply right 1 mile to Route 113. Bear left onto the well-used trail as it rises quickly through the thinning forest. After passing a number of limited viewpoints and climbing over exposed granite, the marked trail reaches the south summit of East Royce in 0.3 mile. Enjoy the excellent views south and west, as well as ample picnic spots. From the south summit, an unmarked but clearly obvious route leads 0.2 mile north to the mountain's 3114-foot high point, where there are more expansive scenes including the prolific mountains of western Maine.

When you have had your fill, retrace your steps to the Brickett Place. If you want a more adventurous return trip, take the East Royce Trail 1.5 miles to Route 113. Across the road, the Spruce Hill Trail connects with the Bickford Brook Trail for a 3.1-mile climb to the open top of Speckled Mountain. (See the USGS maps.) Follow the Bickford Brook Trail 4.3 miles to Brickett Place to complete a challenging, 12.5-mile trek. Similarly, a quiet 11.5-mile loop (which includes a 1-mile road walk) can be completed by heading south 2.1 miles to West Royce. Follow the Basin Rim Trail 2.5 miles to Rim Junction. Turn left on the Basin Trail, which descends 2.3 miles west toward the Basin and Cold River campgrounds.

MAINE COAST

Evergreens line the Penobscot Mountain Trail, Acadia National Park.

A prominent rocky shoreline is often used to describe the Maine coast, it is a shoreline like no other in the eastern United States. Highlighted by 30,000-acre Acadia National Park, the 5000-mile-long Maine coast also includes a number of state and privately owned conservation areas as well. Woven throughout this fabric of conserved land are working fishing villages, scenic lighthouses, 4000 islands, and some of the finest seafood restaurants in the country.

Maine coastal hikes provide cool summer venues, but are often more intriguing during the off-season when the crowds have subsided. However, regardless of the time of year, a hiking adventure on the Maine coast will offer incredible views, abundant wildlife, vibrant colors, and sufficient challenge.

77 CAMDEN HILLS

Distance: 5.4 miles round-trip
Hiking time: 4 hours
Difficulty: Moderate
Low point: 230 feet
High point: 1380 feet
Season: Year-round
USGS map: Camden, ME
Information: Maine Bureau of Parks and Lands

Getting there: From Route 1 in Camden, follow Route 52 north 1.2 miles to the Camden Hills State Park trailhead on the right. Parking is available along the east side of the road.

A hike to either the picturesque summit of Mount Battie or to Mount Megunticook's dramatic Ocean

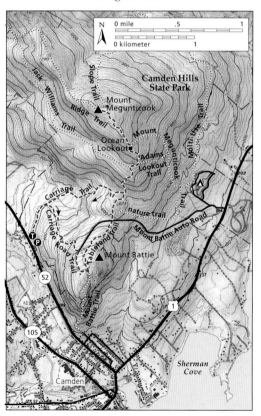

Lookout would alone be a rewarding day in Maine's Camden Hills State Park. This half-day circuit combines both of these signature features on trails that peacefully ascend the lush forested landscape, visit alluring geologic formations, and resound under a chorus of melodious songbirds. Taking advantage of mostly moderate terrain, this adventure is appropriate for hikers of all ages.

Head northeast up the Carriage Road Trail and in 0.3 mile reach a junction. Veer right and begin a modest ascent up the west side of Mount Battie, following the former carriage route most of the way. Roughly halfway up the gentle slope, the winding, 0.8-mile path passes a large boulder on the left. Swinging east, climb to Mount Battie Auto Road and turn right. Stay on the side of the paved road for the final 0.1 mile to the top. At 800 feet above sea level, Mount Battie provides splendid views of Camden Harbor and Village far below. From the top of an old stone tower, more extensive scenery can be enjoyed, including the islands and sprawling peninsulas of Penobscot Bay.

The journey continues down the 1.5-mile Tableland Trail, which leaves north from the center of the summit parking area. Across thinly forested ledges, drop gradually while paralleling the road. Over a final ledge and down a steeper pitch, carefully make your way across the pavement. Rolling over a couple of small ridges, pass a junction with the Nature Trail, and soon arrive at another intersection. Leading left, the Carriage Trail drops 1.2 mile back to Route 52, providing a quicker end to the day's travels. To complete the longer sojourn, continue straight on the Tableland Trail.

A cold winter day on Mount Battie's Carriage Road Trail

Beginning the first of two significant climbs, the Tableland Trail leads up a rock-covered path before reaching a plateau. Stay right at an intersection with the Jack Williams Trail and scramble up the increasingly steep slope. Through stunted oak forests, the route swings northwest with ever-expanding vistas. Watch your step as you approach the top of the Ocean Lookout, as it is perched on the edge of precipitous cliffs. The open ledge provides incredible 270-degree views from Acadia National Park to Ragged and Bald Mountains.

Before descending, follow the Ridge Trail north as it climbs 0.4 mile from the lookout to the wooded summit of Mount Megunticook—the highest point in the park. Return 1.1 miles back to the Carriage Trail, turn right, and begin a modest descent. The path goes under an intriguing rock face and passes a small cascade before dropping steadily to the valley floor. A number of small brook crossings require some care, but generally the water is not too high. The final 0.5 mile is along flat terrain as you join the Carriage Road Trail for the final stretch to the highway.

The loop hike to Mount Battie alone is 3.1 miles, while the trip to Megunticook only is 4.6 miles round-trip. For a longer 7-mile hike, consider following the Ridge Trail north of Megunticook's summit for 1.2 miles before curling back on the 1.7-mile Jack Williams Trail. Both offer sporadic views and enjoyable travels.

78 BALD ROCK MOUNTAIN

Distance: 3.5-mile loop
Hiking time: 3 hours
Difficulty: Moderate
Low point: 260 feet
High point: 1100 feet
Season: Year-round
USGS map: Lincolnville, ME
Information: Maine Bureau of Parks and Lands

Getting there: From Route 1 in Lincolnville Beach, follow Route 173 west 2.2 miles. Turn left onto Youngstown Road. From the junction of Routes 52 and 173 south of Lincolnville Center, follow Route 173 east 2.9 miles before turning right onto Youngstown Road. Once on Youngstown Road, the parking area is immediately on the left.

Blue blazes lead up the Bald Rock Mountain Trail.

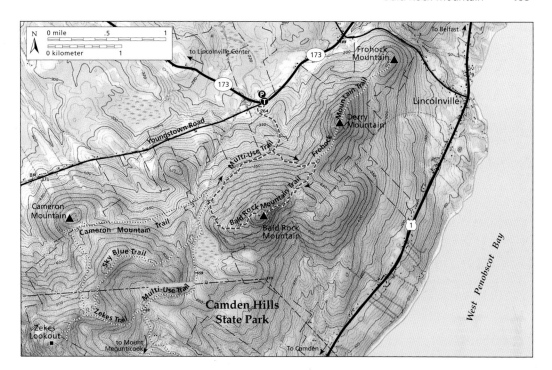

One of the finest ocean views in New England, Bald Rock Mountain is an excellent hiking option any time of the year. The summit's open ledges, while shielded to the north, provide an awesome scene of Penobscot Bay's icy blue waters, countless dark green islands, and the rocky peaks of Acadia National Park in the distance. Accessible by two gradual trails, Bald Rock is an ideal choice for family outings in any season.

At the gate, begin along the wide Multi-Use Trail (most often used by hikers). The gradual path eventually veers right. At the base of a long incline, turn left on the Frohock Mountain Trail and climb more aggressively up the rocky hillside. Quickly the trail levels off and reaches an intersection. To the left a quiet, 1-mile path leads over a low ridge with limited views and then descends to the wooded summit of Frohock Mountain—a pleasant diversion for those seeking solitude. Stay right and follow the blue-blazed route as it moderately winds up the northeast ridge of the mountain. At a second worn-down shelter, the trail proceeds up the rocky slope and soon emerges onto the open summit ledges.

A popular location, Bald Rock Mountain is large enough to accommodate many hikers. On a clear day, the summit begs you to lounge for hours. Gaze upon the schooners riding the whitecaps of Penobscot Bay, past the serene shores of the Fox Islands (North Haven and Vinalhaven), beyond the Blue Hill Peninsula, and out to the distant summits of Isle au Haut and Mount Desert Island. There is no better place to dream of future adventures along the Maine coast.

For the descent, pick up the blue-blazed trail that departs the northwest corner of the summit. With the smell of balsam fir in the air, watch your footing at first. However, quickly the tread improves and after descending a rock staircase, the path reaches a stand of tall white pines and ends at the Multi-Use Trail. Turn right and follow the wide route for a relaxing 1.3-mile conclusion to the day's journey.

If you are looking for a longer adventure on a future Camden Hills trek, consider following the Multi-Use Trail farther west to access a number of routes that can easily lead to loop hikes of up to 10 miles. These lesser-used trails visit a number of scenic features, including Cameron Mountain, Zekes Lookout, and Mount Megunticook.

79 ISLE AU HAUT

Distance: 4.8-mile loop
Hiking time: 4 hours
Difficulty: Moderate–Strenuous
Low point: 0 feet
High point: 309 feet
Season: May–October
USGS map: Isle au Haut West, ME
Information: Acadia National Park (fee)

Getting there: Follow Route 15 south from Blue Hill. After crossing the Deer Isle Bridge, drive 11.2 miles into Stonington and turn left onto Sea Breeze Avenue. The Isle au Haut Ferry Terminal and parking is 0.1 mile ahead. For the latest information, schedule, and rates, visit www.isleauhaut.com.

Located more than 5 miles south of Deer Isle (south of the Blue Hill Peninsula), Isle au Haut is an 8000-acre island with less than 100 year-round residents. Roughly 60 percent of the 6-mile-long-by-2-mile-wide island is owned and managed by Acadia National Park and, unlike the land located on Mount Desert Island, the Isle au Haut section of the park is far less manicured and much wilder. The island is accessible via a passenger-only ferry service that operates out of Stonington, and offers 18 miles of hiking trails that weave through shady forests, to quiet coves,

The view south across Squeaker Cove from the Goat Trail

over open ledges, and across surf-pummeled headlands. There are many ways to enjoy Isle au Haut, and this 4.8-mile circuit is a wonderful introduction to its splendor.

The loop begins at the Duck Harbor Campground, a location that is reached in a number of ways. From May to October the ferry service makes scheduled stops at the harbor—typically late morning and late afternoon—allowing for roughly four hours of exploration. This ferry route is also ideal for those camping overnight (contact Acadia National Park for more information; sites are available by reservation only). Additionally, it is possible to take an early-morning ferry to the town landing and then hike 4.1 miles south on the Duck Harbor Trail. To return to the mainland by the end of the day, you can either grab the late-afternoon ferry in Duck Harbor or hike back to the town landing. The 4.1-mile hike is a bit rough, but generally level; it should take two to two-and-half hours to complete.

Once you have made your way to the campground, take the path east to Western Head Road. Turn right and follow the wide route 0.8 mile to the start of the Western Head Trail. Swinging southwest, this undulating trail soon leads to a small cobble beach. Veer left and for the next mile proceed along or parallel to the scenic shoreline. Take your time to explore the many beaches and headlands along the way. The path has only minor elevation changes, but the footing is uneven in places.

Upon reaching the start of the Cliff Trail, an unmarked path leads right to a secluded beach near the Western Ear. During low tide it is possible to explore the nearby island, but beware of rising water. Pick up the Cliff Trail as it leads north. Taking you at first around a ledge and through the forest, the trail soon emerges onto the island's most scenic section. For the next 0.5 mile, the trail hugs the rocky shoreline while offering repeated scenes of waves crashing into granite bluffs and funneling through narrow coves.

At the eastern end of Western Head Road, assess the time and ferry schedule. Consider returning 1.3 miles along the road back to Duck Harbor if necessary. Otherwise, follow Western

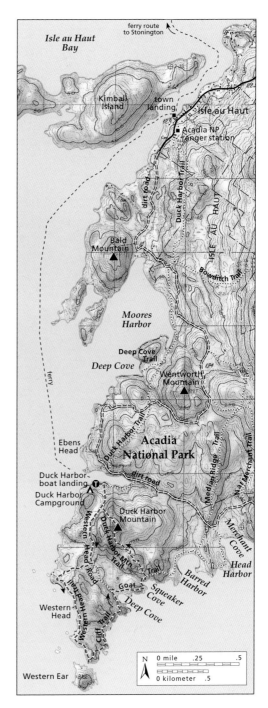

Waves pummel the shore along the scenic Cliff Trail.

Head Road a few hundred yards to the southern end of the Goat Trail. Turn right and follow the path past a large cobble beach and then quickly down to Squeaker Cove. North of here, the Goat Trail continues pleasantly along the coastline, reaching a dirt road in a little more than 1 mile. Following the dirt road west leads back to Duck Harbor in less than 1 mile.

For a more challenging trek back, pick up the Duck Harbor Mountain Trail as it wastes little time scrambling up the granite hillside. The rugged trail climbs up and over a number of bald knobs, descends into narrow gaps in the ledge, and occasionally requires the use of hands. In 0.8 mile, ascend the final section to the open summit and enjoy excellent views of the island and its surroundings. On the western horizon the Camden Hills rise over the Fox Islands.

Dropping quickly, the trail remains in the open for a bit, but soon descends down the rocky path to Western Head Road. Turn right to reach Duck Harbor dock, five minutes away.

80 THE BEEHIVE AND GREAT HEAD

Distance: 4 miles round-trip
Hiking time: 3.5 hours
Difficulty: Moderate–Strenuous
Low point: 0 feet
High point: 546 feet
Season: May–November
USGS map: Seal Harbor, ME
Information: Acadia National Park (fee)

Autumn colors brighten the view south towards Otter Cliff.

Getting there: From Acadia National Park's Hulls Cove Visitor Center north of Bar Harbor, follow Park Loop Road south 3 miles and then turn left. Follow the one-way road south 5.4 miles. Continue 0.5 mile past the entrance station and veer left into the Sand Beach parking area. Alternatively, from June to October take advantage of the free Island Explorer Shuttle buses that stop at this parking area throughout the day (visit www .exploreacadia.com for route and schedule information).

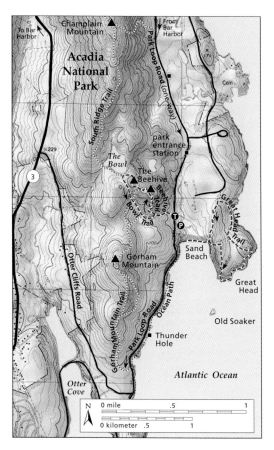

One unique feature of Acadia National Park is its many vertical trails requiring hikers to ascend steel rungs affixed to solid granite rock faces. Although not an ideal choice for explorers wary of heights, for others seeking excitement on Mount Desert Island, opting for one of the park's fist-clenching ascents is a must. This popular climb up the aptly named Beehive is a short but sweet choice. Combine it with a stroll across nearby Sand Beach and the rocky promontory of Great Head for a wonderful half-day adventure on one of Maine's most frequently visited shorelines.

Begin by following the parking entrance back to Park Loop Road. Turn right to quickly reach the Bowl Trail on the left. The rocky path begins at a moderate grade as it quickly heads toward the base of The Beehive. In 0.2 mile veer right onto the Beehive Trail—now the fun begins. Slowly winding up the increasingly sheer mountain face, the route crosses metal bridges, rises up iron rungs, and hugs the granite walls closely. Passing one incredible vista after another, watch your step and take your time. From Schoodic Point to Otter Cliffs, the views are breathtaking (and the drops heart-pounding).

The 0.3-mile ascent eventually ends atop The Beehive's south peak, with excellent albeit less-dramatic views. Continue along the ridge north to a second peak and wonderful views of Champlain Mountain. Dropping rapidly, the rocky path descends to The Bowl, a beautiful pond nestled high on the ridge. Stay left around the pond's south shore to arrive at an intersection. To the right, an attractive trail leads 1.4 miles to the top of Champlain Mountain, an excellent extension to the day's adventure. Turn south and descend into

a lovely birch forest. Stay left on the Bowl Trail and drop into a small basin.

Follow the trail back to Park Loop Road and the Sand Beach lot. Once there, take the staircase that leads to the beach and head east across the sandy expanse. Enjoy the impressive views looking back to The Beehive. At the far end of the beach, pick up the Great Head Trail as it crosses a small outlet stream and quickly rises away from the water. Stay right at the first intersection and climb steadily up the peninsula's granite ledges to numerous splendid vistas. Watch your footing as you rise to a high point and trail junction (to the left a scenic path leads 0.2 mile east before dropping abruptly to another section of the Great Head Trail). Continue right and descend to additional ocean views. Soon, the route bends left and leads up to 145-foot high Great Head. Surrounded by pounding surf and soaring seagulls, this is a cool, relaxing spot to gaze upon the immense ocean. Bear left as the trail swings gently north and passes the intersection with the route that cuts through the middle of the peninsula, a route that offers a shorter but more challenging return to Sand Beach. For a more relaxing conclusion to the hike continue straight and turn left at a second junction. Here a level path leads easily back to the scenic beach.

If you have not had your fill for the day, consider following the Ocean Path. Leading west from the Sand Beach parking area, it swings past popular Thunder Hole to Otter Cliffs over flat landscape.

81 CADILLAC MOUNTAIN

Distance: 6.4-mile loop
Hiking time: 5 hours
Difficulty: Moderate–Strenuous
Low point: 190 feet
High point: 1532 feet
Season: May through November
USGS maps: Seal Harbor, ME; Bar Harbor, ME
Information: Acadia National Park (fee)

Cadillac's summit rises above the North Ridge.

Getting there: From Acadia National Park's Hulls Cove Visitor Center north of Bar Harbor, pick up Park Loop Road and drive 3 miles south. Turn left onto the one-way road leading toward Sand Beach. In 0.9 mile, park at the Gorge Path trailhead located on the right. Alternatively, from June to October take advantage of the free Island Explorer Shuttle buses that pass this parking area throughout the day (visit www.exploreacadia.com for route and schedule information).

The highest point on America's Atlantic coastline, Cadillac Mountain is a must-visit destination. While there are many options to consider, this one combines the best of what the mountain offers, including: a long, exposed scenic ridgeline; a deep, glacier-carved gorge; small cascades; and an occasional scramble up Acadia National Park's famous granite slopes. While not easy, together these features can be enjoyed along a 5-mile loop appropriate for healthy hikers of all ages.

Starting on an old road, the Gorge Path ascends gradually up semi-exposed ledges with limited views. Descending abruptly, the route crosses a small stream and reaches a junction with the Hemlock Trail. Continue straight into the darkening evergreen forest and follow the narrowing path as it enters the lower sections of the gorge. Slowly work your way up, paralleling the small stream, occasionally crossing it. The footing can be a bit slippery when wet, but the trail is adorned with numerous rock steps to aid the way. As the climb ensues, leave behind a series of small cascades and enter a world surrounded by steep rock walls. Upon reaching the final and most impressive of these, the trail quickly climbs out of the shade, reaching a four-way intersection in the saddle between Dorr and Cadillac Mountains.

Turn right and carefully scramble up the rocky slope, stopping now and then to enjoy an expanding view of the ocean. With each step, the scenery becomes more impressive. Before you know it, the sounds and crowds of the Cadillac summit area are in reach. For an informative description of the area's sights and natural history, follow the loop trail that circles around the top and culminates at the high point. Please remain

on the hardened path throughout to help protect the mountain's fragile plants.

For the descent, pick up the North Ridge Trail, which leaves near the auto road exit. This 1.8-mile trail remains almost entirely in the open—something to keep in mind should skies appear threatening. On a clear day, however, the never-ending vistas are breathtaking, from the blue waters of Frenchman Bay to the distant interior mountains and hills (including Katahdin on very clear days). A few sections require extra care, but for the most part the trail is straight-forward. Upon reaching Park Loop Road, turn right and follow the pavement 0.5 mile back to the Gorge Path trailhead. If using the Island Explorer Shuttle, wait here—the North Ridge Trailhead is a regular stop on its rounds.

For an alternative hike that avoids the crowds and chaos that can sometimes overwhelm Cadillac Mountain, opt instead to hike Dorr Mountain. Using Dorr Mountain's North Ridge Trail and the Hemlock Trail, a quieter, and nearly as scenic, 3.6-mile loop can be completed from the Gorge Path trailhead.

82 THE BUBBLES AND PEMETIC

Distance: 6.4-mile loop
Hiking time: 5 hours
Difficulty: Moderate–Strenuous
Low point: 280 feet
High point: 1234 feet
Season: April through November
USGS maps: Southwest Harbor, ME; Seal Harbor, ME
Information: Acadia National Park (fee)

Getting there: From Acadia National Park's Hulls Cove Visitor Center north of Bar Harbor, pick up Park Loop Road and drive 3 miles south. Stay right on the road toward Jordan Pond. In 2 miles turn left into the Bubble Pond parking area. Alternatively, from June to October take advantage of the free Island Explorer Shuttle buses that stop at this parking area throughout the day (visit www.exploreacadia.com for route and schedule information).

Ideally located amidst Acadia's highest peaks and most sparkling lakes, this scenic loop to very popular as well as not-so-crowded corners of the park is a nonstop photographic journey. The hike traverses ever-changing terrain, offering numerous extensions and shortcuts. Choose this circuit from the arrival of the first songbirds until the final vibrant leaf has fallen to the ground. Along the way, take time to gaze at the reflections in Eagle Lake, feel the breezes sweeping across Jordan Pond, and escape into the limitless panorama engulfing Pemetic Mountain.

From the parking area, cross the park road and follow the carriage road north 0.3 mile. At an intersection, bear left and quickly reach the Eagle Lake Trail on the right. The path leads to the expansive lake, swings west, and begins a 1.5-mile trek hugging the shoreline. Gentle footing leads past the Jordan Pond Carry Trail as the route winds north. Remain near the lake and enjoy the endless outlooks, but take your time over the increasingly rocky pathway. Passing through an evergreen tunnel, you reach the North Bubble Trail.

Turning left, begin a steady 0.4-mile climb through thinning forests to wide-open 588-foot Conners Nubble. One of the least-visited summits in the park, the peak provides impressive views of the sprawling lake below. Dropping rapidly west, cross the carriage road and begin a 0.8-mile climb up the North Bubble ridgeline. Once again, the path proceeds through increasingly

A wooden ladder leads up a gorge on the Pemetic Trail.

sparse vegetation as it winds up granite slopes to the edge of a dramatic cliff top with excellent views of Cadillac and Pemetic Mountains. Following a brief drop, the trail rises to the top of North Bubble. Standing 872 feet above sea level, this scenic mountain offers fine snapshots of Jordan Pond and Cliffs.

Slithering to the south, the path descends to a junction with the popular Bubble Rock Trail. To the right, scenic South Bubble Rock and its signature glacial erratic can be reached in 0.3 mile—well worth the extra effort. Dropping to the left, the trail descends to a large parking area. Carefully make your way across the paved

road to the start of the 0.6-mile Pemetic Trail, the most difficult climb of the day. Catch your breath before tackling the steep pitch. Partway up the rocky slope, the main route splits. To the right is the most straightforward option, while the route left cuts through a deep gorge aided by ladders. The two soon become one again as the ascent slightly eases. Pass an intersection with the Pemetic East Trail and scramble the final 0.1 mile to the barren 1234-foot high point, the most expansive viewpoint of the day.

Return to the 1.2-mile Pemetic East Trail and bear right. The route winds gently along the top of the ridge, passes a few vistas, and then descends more aggressively through the thickly forested slopes. After leveling off, hike across the carriage road to the impressive shores of Bubble Pond, where the western wall of Cadillac Mountain rises abruptly east. Swing north to reach the parking area.

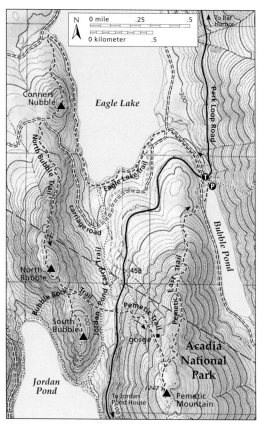

83 SARGENT MOUNTAIN

Distance: 7.3 miles one-way with shuttle
Hiking time: 6 hours
Difficulty: Moderate–Strenuous
Low point: 60 feet
High point: 1379 feet
Season: April–November
USGS map: Southwest Harbor, ME
Information: Acadia National Park (fee)

Getting there: The described one-way shuttle hike can be made using the Island Explorer Shuttle bus, available in June, July, and August. From the Bar Harbor village green, take an Island Explorer bus en route to Brown Mountain and ask to be dropped off at the Giant Slide Trail. The hike ends at Jordan Pond where you can pick up a second bus for the return trip to Bar Harbor (visit www .exploreacadia.com for route and schedule information).

Or to set up a car shuttle, reach the Jordan Pond trailhead (the endpoint of the hike) by following Park Loop Road. Begin at the Hulls Cove Visitor Center and drive 3 miles south. Stay right and continue 4.5 miles to the hiking parking lot entrance on the right. To reach the Giant Slide trailhead and the start of the hike, begin in Somesville at the junctions of Routes 3, 102, and 198. Follow Routes 3/198 east toward Northeast Harbor and drive 2.3 miles to the trailhead on the left; park on either side of the road.

Acadia National Park is dissected by a series of parallel ridgelines. Carved by receding glaciers and stripped by the infamous 1947 fire, these polished-granite mountains showcase exquisite seacoast scenery. Enshrouded with ocean breezes that carry the fresh scent of prolific pine needles, each of these ridges has something unique to offer; however, the finest, most rewarding trek scales the barren summits of Sargent and Penobscot Mountains. While this recommended hike begins and ends at different trailheads, many alternative trips, including

Summer fog blankets Sargent Mountain Pond.

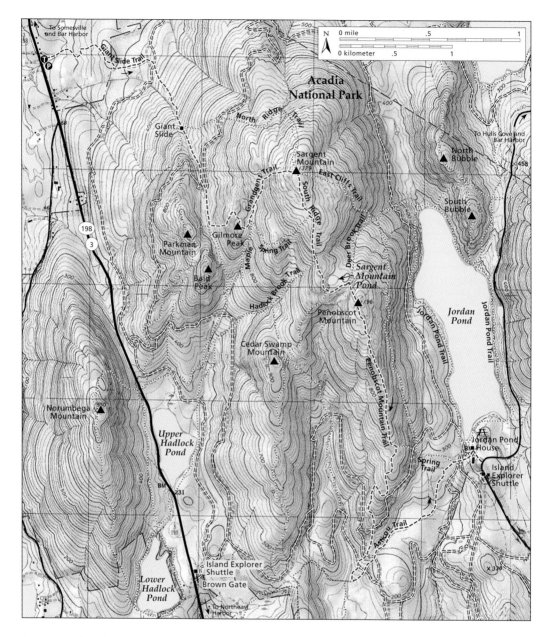

loops, can be planned by utilizing either trail-head alone.

From the Route 3/198 trailhead, head onto the Giant Slide Trail. Recently relocated, the path begins on private land protected by a conservation easement. Be sure to follow the signs closely as you wind up a lush moss- and lichen-covered ledge. Swinging right and rejoining the original way, enter the park and continue the gradual ascent. After crossing a carriage road, the trail soon reaches the base of the Giant Slide. As the walls begin to close in, snake over rock, cross the tumbling stream, sqeeze through tight crevices, and carefully make your way to a four-way intersection deep in the heart of the chasm. Continue straight through a small tunnel and quickly climb out of the slide. Across a second carriage road, the Giant Slide Trail descends briefly to a second four-way intersection.

Turning left onto the Grandgent Trail, the hike climbs more aggressively and soon emerges onto wide-open Gilmore Peak, offering the first of many ocean views. Dropping to the east, stay left at an intersection with the Maple Spring Trail. Paralleling a small wetland, the path winds gradually, then turns right up the steep slope. Rising through the receding tree line, the trail makes its way to a large cairn that marks the top of 1379-foot Sargent Mountain, the highest point in Acadia not accessible by road. Offering 360-degree views, Sargent is arguably the most scenic spot in the park.

Now begins a relaxing jaunt south across the ridge. For 0.7 mile the path weaves through the open air across the smooth granite. Pick up the Penobscot Mountain Trail by turning left toward Sargent Mountain Pond. Pass along the serene pond's shore, and then drop into a narrow saddle. Stay straight and climb to the treeless summit of 1194-foot Penobscot Mountain. Head south down the open ridge, once again over relaxing terrain. In 1.1 miles, at tree line, stay right on the Penobscot Mountain Trail and proceed over the newly reopened route. Winding in and out of sparse vegetation, this scenic path passes a handful of outlooks before descending over forested ledges, across three carriage roads, and ending at the Asticou Trail.

Veer left onto the Asticou Trail. After a short climb up to and over two carriage roads, the route follows a mostly flat grade for 1.2 miles to the Jordan Pond House. After enjoying the relaxing conclusion to the hike, grab a bite to eat at the historic building and check out the pond's picturesque shoreline. Island Explorer Shuttle buses connect the Jordan Pond House with Bar Harbor's village green frequently throughout the day.

There are countless alternative hikes available in this area. Options to consider without using the bus service include ascending Sargent as described and descending the North Ridge Trail. Similarly, a rewarding circuit can be completed by following the Jordan Pond, Deer Brook, and East Cliffs trails to Sargent Mountain. Return to Jordan House as described above.

Penobscot Mountain's barren slopes provide sweeping views.

84 FRENCHBORO

Distance: 6.2-mile loop
Hiking time: 5 hours
Difficulty: Moderate–Strenuous
Low point: 0 feet
High point: 70 feet
Season: May–November
USGS map: Frenchboro, ME
Information: Maine Coast Heritage Trust

Getting there: From the junction of Routes 102 and 102A in Bass Harbor, follow Route 102A south 0.8 mile. Turn right and head 0.4 mile to the state ferry terminal and parking area (the lot occasionally fills during the summer, but other parking is available nearby). The Maine State Ferry Service provides round-trip passenger-only service to the (Frenchboro/Long Island) town dock every Friday from early April to late November. There is one-way service to the ferry terminal on other days, but the island has limited overnight accommodations (a few long-term rentals).

Looking across Western Cove towards Richs Head

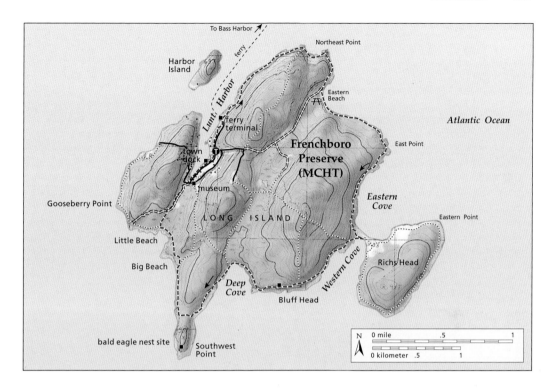

In 2000, Maine Coast Heritage Trust (MCHT), the Island Institute, the Maine Seacoast Mission, and island residents joined together to protect almost 1000 acres in the heart of Frenchboro. Today, this preserve, which comprises two-thirds of the island, is managed by MCHT, a statewide land conservation organization dedicated to "protecting the character of Maine for future generations." Few places embody the character of Maine more vividly than scenic, rock-bound Frenchboro and its working waterfront community.

Home to less than seventy year-round residents and located nearly 7 miles south of the mainland, Frenchboro is an especially alluring destination for those interested in escaping the hordes that descend upon Acadia National Park each summer. Every Friday, from early spring to late autumn, the Maine State Ferry Service departs Bass Harbor at 8:00 AM and returns ten hours later. In between, patrons can enjoy a splendid round-trip cruise through stunning coastal island scenery, as well as a full day to explore Frenchboro's 10 miles of picturesque hiking trails and rugged cobble beaches.

From the town dock, follow the paved road north to the ferry terminal. Pick up the hiking trail on the right. Follow this path, initially across private land, as it skirts the shoreline. Winding back toward the mainland along the ocean's edge, scan the trees and nearby islands for soaring osprey and bald eagles. Soon you enter the MCHT preserve for good and swing around to Northeast Point. In and out of the forest, the trail passes numerous views north toward the summits of Mount Desert Island. Hiking here along this quiet shore, you can only imagine the level of activity building atop Cadillac Mountain, 17 miles away.

Swinging south, arrive at a picnic table near Eastern Beach. Here, the trail proceeds across a wall of stones that separate an inland marsh from the crashing surf. Weaving through evergreens on the far side, the path soon leads to scenic East Point. Hike south over low granite bluffs and then reenter the forest. Before long, the loop leads to the end of a short isthmus, 2.8 miles from the start. This tiny piece of land dividing Eastern and Western Coves, en route to Richs Head, is an excellent place to explore the shoreline and enjoy lunch.

If time permits, consider extending this described loop by completing the recently reopened trail that circles around Richs Head. Outside of the MCHT preserve, this peninsula is protected with a conservation easement held by Acadia National Park. Allow for at least two additional hours to explore this scenic corner of Frenchboro.

The second half of the day's circuit leads south around dramatic Bluff Head. This more rugged side of the island provides exhilarating views of a wild coastline pounded by the open ocean. Around the stunning promontory, the path swings into Deep Cove. Continue in the direction of Southwest Point, then veer inland away from an active bald eagle nest site. Across

the peninsula to Big Beach, the journey heads north along the boulder-filled shoreline and arrives at Little Beach. Take your time enjoying this final coastal stop of the tour.

From Little Beach, a trail leads north back to the village and soon intersects a dirt road. Continue ahead to the paved road. To the left, the street leads to a seasonally open deli and store, which both sell delicious lobster rolls. Follow the pavement right to explore the island's small museum, which is open daily (sometimes staffed). The road that hugs the east side of the harbor leads back to the town dock, where the boat departs at 6:00 PM (5:00 PM in November) to return to Bass Harbor. Check out www.mcht.org for more information on MCHT's conservation activities and other coastal preserves.

Bluff Head stands high above Deep Cove.

85 SCHOODIC MOUNTAIN

Distance: 2.8-mile loop
Hiking time: 2 hours
Difficulty: Moderate
Low point: 120 feet
High point: 1069 feet
Season: April–November
USGS map: Sullivan, ME
Information: Maine Bureau of Parks and Lands

Getting there: From Route 1 in East Sullivan, follow Route 183 north 4.3 miles and then turn left onto a dirt road. Stay on the main road 2.2 miles until it ends at a large parking area.

From the waterfront in Bar Harbor, the shiny granite summit of Schoodic Mountain rises to the north of Frenchman Bay. Frequently seen by Acadia visitors who opt for more crowded trails on Mount Desert Island, Schoodic offers a similar feel with fewer fellow travelers. On the western edge of the Donnell Pond Public Reserved Land, a pocket of conservation totaling more than 14,000 acres, the mountain is accessible via a modest loop that includes a stop at a wonderful freshwater beach. The perfect destination for hikers of all ages, the top of Schoodic Mountain boasts one of Maine's most spectacular ocean views.

The blue-blazed trail departs the western corner of the parking area, near an outhouse. Meander through the thickly forested landscape and across a small brook. Slowly begin a steadier climb and rise past a large boulder on the right. Swinging left, the terrain levels briefly before rising up the rocky hillside. Past an outcrop with views of Black Mountain, rise through the thinning forest canopy onto semi-open ledges. Above, catch the first glimpse of the summit area and soon arrive at a three-way intersection.

Turn left for the 0.4-mile final push to the top. Winding up steeper terrain, the path strikes a pleasant course past ocean and lake viewpoints. Each step brings you higher with fewer trees, until a last effort leads atop the barren summit

area. Save for the communications tower, there is nothing to block the 360-degree views that include the highest summits of Acadia National Park, the Camden Hills, and sprawling Frenchman Bay. Watch your step and do your best to avoid trampling the fragile summit vegetation.

Return to the three-way intersection and head left toward the welcoming shore of Donnell Pond. At first gradual, the descent soon picks up intensity; it's rocky in places, so take your time. The 0.6-mile trail eventually reaches an old woods road. The final dash leads easily toward

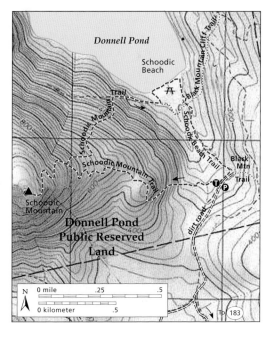

The mountains of Acadia rise beyond Frenchman Bay.

the shore. Turn left before the outhouse and onto the pond's sandy beach. A great place for picnics or a summer swim, Donnell Pond is anchored by 1000-foot peaks on both sides.

At the eastern end of the beach, a 0.5-mile path completes the circuit. Following an old road, the route is straightforward and climbs gently back to the parking area. For return trips to the area, consider an adventure up nearby Black Mountain. From the same trailhead a similar but slightly longer loop leads to this scenic mountain's east summit.

86 CUTLER COAST

Distance: 9.1-mile loop
Hiking time: 7 hours
Difficulty: Moderate–Strenuous
Low point: 0 feet
High point: 210 feet
Season: Year-round
USGS map: Cutler, ME
Information: Maine Bureau of Parks and Lands

Getting there: The Cutler Coast trailhead is located on Route 191 north of Cutler. From Route 1 in East Machias, follow Route 191 east 16.9 miles to the parking area on the right. From Route 189, halfway between Whiting and Lubec, follow Route 191 south 10 miles and turn left into the parking area.

While Maine is famous for its rugged coastline, from June to September many of its most beautiful spots are bustling with activity. In contrast, the 12,000-acre Cutler Coast Public Reserve, located along Maine's less-traveled Bold Coast, offers crowd-free viewing of ocean scenery that is as spectacular as any other in New England. Protected by the state in the 1990s with the help of Maine Coast Heritage Trust and the Land for Maine's Future Program, the Cutler Coast offers hikers the option of a 5.5-mile loop or a more rugged 9.1-mile circuit that includes three primitive campsites. The reserve is a land of rocky cliffs, invigorating ocean breezes, cleansing aromas, and melodious birdcalls. Whether a half day, a full day, or multiple days, a journey to Cutler Coast will dazzle your senses and free your mind.

Follow the evergreen-lined path 0.4 mile to the Inland Trail junction. Continue straight for a relaxing 1-mile trek over a series of small ridges and through boggy areas frequented by moose. The Coastal Trail turns right upon reaching the coast, but first check out the scenic vantage point located on a short spur left. Watch your footing as you descend to an open ledge perched high above the crashing surf below.

Leaving the vista, follow the Coastal Trail southwest high above the shore. Overall the elevation changes little, but the route is far from flat. Passing steep walls and secluded rock beaches, the trail winds through forest and open meadows, passing one dramatic viewpoint after another. At 1.5 miles, the Black Point Brook Cutoff leads 0.8 mile to the Inland Trail. Use this trail to complete a 5.5-mile loop.

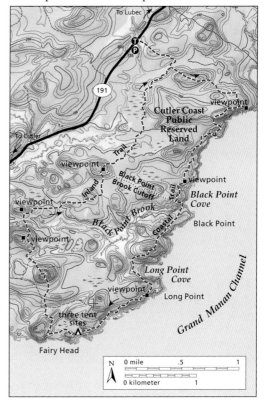

Cutler Coast is a great place to spot wildlife from countless rocky perches.

While the southern section is less dramatic, it is well worth the extra effort. Leaving the stone beach at Black Point Cove (the last reliable fresh, albeit orange, water for campsites that are 2 miles ahead), hike up a small wooden ladder. Across low, rolling terrain, the trail leads ahead to an attractive birch forest lined with ledges and ferns. Here a rock staircase rises up the hillside. Before long you emerge onto the wide-open expanse of Long Point. During warmer months, this is a great location for spotting whales in the distant waves and to gaze upon the steep cliffs of Grand Manan Island in New Brunswick, on the far side of the channel that bears its name.

The Coast Trail soon passes three campsites, each available on a first-come basis. After crossing the outlet of a small bog, the route reenters the woods. This is the start of the Inland Trail (no sign). During late spring and summer, be prepared for insects, as the route passes numerous wetlands. Apart from bugs, the Inland Trail traverses pretty forests and gradually ascends a number of small hills. Each hill has a short spur that leads to limited views. After passing a sizable beaver pond, climb over a semi-open knob and continue straight at the Black Point Brook Cutoff intersection. The path eventually reenters the shade and gradually winds back to the final junction, 0.4 mile east of the parking area.

87 QUODDY HEAD

Distance: 4.2-mile loop
Hiking time: 3 hours
Difficulty: Moderate
Low point: 20 feet
High point: 130 feet
Season: Year-round
USGS map: Lubec, ME
Information: Maine Bureau of Parks and Lands (fee)

Getting there: Beginning at the junction of Routes 189 and 191 in West Lubec, follow Route 189 east 4.2 miles and then turn right onto South Lubec Road. Follow this road 4.7 miles to the parking area on the right.

Ironically, West Quoddy Head forms the eastern most spot in the United States—its eastern brother is located across the border on Campobello Island. Rising 190 feet above the ocean, this oft fog-shrouded peninsula is a natural treasure along Maine's Bold Coast. Purchased by the state in 1962, Quoddy Head State Park is comprised of 532 acres of rugged headlands, more than 4.5 miles of hiking trails, and a picturesque lighthouse built in 1858. Open throughout the year, Quoddy Head is a wonderful spot to witness the raw power of the Maine coast, enjoy glimpses of its many wild creatures, and observe diverse vegetation.

From the parking lot and picnic area, follow the Inland Trail west along flat ground. Reaching a small cove at the base of a dramatic ocean cliff, the path quickly rises to a trail junction. Stay right on the Inland Trail as it slowly levels off and arrives at the start of the Bog Trail. Turn northwest and wind through the tunnel of evergreen trees. At an intersection with the Thompson Trail, stay right and follow the main path onto a long boardwalk that weaves over the acidic bog. Keep your eye open for pitcher plants, baked-apple berry, and other vegetation common to more northern environs. After circling through the open

West Quoddy Head, the nation's easternmost point

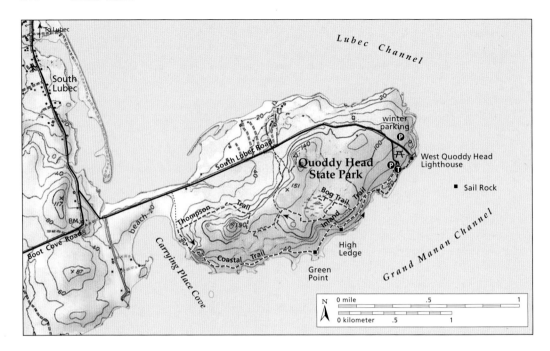

expanse, return to and then join the Thompson Trail on the right.

The 1.2-mile Thompson Trail cuts through the heart of the peninsula. After crossing wetland areas, the path soon joins an old road. Veering right, climb up and over a small ridge. Before long, the wide path ends at the Coastal Trail near the shores of Carrying Place Cove. Named by boaters seeking to avoid the stronger currents to the east of Quoddy Head, the cove has a nice beach for exploring.

The 2-mile return journey along the Coastal Trail is the highlight of the day's trek, with one spectacular view after another. While the elevation change is minor, the path is not flat, a point quickly understood while ascending a low, rocky knoll. Take your time, explore the many promontories, and enjoy the splendid ocean scenes. Across the blue expanse lie the impressive cliffs of New Brunswick's Grand Manan Island; nearby the gnarled shoreline provides ideal photographic opportunities; and

in between scan for seals, ducks, lobstermen, and the occasional whale.

Just beyond scenic Green Point, arrive at a junction with the Inland Trail—the most direct route to the parking area. Continue the adventure right on the Coastal Trail. Swing east, climb past High Ledge with its view of the distant lighthouse, and cautiously make your way along the prominent headlands. Rejoin the Inland Trail and hike down around the cove, but this time stay right along the water's edge. Follow the flat path past the parking area to the scenic West Quoddy Head Lighthouse, the nation's easternmost point.

If you are visiting Lubec overnight, there are many other places to visit, including the Roosevelt Cottage on Campobello Island, with its adjacent trails in Roosevelt Campobello International Park, and Cobscook Bay State Park. For more hiking information, purchase a Cobscook Trails Guide at a local store or by contacting the Downeast Coastal Conservancy (www.downeastcoastalconservancy.org).

NORTHERN MAINE

A rock-bound path leads up Sunday River Whitecap, Grafton Loop Trail.

A land of endless forests, bountiful lakes, rushing rivers, and rolling mountains, northern Maine is wilder than any other place in New England. Its hiking crown jewels, 200,000-acre Baxter State Park and the Appalachian Trail corridor, are surrounded by a patchwork of conservation lands that continues to grow each year.

A region that has always been more famous for its booming timber industry, northern Maine offers a great variety of hiking opportunities to those who are patient enough to uncover them. Visit here during the summer and fall, when trails are more accessible, moose more visible, weather more comfortable, and amenities more available. Be prepared for fewer comforts and conveniences, but revel in greater expanses and remoteness.

88 MAHOOSUC NOTCH

Distance: 11-mile loop
Hiking time: 8 hours/2 days
Difficulty: Very strenuous
Low point: 1620 feet
High point: 3740 feet
Season: June through October
USGS maps: Success Pond, NH; Old Speck Mountain, ME
Information: Maine Bureau of Parks and Lands

Getting there: From the western junction of Routes 2 and 16 in Gorham, follow Route 16 north 4.5 miles into Berlin. Turn right, cross the river, and in 0.8 mile go straight at the lights. Follow the road 1.1 miles around the mill and turn right onto Success Pond Road, near the sign for "OHRV PARKING." Remain on the main dirt road 10.9 miles and turn right onto a side road signed "NOTCH TRAIL." Drive 0.3 mile and turn right across a small bridge. Continue 0.2 mile to the parking area on the right.

Many Appalachian Trail (AT) thru-hikers consider the 27-mile traverse of the Mahoosuc Range to be the most difficult section of the more than 2000-mile journey from Springer Mountain to Mount Katahdin. While steep, rocky, and very demanding, the Mahoosuc mountains are more noteworthy for their serenity, commanding vistas, and pristine waters. This 11-mile loop showcases the best of what this rugged mountain ridge has to offer, including a relentless journey through the labyrinth of caves and boulders of Mahoosuc Notch.

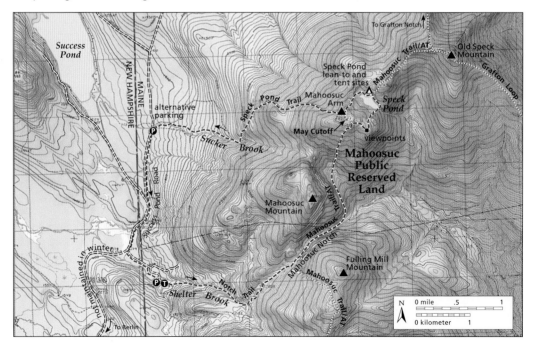

Opposite: *A hiker snakes through the heart of Mahoosuc Notch.*

The hike begins peacefully on the 2-mile-long Notch Trail. Across private lands, the route hugs Shelter Brook. After a second stream crossing, the path veers sharply left and enters the Mahoosuc Public Reserved Land. Managed by the Maine Bureau of Parks and Lands, the reserve and adjacent Grafton Notch State Park comprise more than 30,000 acres of conserved lands and numerous hiking trails. Beyond the public land boundary, reach the head of Mahoosuc Notch at an intersection with the Mahoosuc Trail/AT. Stay straight and enter the narrow seam between two sheer mountain faces. The 1.1-mile scramble through the notch is infamous for its difficulty and early summer snow. Take your time and enjoy the raw beauty. Cold breezes interrupt the heat as air from ice-filled chasms reaches the surface. Below, the brook gurgles, hidden from view. Ducking through caves, squeezing between boulders, and stretching over deep cavities, carefully make your way through.

Upon emerging from the notch, bear left and rise to a stream crossing. If the hike thus far has not tired you, the next mile will. Up the steep pitch of Mahoosuc Arm's south slope, the rocky pathway is relentless. Slowly emerge onto the first of many expansive vistas. Cresting the ridge, the impressive face of Old Speck comes into view. Continue past the 0.3-mile May Cutoff (the official summit of Mahoosuc Arm, a New England Hundred Highest Mountain, is located 0.1 mile west) and follow the white blazes to Speck Pond. Nestled high on the range, this tranquil body of water is an ideal spot to lounge. Continue across the outlet to a junction near the Speck Pond campsite. Managed by the Appalachian Mountain Club, the site is available for a small fee on a first-come basis.

Bear west onto the Speck Pond Trail. Around the pond's north side, the route begins a short climb and in 0.5 mile passes the western side of the May Cutoff. Follow the Speck Pond Trail ahead 3.1 miles to Success Pond Road. Some of the trail cuts through actively managed private forestland. After a gradual descent, the final section follows Sucker Brook over level terrain. The hike's conclusion ends unceremoniously by turning left and following Success Pond Road 1.3 miles to Notch Trail.

This 11-mile loop can be completed in one day, or you can use the Speck Pond campsite for a two-night adventure. Extend the overnight hike by 2.8 miles by adding Old Speck Mountain's summit to the itinerary. If you are looking for a shorter day trip, hike only into the notch, a 6-mile round-trip excursion; or combine Speck Pond and Mahoosuc Arm using the May Cutoff for a 7.9-mile journey.

89 GRAFTON LOOP

Distance: 38.6 miles one-way with shuttle
Hiking time: 3–4 days
Difficulty: Strenuous
Low point: 700 feet
High point: 4170 feet
Season: Year-round
USGS maps: Puzzle Mountain, ME; Old Speck Mountain, ME
Information: Maine Bureau of Parks and Lands

Getting there: From the junction of Routes 2 and 26 in Newry, take Route 26 northwest 4.7 miles to the parking area on the right. (Note: Parking is not allowed at the western trailhead 0.6 mile south on Route 26.)

Recently completed, the Grafton Loop combines 30 miles of new hiking terrain with 8.6 miles of preexisting Appalachian Trail (AT) mileage to form a fabulous backpacking circuit in western Maine. In addition to offering overnight

Puzzle Mountain's views include Grafton Notch and the Presidentials.

opportunities at eight camping locations, the loop also provides a variety of shorter options from half-day to full-day adventures. This lightly traveled trail weaves beneath towering yellow birches, along cascading mountain streams, and across moss-filled ridgelines to spectacular bald peaks and surreal summit vistas. The Grafton Loop, while challengingly steep on occasion, generally provides an ideal pathway for backpack toting and quiet contemplation.

Approaching the loop as a four-day excursion, ascend east up Puzzle Mountain. The first 10.1 miles of the trail's eastern branch traverse private property. Please respect the wishes of these generous landowners; remain on the trail and camp only at the Stewart campsite.

At increasingly more pronounced grades, the path rises. Veering northwest, pass a register box and enter the Stewart Family Preserve, a 485-acre property owned by the Mahoosuc Land Trust that encompasses the Puzzle Mountain summit area. Under the dark evergreen canopy, the trail climbs steeply past chiseled rock and soon reaches Picnic Ledge's dramatic views of Grafton Notch. Catch your breath; the final 0.8-mile stretch to Puzzle Mountain's western peak is challenging. Make your way up the widening, exposed granite to the open summit and exquisite views in most directions.

Continuing east, the trail descends into a small depression before rising to more ledges near the mountain's north peak. Take one last

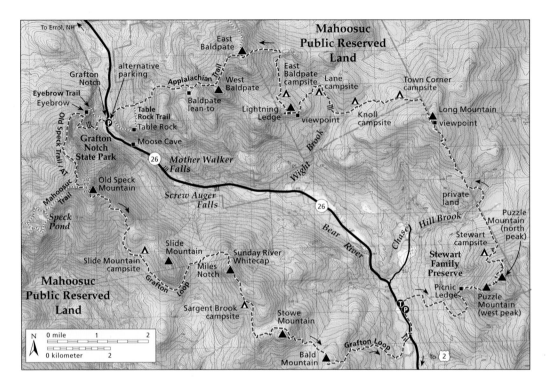

glimpse of Grafton Notch, then drop below tree line and make your way gradually to the Stewart campsite (the first of seven developed campsites on the new trail). Each campsite offers a privy, nearby water, and flat spots to tent.

Weaving downward, the route exits the Stewart Preserve and reaches a yellow-blazed town line. Follow this boundary for the better part of the next 4 miles. After rapidly dropping to a small stream, ascend to, then follow a woods road east 0.2 mile. Bear left and slowly wind up the gentle southern slope of Long Mountain. Passing by and occasionally through forest management areas, scan for moose browsing on the growing vegetation. Crest the summit ridge and pass a spur right to a bench and nice vista at mile 9.4. The trail skirts the wooded summit and descends to the state's Mahoosuc Public Reserve. Turn left and reach the path to the Town Corner campsite. At 10.4 miles from the start, this is an excellent place to spend the first night.

Begin day two by dropping west into a pleasant stream valley. Past a spur to the Knoll campsite, the trail bears right, heads up an adjacent

tributary, and quickly leads to a picturesque cascade. Above the falls, cross the stream twice and at mile 13.2 reach the Lane Campsite Trail. After a final crossing, the route leads out of the valley to Lightning Ledge ridge. Beyond an unmarked spur left to a stunning view across the deep valley, the trail wraps beneath Lightning Ledge's impressive rock wall before more gradually ascending to its partially open summit.

Descend 0.3 mile, cross a small rocky stream, and arrive at the East Baldpate campsite area. This is a good place to refuel before tackling the ensuing 2.3-mile ascent. Beginning slowly under a shady canopy, the trail becomes mossier and steeper. Before long, emerge atop East Baldpate's open summit with its expansive views in all directions. Turn left on the AT and venture across the exposed granite. Gaze upon the seemingly endless lakes and mountains of western Maine, but watch your step on the steep incline. Through a semi-open saddle and past a high alpine bog, the scenery continues up the abrupt slope of West Baldpate. At the mostly open summit, take in the day's final views before dropping 0.8 mile to the Baldpate lean-to. This final part of day two's 8.4-mile hike is partially eroded and can be slippery (it is in the process of being rerouted).

After a peaceful night's rest, follow the AT west 2.3 miles into Grafton Notch. The straightforward descent begins gradually while skirting alongside the ridge. After passing the Table Rock Trail, which leads left 0.5 mile to a spectacular viewpoint, the drop becomes steadier. Safely cross busy Route 26 and then go past a large parking area. To the right, a path leads to the scenic Eyebrow before rejoining the AT. Swing left, remaining on the AT (Old Speck Trail), and then methodically head up a series of rock steps that parallels a cascading brook. Level briefly, cross the running water, and rise onto ledges with views of Old Speck. For the next 2.5 miles the path climbs steadily. Pass the Eyebrow Trail's upper branch and plod up the imposing ridgeline. Sporadically, the trail arrives at outcrops with increasingly delightful views. Just beyond the final one, you reach the western branch of the Grafton Loop.

Veer east and proceed gently 0.3 mile to the 4170-foot summit of Old Speck Mountain. Marred by a cutting that provides western views, the summit is best enjoyed by scaling the ladder that leads to the top of a small tower. Especially impressive are the views looking deep into Mahoosuc Notch and south to the massive Presidential Range. Continue on the blue-blazed trail as it winds down the eastern ridge of the mountain. Through fern-draped forest, the path swings right in a low saddle and drops off the ridge. Make your way gradually to night three's locale, the Slide Mountain campsite (9.3 miles from the Baldpate lean-to).

Day four's 10.5-mile journey starts in a pleasant hardwood forest. Sweeping around Slide Mountain, the path leads across old woods roads. Climb briefly to the ridgeline and then drop quickly into Miles Notch. Once through the flat depression, the route soon leads uphill again, then through thinning forests to emerge onto the open lower ledges of Sunday River Whitecap— arguably the most beautiful mountain on the four-day journey. Follow the gracefully weaving path across the opening landscape. Please remain on the trail, marked with a rock border and occasional boardwalk, to protect the fragile vegetation. Each step to the 3335-foot summit

brings broader views and shots of adrenaline. Take your time atop the Whitecap; the final 7.1 miles are nice, but this is the last spectacular feature on the trek.

Dropping right, the path reenters the forest and passes a spur to the Sargent Brook campsite. Continue to semi-open ledges on Stowe Mountain. After descending into a deep chasm, passing a secluded wetland, and climbing briefly, the trail begins a short, steep descent. Across a long saddle, the path rises to the wooded top of Bald Mountain. Veering left, the route reaches the banks of a mountain stream, which it follows and crosses repeatedly for a couple of miles. While not dramatic, the stream's pools and flowing water are welcome company. Nearing Route 26, swing left onto a road used by snowmobiles. The wide path leads over fields and across the Bear River Bridge. Turn left and continue to a dirt road that leads east to Route 26, 0.6 mile south of the parking area. Carefully follow the road north to complete the circuit.

If multi-day adventures are not your thing, consider the following day trips on the loop: 2.4 miles round-trip to Table Rock or The Eyebrow; 6.4 miles round-trip to Puzzle Mountain's west peak; 8 miles round-trip to East Baldpate; 8 miles round-trip to Old Speck Mountain, or 14.2 miles round-trip to Sunday River Whitecap.

By early summer a snowshoe hare's coat has turned from white to brown.

90 TUMBLEDOWN MOUNTAIN

Distance: 5.5-mile loop
Hiking time: 4.5 hours
Difficulty: Strenuous
Low point: 1115 feet
High point: 3060 feet
Season: May through October
USGS map: Roxbury, ME
Information: Maine Bureau of Parks and Lands

Getting there: From Weld, follow Route 142 north 2.3 miles and turn left. Drive 0.5 mile, then veer right onto a dirt road (Byron Notch Road). In 2.3 miles stay right at the intersection. The trailhead is located 1.6 miles ahead, with parking on either side of the road. From Route 17 in Byron, follow Byron Notch Road 5.8 miles east to the Brook Trail parking area.

No hiking tour of western Maine would be complete without scaling Tumbledown Mountain's rocky ridge. Surrounded by higher peaks to the north, Tumbledown compensates for its relatively diminutive height with captivating natural features including a high-elevation pond and sheer cliff faces. It is no wonder that the mountain has

become the centerpiece of a major conservation effort. Spearheaded by the Tumbledown Conservation Alliance and the Trust for Public Land, with help from the Land for Maine's Future Program and the Federal Forest Legacy Program, a coalition of groups are seeking to protect more than 25,000 acres of prime recreational land. This challenging 5.5-mile circuit vividly showcases the fruits of their labor.

The day's journey ascends the very steep Loop Trail, crosses the scenic Ridge Trail, and concludes along the shady Brook Trail. However, begin the adventure by heading west on an uninspiring 1.3-mile walk along Byron Notch Road. The walk, slightly uphill, serves as a warm-up for the climb ahead.

Upon reaching the Loop Trail sign, turn right and proceed up gentle grades. In 1 mile the path reaches Tumbledown Boulder, an immense rock that marks a transition on the day's trip. Beyond, the route becomes more challenging. Begin a short, steep ascent. Paralleling an exposed ledge, the 0.3-mile climb ends atop a small open ridge and views of Tumbledown Mountain's imposing southern wall. Descend briefly and then begin a final, relentless 0.6-mile ascent to the main ridge. Methodically make your way up the increasingly vertical and narrowing trail. As the final ledges envelop and seemingly block the way, scale a rock wall via iron rungs that lead through a small cave (not suitable for dogs or small children) and arrive at a junction with the Ridge Trail.

From a small saddle, the Ridge Trail leads left 0.1 mile to the rocky summit of Tumbledown's West Peak—well worth the small effort. To the

A rare quiet summer day at Tumbledown Pond

right, follow the path 0.2 mile as it scrambles up small ledges to the wide-open East Peak. Here there are tremendous views, especially southwest toward the White Mountains and east toward sprawling Webb Lake. Continue along the Ridge Trail and drop 0.4 mile across mostly open terrain to scenic Tumbledown Pond. This popular and slightly over-loved water body is nonetheless a very picturesque location and a great place to relax on a warm summer day.

The 1.5-mile descent follows the Brook Trail, which begins on the pond outlet's east side. Along the first 0.5 mile, the footing is uneven and rocky. After crossing the bubbling stream, descend to an old woods road. From here, enjoy a straightforward conclusion to a tremendous day on Tumbledown Mountain.

For an alternative hike that avoids both the road walk and the very steep Loop Trail, use only the Brook and Ridge Trails. By returning on the same route, it is 4.4 miles round-trip to the East Peak. A third option can be completed by following a newly created one-mile path that connects the Brook trailhead with the Parker Ridge Trail. Turn left and ascend 1.8 miles steeply up the scenic ridge before descending to Tumbledown Pond. Scale the East Peak and then return along the Brook Trail to complete a 5.1-mile circuit.

91 SADDLEBACK MOUNTAIN

Distance: 11.6 miles round-trip
Hiking time: 9 hours
Difficulty: Strenuous
Low point: 1590 feet
High point: 4116 feet
Season: Year-round
USGS map: Saddleback Mountain, ME
Information: National Park Service

Getting there: The parking area is located on the south side of Route 4, 9.5 miles east of downtown Rangeley and 12.4 miles west of Phillips.

One of Maine's most striking Appalachian Trail (AT) sections, the march to the summit of

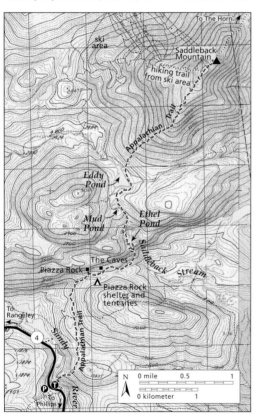

Saddleback grows more alluring with each step. At first, fascinating geologic formations give way to wildlife-rich ponds. With the ponds' reflections etched in your mind, you traverse a mile-long ridge of sparse, stunted trees; soft, windswept sedges; and ever-expanding, breathtaking mountain scenery. Culminating atop the wide-open 4116-foot summit, the journey takes in seemingly boundless views as invigorating as they are beautiful. A hike to Saddleback is physically demanding, but the dividends are far greater.

The trek begins on the north side of Route 4 and descends swiftly to the Sandy River. Cross the bridge near an old mill site and ascend the low hillside. In 1.2 miles, the route traverses a dirt road and then proceeds along the side of a dark forested slope. Dropping to a small brook, swing right into a more inviting landscape and quickly reach the Piazza Rock campsite. Managed by the Maine Appalachian Trail Club (MATC), the site contains a lean-to and tent sites that are available on a first-come basis. To the left, a 0.1-mile steep climb wraps beneath and then to the top of the campsite's dramatic namesake natural feature. Jutting out of the hillside amidst a sea of adjoining boulders, Piazza Rock is quite impressive. North of the campsite, a second spur leads left to a labyrinth of small caves that offers a second intriguing diversion.

Continuing along the AT, the path's relaxing grade soon meets a steadier ascent. Weaving up a series of switchbacks, rise along the steep slope to a small basin and the dark, blue waters of Ethel Pond, the first of three moose-friendly

A crisp fall day on Saddleback Mountain's scenic summit ridge

water bodies. The next mile climbs modestly, but the treadway is uneven and demanding. After plodding along, then across Saddleback Stream, the path skirts boggy Mud Pond and then reaches Eddy Pond's more scenic shoreline.

Now only 2 miles from the summit, cross another dirt road and begin a more aggressive climb up the challenging slope. While the incline is difficult, the path's smooth granite surface is accommodating on the feet. Watch your step if the way is wet or icy; otherwise, enjoy the shrinking tree heights as the route bursts into the open air. The final mile snakes around ledges, through fields of fragile alpine vegetation, and past one

stunning outlook after another. Use caution here during inclement weather—there is little protection. Pass over a southern knob, where a trail leaves left to the ski area. Continue through a low saddle and up to the high point. The nearby scenes of Rangeley Lake, Mount Abraham, and Sugarloaf are spectacular, with distant views stretching to Québec and the White Mountains.

If you have time and energy, consider extending the day's hike 3.2 miles round-trip and head north on the AT to The Horn, a challenging but spectacular 1.6 miles of trail. (See the USGS map.) While difficult, the rewards are great. In either case, retrace your steps south to wrap up the day's adventure.

92 MOUNT ABRAHAM

Distance: 9 miles round-trip
Hiking time: 7 hours
Difficulty: Strenuous
Low point: 1180 feet
High point: 4049 feet
Season: May through October
USGS map: Mount Abraham, ME
Information: Maine Bureau of Parks and Lands

Getting there: From the junction of Routes 27 and 142 in Kingfield, drive west. After crossing over the West Branch of the Carrabassett River, turn left in 0.2 mile onto West Kingfield Road. Drive 3.7 miles (in 3 miles the pavement ends) and veer right. Stay on the main dirt road, and in 2.2 miles veer left. After crossing two small bridges, stay right and drive 0.6 mile to a T intersection and the trailhead. Park here, off the road.

The boulder-draped summit of Mount Abraham is a distinctive feature of Maine's western mountains and one of the most scenic spots in New England. Located near the main mountain ridge traversed by the Appalachian Trail, Mount Abraham provides tremendous nearby views of Saddleback, Sugarloaf, and Bigelow Mountains. From the 360-degree summit vantage point

seemingly endless ridges, valleys, and lakes trail off into the distance. At your feet lie fragile alpine flowers, stunted evergreen trees, and the scatterings of glaciers that receded thousands of years ago. Mount Abraham is a challenging climb but offers rewards that will last a lifetime.

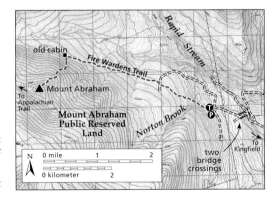

Covered in rocks, Mount Abraham offers exceptional views.

The 4.5-mile hike follows the Fire Wardens Trail as it winds through the 6214-acre state-owned Mount Abraham Public Reserved Land. Protected in the late 1990s with the help of the Land for Maine's Future Program, the Maine Appalachian Trail Land Trust, the Appalachian Trail Conservancy, and the Maine Chapter of The Nature Conservancy, the reserve encompasses most of the northeastern side of the mountain as well as the summit. After paralleling Norton Brook, the trail bears right, crosses the running water, and ascends gradually along old woods roads. Follow the slightly eroded path for nearly 1 mile to a road crossing. Accessible by car, this dirt road was built by a previous landowner and may not be maintained by the state in the future. Some hikers park here to eliminate 2 round-trip miles from the trek.

Pick up the trail on the far side of the road and continue 1.9 miles along moderate terrain. The path gains little elevation, but is not flat as it traverses a number of small streams and depressions along the way. The route eventually reaches the worn-down cabin previously used by the fire warden. While not safe to use today, the cabin provides an excellent location to stop and energize for the 1.5-mile climb that follows.

Gaining more than 1800 feet, the final section wastes little time scaling the steep mountain terrain. After leaving a dark stream valley, follow the aggressive trail through the thick evergreen forest. With persistence and time, you'll reach the base of an extensive talus slope. Here the climb does not let up, but with ever-expanding views, the effort becomes increasingly more rewarding. As the trail weaves in and out of the shrinking forest, use caution on the loose rock. Also be alert of changing weather conditions; there is little protection.

Before you know it, the dilapidated summit fire tower is in view. Enjoy the sweeping views of nearby 4000-foot peaks and Abraham's long boulder-filled ridgeline to the east. For future reference, note the scenic path leading west toward the Appalachian Trail, an excellent diversion along the popular backpacking route. When you have had your fill, retrace your steps to the car.

93   BIGELOW RANGE

Distance: 14-mile loop
Hiking time: 10 hours/2 days
Difficulty: Strenuous
Low point: 1225 feet
High point: 4145 feet
Season: May through October
USGS maps: The Horns, ME; Sugarloaf Mountain, ME
Information: Maine Bureau of Parks and Lands

Getting there: From Kingfield, take Route 27 north. Continue 3.3 miles past Sugarloaf Ski Area and turn right onto a dirt road (just west of where the Appalachian Trail crosses Route 27). Follow the dirt road 1 mile to an Appalachian Trail parking area on the left.

The centerpiece of a 36,000-acre preserve permanently protected by Maine voters in 1976, Bigelow Mountain's scenic ridgeline is an assortment of breathtaking views, idyllic ponds, and abundant wildlife. Once proposed as another big ski area in northern New England, Bigelow Mountain is now a popular destination for hikers and backpackers. Managed by the state for multi-use, including timber management, the Bigelow Preserve offers a great variety of options. This full-day or two-day loop traverses the ridge's most popular locations, but visits quieter locations as well.

Begin by following the dirt road east 0.6 mile to a parking area and the start of the Fire

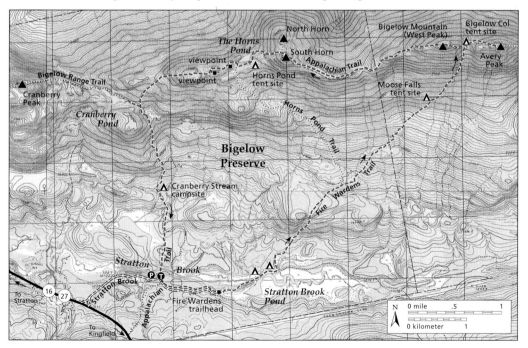

Opposite: *From the west, the Horns stand high above their namesake pond.*

The Horns are two of many peaks visible from Bigelow's West Peak.

Wardens Trail. Veer left, hike 0.5 mile, and cross the Stratton Brook. The route follows a narrowing roadway along the sprawling wetland for 0.7 mile, then bends sharply left onto a more rustic footway. Continue 2.5 miles up a small incline, past the Horns Pond Trail intersection, and then steadily to the Moose Falls campsite. Maintained by the Maine Appalachian Trail Club (MATC), this is the first of four tenting locations on the journey, each available on a first-come basis.

It is time to tackle the hike's most demanding section, a grueling mile-long ascent to the ridgeline. Using rock steps leading up the steep mountainside, slowly make your way into a cozy saddle, the home of a second MATC campsite and a junction with the AT. After catching your breath, head east on the AT and scramble 0.4 mile to the barren, alpine summit of 4088-foot Avery Peak. Named after Maine native Myron Avery, arguably the visionary most responsible for the creation of the AT, the scenic peak appropriately enjoys expansive views that, on the clearest days, stretch from Mount Katahdin to Mount Washington. Return to the saddle and hike west along the AT 0.3 mile to the often-windswept West Peak. The highest point on Bigelow Mountain, the 4145-foot summit provides an awe-inspiring 360-degree panorama, including stunning scenes of Flagstaff Lake.

Follow the white-blazed trail west down the exposed rock, reenter the forest, and begin a steady descent. The journey soon eases into a relaxing ridge walk, but is eventually interrupted by a short scramble to South Horn's scenic pinnacle. Steeply down the opposite side, pass a 0.2-mile spur leading right to North Horn's impressive summit vista. Continue descending to a MATC campsite, where two paths lead right to placid The Horns Pond, nestled beneath imposing ledges.

Resume the journey west along the AT. Past the Horns Pond Trail junction, the route swings right and climbs to two splendid aerial views of the pond. Leveling off, follow the path through the boreal forest to a spur left and views of Sugarloaf. Beyond, descend rapidly past large rocks and tiny caves to a trail junction. Follow the Bigelow Ridge Trail right 0.1 mile to the sparkling blue waters of Cranberry Pond. This trail continues 1.6 miles around ledges, over small ridges, and steeply to Cranberry Peak's open summit—a worthwhile adventure if time and energy allow. From the pond, return 0.1 mile to the AT and turn right. The final 2.4-mile leg begins with a steady descent to the Cranberry Stream campsite, but soon moderates. A short climb leads back to Stratton Brook Road.

For a less-strenuous, yet attractive alternative Bigelow Range hike, scale Cranberry Peak alone. This 8.2-mile option, while challenging, can be completed in five to six hours. A slightly easier and shorter 13.2-mile loop can also be completed beginning at the Fire Wardens trailhead and descending the Horns Pond Trail.

94 MOUNT KINEO

Distance: 3.8 miles round-trip
Hiking time: 3 hours
Difficulty: Moderate–Strenuous
Low point: 1030 feet
High point: 1806 feet
Season: May through October
USGS maps: Mount Kineo, ME; Brassua Lake East, ME
Information: Maine Bureau of Parks and Lands

Getting there: Drive north on Routes 6/15 from Greenville. Continue 1.5 miles past Moosehead Lake's west outlet and turn right. Follow the road 0.3 mile to the Rockwood boat launch. The trailhead is located across the lake on a peninsula. For a fee, a private boat runs hourly from 8:00 AM to 5:00 PM in July and August. From Memorial Day through June and September through Columbus Day the boat runs every 2 hours from 9:00 AM to 5:00 PM. Crossing the water by canoe or kayak is possible but can be dangerous. The lake freezes solidly in the winter, allowing foot access. The shortest distance across is 0.7 mile.

Standing atop Mount Kineo's summit tower, you are blessed with an extraordinary panorama of endless blue waters, lush green hillsides, and distant rocky mountaintops. Even more dramatic than the summit vista are Kineo's 700-foot cliffs, which emerge from the deepest depths of New England's largest lake. Native Americans, who searched for stone tools at its base, believed Kineo was the remains of a large cow moose slain by a god. In 1990, the mountain that inspired this legend and more than 800 acres surrounding it were permanently protected by the state, with assistance from the Maine Chapter of The Nature Conservancy and funding from the Land for Maine's Future Program. Thanks to these efforts, hikers can continue to scale Kineo's legendary slopes and enjoy one of the most spectacular views in New England.

From the dock, turn left onto the Carriage Trail, which, with minor elevation changes, closely follows the lake's picturesque shoreline.

Continue beneath the base of a talus slope, past the mountain's lower cliffs, and to the start of the Indian Trail.

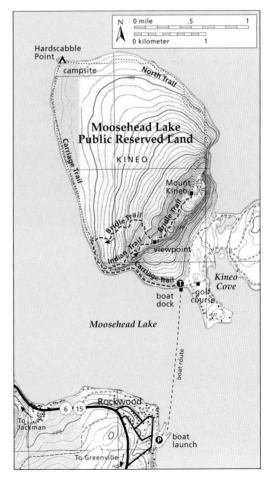

Turn right and begin an aggressive 0.4-mile climb up the steep mountain slope. Closely hugging the edge of the rising cliff side, the challenging path offers one spectacular vista after another. (Take extra care and watch children closely; the trail often approaches precipitous drops). Beyond a grassy ledge, with stunning views of the lake below, arrive at a junction with the Bridle Trail, and swing right. Up and over a small knoll, the route soon ascends to the wooded summit and the base of a tall observation tower. Scale the five sets of stairs that lead above the canopy to behold the breadth of Moosehead Lake and its boundless surroundings. On a clear day, enjoy the views of Baxter State Park rising in the east, beyond the Spencer Mountains.

The 2.2-mile return to the dock should take roughly 90 minutes (allow plenty of time, to avoid missing the last boat). On the descent, skip the Indian Trail, and remain exclusively on the more gradual and more forested Bridle Trail. In less than a mile, arrive at the shoreline. Turn left on the Carriage Trail to reach the dock.

For a 5.5-mile hike, opt for the less-traveled North Trail, reached by following the Carriage Trail to Hardscrabble Point (the site of a primitive tenting area). This quieter alternative traverses miles of flat terrain before steeply climbing the mountain's forested north ridge. If time permits, grab lunch at the nearby golf course restaurant—it is a relaxing place to hang out while waiting for the next boat departure.

Looking back at Kineo's dramatic cliffs after a day on the mountain

95 BIG MOOSE MOUNTAIN

Distance: 5.8 miles round-trip
Hiking time: 4 hours
Difficulty: Moderate–Strenuous
Low point: 1340 feet
High point: 3100 feet
Season: May–November
USGS map: Big Squaw Pond, ME
Information: Maine Bureau of Parks and Lands

Getting there: From Greenville, follow Routes 6/15 north. After crossing under the railroad tracks in Greenville Junction, drive 3.5 miles to a dirt road on the left. Turn here, and drive 1.4 miles to the parking area on the right.

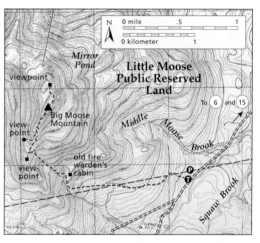

The highest peak in Maine's 15,000-acre Little Moose Public Reserved Land, Big Moose Mountain rises prominently west of Greenville, above the vast shores of Moosehead Lake. Formerly Big Squaw Mountain, the state renamed it and other similarly named natural features in the late 1990s to erase from Maine's maps the pejorative word once used to describe Native American women. By any name, Big Moose Mountain is worthy of exploration. This pleasant trek to its pointy summit and three scenic vistas includes incredible views of distant heights, unending forests, and expansive blue waters.

Heading northwest from the parking area, the trail ascends gradually 0.2 mile to the original route used to access the summit tower. Built in 1905, the Big Moose fire tower was the first one constructed in the United States. Along with most of its brethren, it has long been abandoned thanks to the advent of the airplane and other firefighting technology. Turn left and rise 1 mile along moderate grades, before swinging right near the side of a small brook. A short climb leads to the former fire warden's increasingly rustic cabin. While no longer maintained, the structure serves as a convenient resting spot near the hike's halfway point.

Similar to the paths that depart most fire wardens' cabins, this trail begins an arduous climb up a demanding slope. After crossing a small stream, plod up a long series of rock steps. With persistence, the incline eases near a spur left. Follow the short path to a rock outcrop with splendid views east toward Lily Bay. Rising steadily, but less steeply, the main route passes a second spur on the left. This time, the side trail drops quickly to a western outlook, with distant scenes of Bigelow Mountain and its many rounded neighbors. Push up the final 0.5 mile to the mountain's high point and the remains of its historic tower.

With limited visibility from the mostly wooded peak, descend 0.2 mile to the north. A narrow path leads to an open shoulder with incredible views of Moosehead Lake 2000 feet below, the Spencer Mountains on the far shore, and towering Mount Katahdin in the distance.

The sun burns through early morning fog.

To the north, swaths of forestland dotted with lakes stretch from Mount Kineo to the Québec border. Beautiful throughout the summer, the views from Big Moose are especially tantalizing in late September when peak foliage artistically paints the landscape. Return along the same trail to conclude a glorious adventure in the heart of northern Maine.

96 GULF HAGAS

Distance: 9-mile loop
Hiking time: 7 hours
Difficulty: Moderate–Strenuous
Low point: 650 feet
High point: 1160 feet
Season: May through October
USGS map: Barren Mountain East, ME
Information: KI–Jo-Mary Multiple-Use Forest (fee), Appalachian Mountain Club

Getting there: From Brownville Junction, follow Route 11 north 4.8 miles and then turn left onto Katahdin Ironworks (KI) Road. Follow this logging road 6.3 miles to a gatehouse. Stop and pay the entry fee. Drive 2.4 miles ahead and stay left at a fork in the road. Cross the Pleasant River in 1.4 miles. In 2.9 miles pass a large parking lot on the right (alternative access point). Continue straight 4.3 miles to a three-way intersection. To reach this same intersection from downtown Greenville, follow Pleasant Street past the municipal airport and in 3.6 miles cross Big Wilson Stream. Continue up the logging

road (Greenville Road) 8.6 miles to Hedgehog Checkpoint. Stop and pay the entry fee. In 1.9 miles arrive at the intersection. From the three-way intersection follow Upper Valley Road north 1 mile to the trailhead and parking area. Remember that logging trucks always have the right-of-way on these private roads.

Described as the "Grand Canyon of Maine," Gulf Hagas is a deep gorge where rushing water slowly carves the slate walls that surround it. This scenic loop meanders through pleasant forests, to the edges of steep precipices, and amid

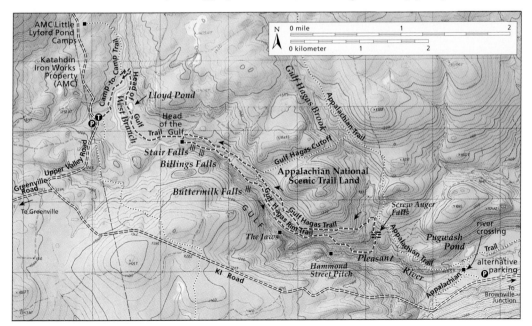

Billings Falls, one of many unique features in Gulf Hagas (Photo by Maria Fuentes)

the refreshing spray of crashing waterfalls. Gulf Hagas is unlike any other place in New England. Save for the dynamite that once aided the logging drives that took place here, it is a location that continues to change slowly, in fact, negligibly, over the course of a human lifetime.

Traditionally, hikers have accessed the gulf from the east. A slightly shorter but more adventurous route, the eastern access follows the Appalachian Trail and includes a sometimes challenging river crossing. In 2003, the Appalachian Mountain Club (AMC) acquired 37,000 acres that abut Gulf Hagas to the west, as well as a number of sporting camps they now manage for overnight visits. Since acquiring the property AMC has also developed more than 50 miles of trails in the area including a new Gulf Hagas access point from the west. The day's journey begins here.

Head east on the wide path that quickly intersects the Camp-to-Camp Trail. Stay left and proceed 0.5 mile over level terrain. After passing a small wetland, the route reaches a dirt road. Turn right and follow the road over a bridge that spans the West Branch of the Pleasant River. This is the start of the 1.3-mile Head of Gulf Trail. Once across the rushing water, continue up the narrowing road. Soon the trail swings sharply right and begins a more welcoming course. With little elevation change, hike south past Lloyd Pond, a short spur right to the river, and eventually to a trail junction.

Turn right onto the Gulf Hagas Rim Trail and descend 0.1 mile to the Head of the Gulf—now the real fun begins. For nearly 3 miles the Rim Trail sinks deeper into the rugged chasm. As you wind over the undulating terrain, use extra care on the slate bedrock that abounds; it can be quite slippery when wet. Take advantage of the many side trails and vistas that showcase Stair Falls, Billings Falls, Buttermilk Falls, The Jaws,

Hammond Street Pitch, and countless other unnamed natural features. Eventually the path veers away from the river and begins to climb along Gulf Hagas Brook. After passing charming Screw Auger Falls the Rim Trail ends at a large boulder with a commemorative plaque.

To the right, the Appalachian Trail leads 1.5 miles to the more popular eastern access point. Turn left and follow the Gulf Hagas Trail (sometimes called Pleasant River Road). With modest elevation gain, this 2-mile route provides a straightforward return to the Head of Gulf Trail and the start of the 1.8-mile conclusion to the day's trek.

For those seeking a shorter, 6-mile excursion into the gulf, consider using the 0.1-mile connector trail that leads northeast from Buttermilk Falls. This less-strenuous alternative still includes the most scenic portions of the Gulf Hagas Rim Trail.

97 DOUBLETOP MOUNTAIN

Distance: 8 miles one-way with shuttle
Hiking time: 7 hours
Difficulty: Strenuous
Low point: 1055 feet
High point: 3488 feet
Season: May–October
USGS map: Doubletop Mountain, ME
Information: Baxter State Park (fee)

Getting there: From Exit 240 on Interstate 95, follow Route 11 west. Drive 11.3 miles into Millinocket and turn right at a T intersection, onto Katahdin Avenue. In 0.2 mile, turn left onto Bates Road (becomes Baxer Park Road). Continue 16.7 miles to Togue Pond gatehouse. After registering, follow Perimeter Road west 10.3 miles. If you are accessing the southern trailhead, turn left to Kidney Pond Campground—the day-use parking is located 1.4 miles on the right. If you are heading to the northern trailhead, continue straight 6.3 miles, and then turn left into Nesowadnehunk Field Campground—the day-use parking is located 0.2 miles on the right.

Rising like a giant prism on Baxter State Park's western boundary, Doubletop's ledge-scarred slopes and rocky summit outcrops are a formidable backdrop to this exhilarating northern New England hike. Accessible by two trails, a challenging ascent from the south and a more

Doubletop stands majestically above Deer Pond.

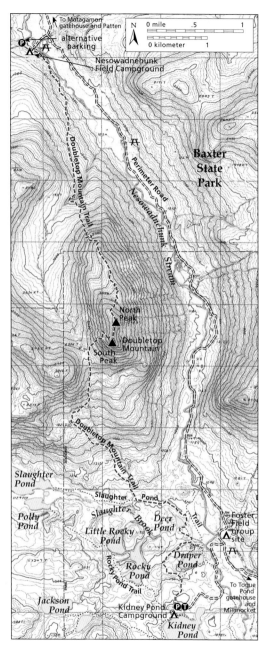

Embarking through a tunnel of evergreen trees, the path departs the southern trailhead and weaves past a 0.1-mile spur right to scenic Draper Pond before descending to a crossing of Slaughter Brook. Proceed over level terrain to the shore of Deer Pond and a stunning view of Doubletop's pyramid-shaped southern face. Circling the shoreline, the route soon intersects the Slaughter Pond Trail and coincides with it 0.7 mile left to an old logging camp area. Turn right onto the Doubletop Mountain Trail and begin a modest 1.2-mile ascent near a small brook, and cross it four times. The slope becomes increasingly steeper with ledges looming above. Here, the trail veers sharply northeast passing beneath large boulders. Watch your footing as the surface becomes rougher and wetter, before a steady climb to a large saddle on the ridge.

The final 0.8-mile, 900-foot climb to Doubletop's South Peak is a great test of endurance, patience, and skill. In addition to carefully placed strides, the relentless ascent requires frequent upper-body use. Hang in there; the perseverance soon pays off with captivating views of Mount Katahdin and its surroundings. Doubletop's barren South Peak, perched high above precipitous cliffs and steep slopes, also offers incredible scenes of lakes, rivers, and mountains in all directions.

Journey across the narrow summit spine 0.2 mile to the mountain's slightly higher North Peak. The former site of a fire tower, this less dramatic but equally beautiful location provides a slightly different perspective and the day's final expansive views. The 3.1-mile descent to the north begins quickly with a 0.5-mile drop; however, the route soon flattens and leads 1 mile pleasantly across the ridge. After a second, aggressive 0.5-mile descent, cross a bubbling, mountain brook and begin a modest 0.7-mile hike to the banks of Nesowadnehunk Stream. Stay left and follow the stream 0.5 mile to the campground that bears its name. Continue a few hundred yards to the day-use parking area located near the ranger station.

If limited to one car, choose the southern route for the most challenge and natural features—9.8 miles round-trip to the North Peak. For a shorter, more straightforward hike, approach from the north—6.6 miles round-trip to the South Peak.

gradual, shorter trek from the north, the most ideal journey would be to combine both by using two cars. The described hike assumes such an arrangement; however, being limited to one trail or the other will not materially detract from the awesome summit views attainable from either end.

98 KATAHDIN LAKE

Distance: 6.6 miles round-trip
Hiking time: 4 hours
Difficulty: Moderate
Low point: 1015 feet
High point: 1270 feet
Season: May through October
USGS map: Mount Katahdin Lake, ME
Information: Baxter State Park (fee)

Getting there: Follow the directions in Hike 97 to Baxter State Park's Togue Pond gatehouse. After registering, follow the park road right and drive 6.2 miles to the parking area on the left.

In 2006, the Baxter State Park Authority acquired a 4119-acre parcel of land surrounding most of 649-acre Katahdin Lake. This acquisition, while controversial in some circles, helped to complete the late Governor Baxter's original vision for a park that included Maine's highest summit and the picturesque lake that bears its name to the east. Once visited by President Theodore Roosevelt, the lake enjoys a storied past and has been visited by countless artists seeking to capture one of the most breathtaking views in New England. Now, thanks to the efforts of Maine's public policymakers, the Trust for Public Land, and many generous donors,

Besides offering breathtaking mountain views, Katahdin Lake is a great place to spot wildlife.

Snow lingers atop Mount Katahdin in late May.

Katahdin Lake will remain accessible to countless future generations of outdoor enthusiasts seeking beauty and solitude in Maine's most storied park.

The 3.3-mile hike leads east and follows old woods roads throughout. The grassy path quickly crosses a small tributary and briefly reaches the banks of the main brook. Continue east along the path for about 0.5 mile to a second bridge crossing, this time leading over Sandy Stream.

Follow the trail up a small hillside and across a low-lying ridge. As the thick evergreen tunnel opens up to a hardwood-dominated forest, follow the path downhill in a more northerly direction. The route continues to meander along the rolling landscape, and occasionally through wetlands; take advantage of the boardwalk and watch your step on wet surfaces. In a few places where former woods roads once diverged, the trail is less obvious, but there are ample blue blazes to lead the way.

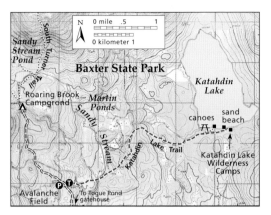

A spur branches left 2.9 miles from the park road. This path leads to the lake and two canoes available for rental (with life jackets) by the park ($1/hour or $8/day). Inquire at the Togue Pond gatehouse about availability. Paddling onto the lake surrounded by a chorus of loons, exploring the many coves in search of foraging moose, and basking in the shadow of Katahdin's impressive eastern slopes are an ideal way to enjoy this spectacular natural area. Be alert to the weather, the lake can get choppy on windy days. The main trail leads right and after one last low ridge abruptly ends at the Katahdin Lake Wilderness Camps. This traditional Maine sporting camp, privately owned and operated, is on leased park land. Idyllically located, the camp provides a good spot from which to enjoy the surroundings. The park hopes to develop additional trails nearby in the years to come. Contact the sporting camp directly regarding overnight stays (www .katahdinlakewildernesscamps.com).

From the western side of the camp, a short path leads to a sandy beach on the lake's south shore. Here there are tremendous mountain views, swimming opportunities, and great picnicking spots. While it's a difficult place to leave, when the time comes, retrace your steps to the parking area.

Moose commonly forage in Katahdin Lake.

99 SOUTH TURNER

Distance: 4 miles round-trip
Hiking time: 3.5 hours
Difficulty: Strenuous
Low point: 1480 feet
High point: 3122 feet
Season: May through October
USGS maps: Mount Katahdin, ME; Katahdin Lake, ME
Information: Baxter State Park (fee)

Getting there: Follow the directions in Hike 97 to Baxter State Park's Togue Pond gatehouse. After registering, follow the park road right and drive 8.1 miles to the day-use parking area on the left.

Note: The hike begins at Roaring Brook Campground, a popular starting point to ascend Mount Katahdin. As such, the limited day-use parking area fills quickly on many summer and early fall days. Be prepared to alter your plans if you are unable to secure a parking spot. Early and late in the season are

good times to visit South Turner, when trails to Katahdin are closed. In addition, South Turner is an excellent hike for those staying overnight at Roaring Brook Campground.

Arguably the finest view of Mount Katahdin, the proximity of South Turner Mountain to Maine's highest point provides an unbelievable vantage point to gaze upon the many ravines and ridges that shape its eastern slopes. The 2-mile trip to the top, although short, is an exhilarating workout. In fact, most of the 1700-foot elevation gain takes place in the final 1.2 miles. Preceding and following the relentless trail to the 3122-foot summit is a relaxing 0.7-mile jaunt past Sandy Stream Pond, where similar Katahdin views abound along with frequent, intimate glimpses of resident moose.

Pick up the trail near the ranger's cabin. After filling in the sign-up sheet, continue straight. At a junction, veer right onto the Russell Pond Trail, where a bridge leads across Roaring Brook. Past a nature trail, the well-maintained path arrives at an intersection. Stay right on the Sandy Stream Pond Trail and meander over a small ridge to the edge of the pond. The trail winds around the eastern shore, and along the way three spurs lead to the water's edge where tremendous views of Mount Katahdin and South Turner Mountain await, the most photogenic spot being Big Rock. Sandy Stream Pond is also an excellent place to witness moose browsing on succulent aquatic plants.

After crossing the pond's outlet, reach the start of the South Turner Trail and turn right. The 1.3-mile route begins gently, but the footing soon becomes rocky, winding through a maze

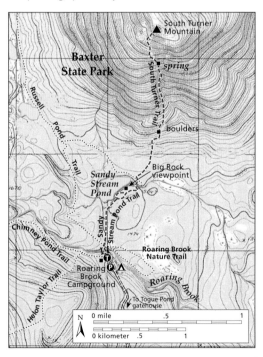

Hikers search for wildlife in Sandy Stream Pond.

of boulders and small ledges. Beyond, the tread improves, but the incline becomes more pronounced. Through a tranquil hardwood forest, the trail methodically ascends rock steps and in 0.9 mile reaches a spur right to a spring.

The final 0.4-mile climb remains as steep; however, with each step the forest slowly opens until culminating at the base of a wide-open talus slope. Here Mount Katahdin consumes the western horizon. Watch your footing on the remaining ascent up the loose, rocky path. At the summit, a small sign marking the high point is encircled with 360-degree views. To the north lies Traveler Mountain and to the south sprawls Katahdin Lake. Catch your breath and enjoy the surrounding landscape, before returning the same way to Roaring Brook Campground.

The white-throated sparrow's "Old Sam Peabody" call is a common tune in Baxter State Park.

100 MOUNT KATAHDIN

Distance: 10.4 miles round-trip
Hiking time: 10 hours
Difficulty: Very strenuous
Low point: 1070 feet
High point: 5267 feet
Season: June through October
USGS map: Mount Katahdin, ME
Information: Baxter State Park (fee)

Getting there: Follow the directions in Hike 97 to Baxter State Park's Togue Pond gatehouse. After registering, follow the park road left, drive 7.7 miles, and turn right into Katahdin Stream Campground. Day-use parking is on the left.

The towering conclusion to the 2174-mile Appalachian Trail (AT), Mount Katahdin stands above Maine amid a sea of lakes, forests, rivers, and rolling hillsides. Rugged, rocky, and raw, the massive peak leaves nearby summits in its shadow, while intoxicatingly luring countless visitors to

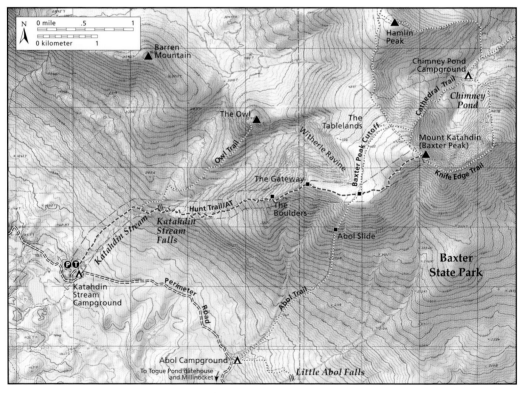

Opposite: *The Tablelands, one of Katahdin's few gradual landscapes*

its dizzying heights. A hike to Katahdin's summit can instill memories to last a lifetime; however, the mountain should be approached with respect. Underestimating the physical and natural challenges presented can result in serious injury or worse. Katahdin is arguably the most strenuous hike in New England, and its weather is unforgiving. Approach the hike with ample preparation and caution, and the reward will be strikingly beautiful vistas, intriguing natural features, and a tremendous sense of accomplishment.

The day's first challenge is to find a parking space. On some nice days, especially weekends, the Katahdin Stream day-use parking area fills early in the morning (the Togue Pond gatehouse opens at 5:00 AM during the summer). Once the lot holds twenty-five cars, it is closed for the day. While Maine residents can secure one of six additional reserved parking spaces by calling in advance, the only other way to guarantee access to the trail is to stay overnight at the campground.

From the campground, pick up the Hunt Trail on the west side of the stream. Named for Irving Hunt, a sporting camp owner who created it in the 1890s, the 5.2-mile path coincides with the northern terminus of the AT. Begin a modest 1.1-mile ascent near the cascading stream. Past the Owl Trail on the left, descend to and then cross a bridge over the rushing water. The route swings left while rising to an impressive view of Katahdin Stream Falls. Once across semi-open ledges, the trail begins a grueling 1.7-mile ascent up the ridge. Make your way past rock crevices and small caves to The Boulders. If weather is threatening, turn back here. Otherwise, rise above tree line with the help of iron rungs and carefully ascend the steep ledges where ever-expanding views accompany each step, including The Owl nearby, and Doubletop in the distance.

The challenging climb moderates across a narrow spine and then scrambles 0.5 mile up to The Gateway, a natural stone entrance for The Tablelands. With a little more than 600 feet of elevation to go, the remaining 1.6-mile stretch begins easily along the moon-like plateau. Hike through an intersection with the Abol and Baxter Peak Cutoff trails. The final push rises steadily to the dramatic summit, perched precipitously above Chimney Pond Basin. With 360-degree views and, most likely, many fellow travelers, enjoy the boundless natural splendor wherever you choose to look. From this location it is easy to grasp why Native Americans referred to Katahdin as the "greatest mountain."

Return as you came, but keep in mind that the rocky trail surface can often be as or more difficult and time-consuming on the descent—so plan accordingly. For variety, opt for a slightly longer hike by descending the very steep 2.8-mile Abol Trail. Very difficult at first, the route down the Abol Slide slowly eases while offering incredible views throughout. Once you reach the campground, follow Perimeter Road 2.2 miles back to Katahdin Stream.

Tame spruce grouse are pleasant members of Baxter Park's boreal forest.

APPENDIX

Acadia National Park
P.O. Box 177
Bar Harbor, ME 04609
Phone: (207) 288-3338
www.nps.gov/acad/index.htm

Appalachian Mountain Club
5 Joy Street
Boston, MA 02108
Phone: (617) 523-0655
www.outdoors.org

Appalachian National Scenic Trail
P.O. Box 50
Harpers Ferry, WV 25425
Phone: (304) 535-6278
www.nps.gov/appa/

Appalachian Trail Conservancy
P.O. Box 807
Harpers Ferry, WV 25425-0807
Phone: (304) 535-6331
www.appalachiantrail.org

Ashburnham Conservation Trust
P.O. Box 354
Ashburnham, MA 01430-0354
Phone: (978) 827-6427
www.AshburnhamConservationTrust.org

Baxter State Park
64 Balsam Drive
Millinocket, ME 04462
Phone: (207) 723-5140
www.baxterstateparkauthority.com/index.html

Berlin Land Trust
P.O. Box 8278
Berlin, CT 06037-8278
Phone: (860) 828-4393
www.berlinlandtrust.org

Block Island Conservancy
P.O. Box 84
Block Island, RI 02807
Phone: (401) 466-3111
www.biconservancy.org

Cape Cod National Seashore
99 Marconi Site Road
Wellfleet, MA 02667
Phone: (508) 771-2144
www.nps.gov/caco

Connecticut Department of Environmental
    Protection
79 Elm Street
Hartford, CT 06106-5127
Phone: (860) 424-3000
www.ct.gov/dep

Connecticut Recreation and Parks Association
1800 Silas Deane Highway, Suite 172
Rocky Hill, CT 06067
Phone: (860) 721-0384
www.crpa.com

Friends of Acadia
P.O. Box 45
Bar Harbor, ME 04609
Phone: (800) 625-0321
www.friendsofacadia.org

Friends of the Wapack (FOW)
P.O. Box 115
West Peterborough, NH 03468
www.wapack.org

Green Mountain Club (GMC)
4711 Waterbury-Stowe Road
Waterbury Center, VT 05677
Phone: (802) 244-7037
www.greenmountainclub.org/

Green Mountain National Forest
231 North Main Street
Rutland, VT 05701
Phone: (802) 747-6700
www.fs.fed.us/r9/forests/greenmountain
   /index.htm

Maine Appalachian Trail Club
P.O. Box 283
Augusta, ME 04332-0283
www.matc.org

Maine Bureau of Parks and Lands
22 State House Station
Augusta, ME 04333
Phone: (207) 287-3821
www.maine.gov/doc/parks

Maine Coast Heritage Trust
1 Bowdoin Mill Island, Suite 201
Topsham, ME 04086
Phone: (207) 729-7366
www.mcht.org

Massachusetts Department of Conservation
   and Recreation
251 Causeway Street, Suite 600
Boston, MA 02114-2104
Phone: (617) 626-1250
www.mass.gov/dcr/index.htm

Mount Grace Land Conservation Trust
1461 Old Keene Road
Athol, MA 01331-9734
Phone: (978) 248-2043
www.mountgrace.org

New Hampshire Division of Parks
   and Recreation
P.O. Box 1856
Concord, NH 03302-1856
Phone: (603) 271-3556
www.nhstateparks.org
www.nhtrails.org/

North Maine Woods
92 Main Street
Ashland, ME 04732
Phone: (207) 435-6213
www.northmainewoods.org

Parker River National Wildlife Refuge
6 Plum Island Turnpike
Newburyport, MA 01950
Phone: (978) 465-5753
www.fws.gov/northeast/parkerriver/

Randolph Mountain Club
P.O. Box 279
Gorham, NH 03581
www.randolphmountainclub.org

Rhode Island Division of Parks and Recreation
2321 Hartford Avenue
Johnston, RI 02919-1719
Phone: (401) 222-2632
www.riparks.com

Rhode Island National Wildlife Refuge Complex
Kettle Pond Visitor Center
50 Bend Road
Charlestown, RI 02813
Phone: (401) 364-9124
www.fws.gov/northeast/ri/rirc.htm

Society for the Protection of New Hampshire
   Forests
54 Portsmouth Street
Concord, NH 03301
Phone: (603) 224-9945
www.spnhf.org/

Stowe Land Trust
P.O. Box 284
Stowe, VT 05672-0284
Phone: (802) 253-7221
www.stowelandtrust.org

A red squirrel enjoys a late day snack.

The Nature Conservancy (TNC)
www.nature.org

Connecticut Chapter
55 High Street
Middletown, CT 06457-3788
Phone: (860) 344-0716

Maine Chapter
14 Maine Street, Suite 401
Brunswick, ME 04011
Phone: (207) 729-5181

Massachusetts Chapter
205 Portland Street, Suite 400
Boston, MA 02114
Phone: (617) 227-7017

New Hampshire Chapter
22 Bridge Street, 4th Floor
Concord, NH 03301
Phone: (603) 224-5853

Rhode Island Chapter
159 Waterman Street
Providence, RI 02906
Phone: (401) 331-7110

Vermont Chapter
27 State Street, Suite 4
Montpelier, VT 05602
Phone: (802) 229-4425

The Trustees of Reservations
572 Essex Street
Beverly, MA 01915-1530
Phone: (978) 921-1944
www.thetrustees.org

Trust for Public Land
New England Regional Office
33 Union Street
Boston, MA 02108
Phone: (617) 367-6200
www.tpl.org

Vermont Department of Forests, Parks, and
  Recreation
103 South Main Street
Waterbury, VT 05671-0601
Phone: (802) 241-3650
www.vtfpr.org/

Vermont Division for Historic Preservation
National Life Building
Second Floor
Montpelier, VT 05620-1201
Phone: (802) 828-3213
www.historicvermont.org/sites/

Vermont Land Trust
8 Bailey Avenue
Montpelier, VT 05602-2161
Phone: (802) 223-5234
www.vlt.org

White Mountain National Forest
719 North Main Street
Laconia, NH 03246
Phone: (603) 528-8721
www.fs.fed.us/r9/white/

Wonalancet Out Door Club
HCR 64, Box 248
Wonalancet, NH 03897
www.wodc.org

INDEX

ABOUT THE AUTHOR

Jeffrey Romano has been hiking for more than thirty years. A lifelong resident of New England, Jeff has lived in four of the region's six states. In addition to scaling New England's 100 highest peaks, he has hiked extensively throughout the wild places of all six states. Born in Connecticut, Jeff grew up in southern New Hampshire. He earned a B.A. in Politics from Saint Anselm College and a J.D. from Vermont Law School. Jeff has worked on a handful of political campaigns and for a number of nonprofit organizations. He currently coordinates public policy activities for Maine Coast Heritage Trust, a statewide land trust that focuses on the conservation of Maine's unique coastline. When not in his office or in the state house in Augusta, Jeff is often found with his family on one of New England's many hiking trails. An avid birdwatcher, he lives in Hallowell with his wife Maria and their son, Anthony. Jeff is also the author of *Best Loop Hikes: New Hampshire's White Mountains to the Maine Coast* (The Mountaineers Books, 2006).

THE MOUNTAINEERS, founded in 1906, is a nonprofit outdoor activity and conservation club, whose mission is "to explore, study, preserve, and enjoy the natural beauty of the outdoors. . . . " Based in Seattle, Washington, the club is one of the largest such organizations in the United States, with seven branches throughout Washington State.

The Mountaineers sponsors both classes and year-round outdoor activities in the Pacific Northwest, which include hiking, mountain climbing, ski-touring, snowshoeing, bicycling, camping, kayaking, nature study, sailing, and adventure travel. The club's conservation division supports environmental causes through educational activities, sponsoring legislation, and presenting informational programs.

All club activities are led by skilled, experienced instructors, who are dedicated to promoting safe and responsible enjoyment and preservation of the outdoors.

If you would like to participate in these organized outdoor activities or the club's programs, consider a membership in The Mountaineers. For information and an application, write or call The Mountaineers, Club Headquarters, 7700 Sand Point Way NE, Seattle, WA 98115; 206-521-6001. You can also visit the club's website at www.mountaineers.org or contact The Mountaineers via email at clubmail@mountaineers.org.

The Mountaineers Books, an active, nonprofit publishing program of the club, produces guidebooks, instructional texts, historical works, natural history guides, and works on environmental conservation. All books produced by The Mountaineers Books fulfill the club's mission.

Send or call for our catalog of more than 500 outdoor titles:

The Mountaineers Books
1001 SW Klickitat Way, Suite 201
Seattle, WA 98134
800-553-4453
mbooks@mountaineersbooks.org
www.mountaineersbooks.org

The Mountaineers Books is proud to be a corporate sponsor of The Leave No Trace Center for Outdoor Ethics, whose mission is to promote and inspire responsible outdoor recreation through education, research, and partnerships. The Leave No Trace program is focused specifically on human-powered (nonmotorized) recreation.

Leave No Trace strives to educate visitors about the nature of their recreational impacts, as well as offer techniques to prevent and minimize such impacts. Leave No Trace is best understood as an educational and ethical program, not as a set of rules and regulations.

For more information, visit www.LNT.org, or call 800-332-4100.

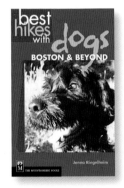

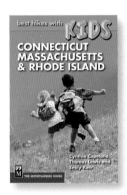